I0187277

Fiqh us-Sunnah

FIQH us-SUNNAH

Supererogatory Prayer

Muhammad Sa'eed Dabas
Jamal al-Din M. Zarabozo
(Translators)

American Trust Publications
721 Enterprise Drive
Oak Brook, IL 60523

Copyright © 1409 / 1989

Reprinted 2012

American Trust Publications
721 Enterprise Drive
Oak Brook, IL 60523

Phone: (630) 789-9191 Fax: (630) 789-9455

All Rights Reserved

No part of this book may be reproduced by any means, nor translated into any other language, without prior written permission from the Publisher.

Library of Congress
Catalog Card Number
85-73207

ISBN No. (Vol. II) 0-89259-077-7
        (Set) 0-89259-033-5

Printed in the United States of America

فَلَا وَرَبِّكَ لَا يُؤْمِنُونَ حَتَّىٰ يُحَكِّمُوكَ
فِيمَا شَجَرَ بَيْنَهُمْ ثُمَّ لَا يَجِدُواْ
فِىٓ أَنفُسِهِمْ حَرَجًا مِّمَّا قَضَيْتَ وَيُسَلِّمُواْ تَسْلِيمًا .

But no, by your Lord!
They do not really believe
unless they make you
(O Prophet) a judge
of all on which they disagree
among themselves,
and then find in their hearts
no bar to an acceptance
of your decision
and give themselves up to it
in utter self-surrender (an-Nisa' 4:65).

TABLE OF CONTENTS

Chapter Three
THE MOSQUES

PLACES WHERE (OFFERING) PRAYER IS PROHIBITED
THE SUTRAH OR PARTITION IN FRONT OF ONE WHO

Chapter Four
WHAT IS ALLOWED DURING THE PRAYER

Chapter Five
ACTIONS WHICH ARE DISLIKED DURING THE PRAYER
(*MAKRUHAT US-SALAH*)

Chapter Six
ACTIONS WHICH INVALIDATE THE *SALAH*

PREFACE

It was a privilege for me to have had the opportunity to study with the author of *Fiqh us-Sunna*, Shaykh Sayyid Sabiq. A review of this work in English recalls fond and special memories of two decades past when I regularly met with Shaykh Sayyid during the book's final writing and editing. Often, we discussed the background and circumstances that led to the emergence of this important work. I believe sharing some of this information, along with comments about the work and its translation, will be helpful to our readers.

In the 1940's, when the modern Islamic movement in Egypt was approaching its height, a new breed of Muslims emerged, shedding fears, yearning to understand Islam, and living its way of life. Hasan al-Banna, the principal figure igniting the movement, wanted to free Muslims from a block obscuring this understanding of Islam called *taqlīd*, or blind, rigid adherence and unyielding allegiance to one or another preferred juristic school, a point of view that gained prevalence throughout the Muslim world in the later centuries. It was exactly for this reason that Hasan al-Banna summoned his brilliant student and associate, Shaykh Sabiq, to re-introduce *fiqh* (Islamic law and etiquette) to the coming generation through the mirror of the Prophet's life-model, upon him be peace. In this light, he examined the *fiqhī* opinions of some of our great jurists, particularly Abū Hanīfa, Mālik, al-Shāfi'ī, and Ahmad Ibn Hanbal. He sought neither to dramatize their differences nor overlook them. The choice of the title *Fiqh us-Sunna* (The Jurisprudence of Sunna), instead of *Fiqh al-Madhāhib*

(The Jurisprudence of the Legal Schools), illustrates the spirit of the approach that runs through the entire work. The author relied on many of the great works of comparative *fiqh*: Ibn al-Qayyim's *Zād al-Ma'ād*; Shawkānī's *Nayl al-Awtār, al-Durar al-Bahīyya*, and *al-Sayl al-Jarār*; Ibn Rushd's masterpiece *Bidāyat al-Mujtahid*; Ibn Qudāma's *al-Mughnī*; and San'ānī's *Subul al-Salām*.

Fiqh us-Sunna, a pioneering effort to offer fair and easy access to diverse opinions of *fiqh*, is not immune to methodological problems or even errors. Its primary shortcoming is its introduction of conflicting juristic opinions without reasonable analysis and explanation.

It should be noted that diverse opinions of *fiqh* may create confusion in some minds not properly prepared to appreciate the accommodating nature of *fiqh*. After all, *fiqhī* opinions are not mere mind games of scholars. They are viable options in the lawful application of Islam, providing the flexibility needed to meet the demands of an ever-changing world—for the individual, for the circumstance, for the generation, and for the Ummah.

The term *fiqh* is derived from the root word *faqiha*, which means "to understand." In its technical usage, it stands for the science detailing Islamic jurisprudence. However, *fiqh's* root meanings are not divorced from its technical sense. Does it not require understanding to discern the *fiqh* governing and regulating public, private, economic, social, political, and spiritual concerns of the Muslim Ummah? Islamic jurisprudence has as its primary function the necessary task of reaching an understanding (*fiqh*) of the *Sharī'a*, the principles, rules, laws, and issues that have been revealed by the Lord of the Worlds to Muhammad, upon him be peace, to convey to humanity.

Opinions and interpretations do, however, vary. Incidents without precedent virtually guarantee that jurists of today will differ on some issues, be they political, sociological, or otherwise. But regardless of how diversity surfaces, the differences themselves are not inherently evil. On the contrary, flexibility is the hallmark of this *Sharī'a* that is ever-revealing itself to humanity. This freedom is of the *fitra* (natural state), while unyielding rigidity only stunts the growth and the contribution of the Muslim Ummah, as it has in the recent past. Reading this book will perhaps give you a feel for this fresh spirit.

As for translation, it is never an easy task. Bringing an Arabic text of *fiqh* into English is all the more difficult. The work of the translators is to be appreciated. Muhammad Sa'eed Dabas, with his training in Arabic, was complemented by Jamal Zarabozo's feel for English. However, special terminologies are in need of some standardization, and the writing style would improve with overall tightening. American Trust Publications should be congratulated for its pioneer effort to provide English readers access to this unique work of *fiqh*.

Finally, let me caution that a close reading of this book will introduce a person to *fiqh* and its related issues, but it will not make him or her a *faqīh* (legist). This certainly is the function of our future institutions, to train eager North American young men and women, and interested elders, in Arabic; the sciences of Qur'an, Sunna, and *Usūl al-Fiqh*; the development of Islamic jurisprudence; and Islam in general. Until then, we lie somewhere between dependence on our scholars of the East, and their works, and our own understanding of contemporary challenges facing all of us in the West.

Ahmad Zaki Hammad, Ph.D

AT-TATAWWU'
SUPEREROGATORY PRAYERS

Their Significance: *At-tatawwu'*, or *nawafil* or supererogatory prayers, have been legislated to make up for any deficiencies left in the performance of *fard salah* (obligatory prayers). In *salah*, there are virtues that are not found in any other form of worship. Abu Hurairah reports that the Prophet *sallallahu alehi wasallam* said: "The first thing that the people will be called to account for on the Day of Resurrection will be the prayers. Our Lord will say to the angels although He knows better: 'Look into the *salah* of my servant to see if he observed it perfectly or been negligent in it. So if he observed it perfectly it will be recorded to his credit, but if he had been negligent in it in any way, Allah would say: See if My servant has any supererogatory prayers. Then if he has any supererogatory prayers, Allah would say: Make up the deficiency in My servant's obligatory prayer with his supererogatory prayers.' Thereafter all his actions will be examined in like manner" (Abu Dawud).

Abu Umamah narrates that the Prophet *sallallahu alehi wasallam* said: "Allah does not listen to anything from His slave as He does to the two *rak'at* (of prayer) that he offers. Mercy descends over the servant's head as long as he remains in prayer" (Ahmad and at-Tirmidhi). As-Sayuti grades it *sahih*. In *al-Muwatta'*, Malik says: "It has reached me that the Prophet said: '(Try to) keep to the straight path although you won't be able to do so completely; and know that the best of your deeds is the *salah*, and only a (true) believer preserves his *wudu*.'" Muslim records from Rabi'ah ibn Malik al-Aslami that the Prophet *sallallahu alehi wasallam* said: "Ask [anything]." Rabi'ah said: "I ask of you to be your companion in paradise." The Prophet said: "Or anything else?" Rabi'ah said: "That is it." The Prophet *sallallahu alehi wasallam* said to him: "Then help me by making many prostrations (i.e., supererogatory prayers)."

Offering Supererogatory Prayers in One's House: Ahmad and Muslim relate from Jabir that the Messenger of Allah said: "If one of you offers his prayers in the Mosque then he should make a portion of his prayers in his house, as Allah has made his prayers in his house a means of betterment (for him)."

Ahmad records from 'Umar that the Messenger of Allah said: "The *nawafil salah* of a man in his house are a light; whoever wishes should lighten up his house."

'Abdullah ibn 'Umar reports that the Prophet *sallallahu alehi wasallam* said: "Make some of your prayers in your houses and do not turn your houses into graves." This statement is related by Ahmad and Abu Dawud. Abu Dawud records from Zaid ibn Thabit on sound authority that the Messenger of Allah said: "A person's *salah* in his house is better than his *salah* in my mosque, except for the *fard salah*."

These *ahadith* prove that it is preferred to say one's *nawafil* prayers in one's house since prayers in one's house are better than those that he performs in the mosque. An-Nawawi says: "The Prophet *sallallahu alehi wasallam* encouraged one to offer *nawafil* in one's house because then the prayers are more private and will have less of a chance of being done for show and will be free from defécts that vitiate good deeds. Furthermore, this will be a blessing for the house as mercy and angels will descend on it while Satan flees from It."

Their Elongation: It is preferred to prolong the reciting by making many *rak'at*. The group, except for Abu Dawud, reports that al-Mughirah ibn Shu'bah said: "The Prophet *sallallahu alehi wasallam* would stand and pray until his feet or shanks swelled. When he was asked about it, he said: 'Should I not be a thankful slave?'" Abu Dawud records from 'Abdullah ibn Hubshi al-Khath'ami that the Prophet *sallallahu alehi wasallam* was asked: "What is the best deed?" He said: "Prolonging the *qiyam*; (standing) [in the prayer]." Then it was asked: "What is the best charity?" He replied: "The sacrifice made by one who has little to give." Then it was asked: "What is the best migration?" He responded: "The migration from what Allah has forbidden." Then it was asked: "What is the best *jihad*?" He replied: "Whoever strives against the polytheists with his wealth and soul." They asked: "What is the most honorable death?" He answered: "He whose blood is spilled and whose horse is wounded."

It is allowed to make supererogatory prayers while in *julus* (sitting): It is acceptable for one to make *nawafil* while sitting even though he has the ability to stand. It is also acceptable for one to make part of such prayers sitting and part of them standing even if all of that is in one *rak'ah*, (i.e., one sits for part of the first *rak'ah* and then stands for the rest of it, or vice versa). All of that is acceptable without any dislike for it. One may sit in any manner one likes although it is preferable to sit cross-legged. Muslim records that 'Alqamah asked 'Aishah: "How did the Prophet perform two *rak'at* while sitting?" She replied: "He would recite while sitting and then when he wished to make *ruku'*, he would stand and bow." Ahmad, Abu Dawud, at-Tirmidhi, an-Nasa'i, and Ibn Majah record that she said: "I never saw the Messenger of Allah ever sitting while reciting during the night prayer until he became old, then he would sit until when about thirty or forty verses were left of his recital then he would stand, finish the recital and make *ruku'*..."

Different Types of *Nawafil*: *Nawafil* may be divided into two types: general and specific prayers. The *nawafil* are said to be those prayers which are in addition to the *fard salah*, as prayed by the Prophet *sallallahu alehi wasallam*.

An-Nawawi says: "If one decides to make *nawafil* prayers and he does not make any intention concerning the number [of *rak'at*] he shall make, then he may end the prayer after one *rak'ah* or make it two *rak'at* or increase it to three or one hundred or one thousand, and so forth. If he prays a number of [*rak'at*], without knowing how many, and then ends the prayer his *salah* will still be valid." There is no difference of opinion on this. The *Shaf'iyyah* are in agreement with it and there is a text attributed to ash-Shaf'i on this point.

Al-Baihaqi records with a chain of narrators, that Abu Dharr prayed many *rak'at* and then concluded his *salah*. Al-Ahnaf ibn Qais asked him: "Do you know if you finished on an odd or an even number?" He replied: "Even if I do not know, Allah knows. I heard my friend Abu al-Qasim say: 'No slave makes a *sajdah* to Allah without Allah raising him a degree and wiping out one of his sins due to it.'" This is related by ad-Darimi in his Musnad with a *sahih* chain, but it should be noted that there is a difference of opinion over the integrity of one of its narrators.

The specific *nawafil* prayers are referred to as *al-sunan ar-ratibah*, or the *sunnah* prayers that have a specific order, number, and so on. These include the *sunnah* prayers of *fajr*, *zuhr*, '*asr*, *maghrib*, and '*isha*.

The Two *rak'at* of *Fajr*: There are a number of *ahadith* that state the virtues of observing the *sunnah* prayer at dawn time. For example: 'Aishah relates that the Prophet *sallallahu alehi wasallam* said about the two *rak'at* before the *fajr*: "They are dearer to me than the whole world." This is related by Ahmad, Muslim, and at-Tirmidhi. Abu Hurairah reports that the Prophet said: "Do not leave the two *rak'at* of the *fajr*, even if you are being attacked by a cavalry." This is confirmed by Ahmad, Abu Dawud, al-Baihaqi, and at-Tahawi. The message of the *hadith* is that one should not leave the two *rak'at* of the *fajr* no matter what the excuse, even while under enemy attack or under most trying conditions. 'Aishah says: "The Messenger of Allah was not so particular about observing any supererogatory prayer as he was in observing the two *rak'at* before *salatul fajr*." This is related by al-Bukhari, Muslim, Ahmad, and Abu Dawud. She also reports that the Prophet said: "The two *rak'at* of the fajr are better than this world and all it contains." This is reported by Ahmad, Muslim, at-Tirmidhi, and an-Nasa'i. Ahmad and Muslim also record that she said: "I have never seen him [the Prophet] more in haste to do a good deed than he was to perform the two *rak'at* before the morning [prayer]."

To Make Them Quickly: It is well-known that the Prophet would make a very short recital in the two *rak'at* before the dawn. Hafsah reports: "The Prophet would pray the two *rak'at* of fajr before the dawn in my house and he would make it very quick." Naf'i states: "'Abdullah [Ibn 'Umar] would also make it very quickly." This is related by Ahmad, al-Bukhari, and Muslim. 'Aishah narrates: "The Prophet would pray the two *rak'at* before the dawn prayer in my house so quickly that I wondered if he had recited the Fatihah in them or not." This is related by Ahmad and others. She also said: "When the Prophet prayed the two *rak'at* before the dawn prayer I estimated the time that he took in recital was like what it takes to recite al-Fatihah. This is related by Ahmad, an-Nasa'i, al-Baihaqi, Malik, and at-Tahawi. It is preferred to recite what has been related from the Prophet *sallallahu alehi wasallam*: 'Aishah reports that the Prophet would silently recite the following in the two *rak'at* before *salatul fajr*:
"Say: O disbelievers," 　　　　　　　　 ﴾قُـل يا أُيُهَـا الكَـافِرُونَ﴿
and
"Say: He is Allah, the One." 　　　　　　﴾قُـل هُــوَ اللهُ أحَـــدٌ﴿
This is related by Ahmad and at-Tahawi. He would recite them after al-Fatihah as there is no prayer without the recital of al-Fatihah, as we have already discussed. She also reports that the Prophet said: "These are the two most blessed *surahs*," and he would recite them in the two *rak'at* before *salatul fajr*. This is related by Ahmad and Ibn Majah. Jabir relates that a man stood to pray the two *rak'at* before the dawn prayer and recited

"Say: O disbelievers!" in the first *rak'ah* until he finished the *surah*. The Prophet said: "That slave knows his Lord." In the second *rak'ah* he recited: "Say: He is Allah, the One"...to the end of the *surah*. The Prophet said: "That slave (of Allah) believes in his Lord." Talhah said: "I love to recite these two *surahs* in these two *rak'at*." This is related by Ibn Hayyan and at-Tabarani. Ibn 'Abbas reports that the Prophet *sallallahu alehi wasallam* would recite the following in the two *rak'at* before the dawn prayer:

"Say: We believe in Allah and what has been revealed to us,"[1] and from *surah* al-'Imran, 'Come to common terms as between us and you.' This is related by Muslim.

﴿قـولـوا آمـنا بالله ومـا أنـزل إليـنا﴾

﴿تعالوا إلى كلمة سواء بيننا وبينكم﴾

In the first *rak'ah*, after al-Fatiha, he would recite the verse: "Say: We believe in Allah, and the revelation given to us and what was revealed to Abraham, Ismail, Isaac, Jacob and the tribes, and [in what] was given to Moses and Jesus, and what was given to the Prophets, from their Lord and we do not differentiate between any of them. And we are Muslims."[2]

﴿قولوا آمـنا بالله ومـا أنـزل إلى إبراهيم وإسماعيل وإسحق ويعقوب والأسباط وما أوتي موسى وعيسى وما أوتي النبيون من ربهم لا نفرق بين أحد منهم ونحن له مسلمون﴾

In the second *rak'ah* he would recite: "Say: O People of the Book, come to a statement that is common between us and you; that we shall not worship any save Allah and we shall not associate any partners with Him and we shall not take others as Lords besides Allah. And if they turn away then say: Bear witness that we are they who have surrendered unto Him."[3]

﴿قل يا أهل الكتاب تعالوا إلى كلمة سواء بيننا وبينكم ألا نعبد إلا الله ، ولا نشرك به شيئاً ، ولا يتخذ بعضنا بعضاً أرباباً من دون الله ، فإن تولوا فقولوا اشهدوا بأنا مسلمون﴾

He also reports, in a version recorded by Abu Dawud, that in the first *rak'ah* the Prophet *sallallahu alehi wasallam* would recite: "Say: We believe in Allah..."

﴿قولوا آمنا بالله﴾

---

[1] Qur'an 2:136
[2] Qur'an 3:64
[3] Qur'an 3:64

In the second *rak'ah* he would recite: "But when Jesus became conscious of their disbelief, he cried: 'Who will be my helpers in the cause of Allah?' The disciples said: 'We will be Allah's helpers...'"[4]

﴿فلما أحس عيسى منهم الكفر قال من أنصـاري إلى الله قال الحـواريون نحن أنصار الله آمنا بالله واشهد بأنا مسلمون﴾

From the report of 'Aishah, mentioned earlier, it is concluded that it is permissible just to recite al-Fatihah in each *rak'ah*.

Supplication after finishing the two *sunnah rak'at* before the *fajr* prayer: An-Nawawi says in *al-Adhkar:* "It is related in the book of Ibn as-Sanni from Abu al-Malih (whose name was 'Aamr ibn Usamah) on the authority of his father that his father had prayed the two *rak'at* of the dawn [before *salatul fajr*] and the Prophet *sallallahu alehi wasallam* was praying the two *rak'at* close to him, and he heard the Prophet say, while sitting:

'O Allah, Lord of Jibrail, Israfeel, Mikail, and Muhammad, the Prophet, I seek refuge in Thee from the Fire,'"...three times.

الـلهم رب جبريل وإسرافيل وميكـائيل ومحمد النبى ﷺ أعوذ بك من النار.

He also records from Anas that the Prophet said: "Whoever says, on Friday morning before the *salatul fajr*,
'I seek the forgiveness of Allah, there is no other god except Him, the Living, the Sustaining, and I repent unto him,'

أستغفر الله الذى لا إله إلا هو الحى القيوم وأتوب إليه .

three times, Allah will forgive his sins even if they were as abundant as the foam on the sea."

Lying down after them: 'Aishah says: "After the Prophet had prayed the two [*sunnah*] *rak'at* of the *fajr*, he would lie down on his right side." This is related by the group. They also record that she reported: "After the Messenger of Allah had prayed the two [*sunnah*] *rak'at* of the *fajr*, he would lie down if I was asleep or would talk to me if I was awake."

There is quite a difference of opinion over this point. Apparently, it is preferred for one to do so if one prays these *sunnah rak'at* in one's house and not in the mosque. Ibn Hajar says in *Fath al-Bari:* "Some of the early scholars were of the opinion that it is preferred to do so if one prays in one's house rather than in the mosque." This has been recorded from Ibn 'Umar. Some of our scholars reinforce this argument by stating that there is no evidence that the Prophet ever did so in the mosque. It has also been

---

[4]Qur'an 3:52

authentically recorded from Ibn 'Umar that "he would throw pebbles at anyone who did so in the mosque," and this was related by Ibn Abi Shaibah. Imam Ahmad was asked about it and he said: "I do not do it but if a person does it, it is good."

Their belated performance: Abu Hurairah reports that the Prophet said: "Whoever fails to pray the two [*sunnah*] *rak'at* of the *fajr* until the sun rises, [he should then] pray them." This is related by al-Baihaqi. About its chain an-Nawawi says it is good.

Qais ibn 'Umar relates that he went to the dawn prayer and found the Prophet praying *fajr*. Although Qais had not prayed the *sunnah* prayer, he joined the Prophet *sallallahu alehi wasallam* and prayed with him. When he had finished *salatul fajr*, he prayed the two *rak'at* (*sunnah*) prayer. The Messenger of Allah passed by him and inquired: "What is this prayer?" Qais then informed him of all that had happened. The Prophet kept silent and did not say anything.[5] This is related by Ahmad, Ibn Khuzaimah, Ibn Hibban, at-Tirmidhi, Abu Dawud, and Ibn Majah. Al-'Iraqi says its chain is *hasan*.

Ahmad, al-Bukhari, and Muslim relate from 'Imran ibn Hussain that, during a journey, the Prophet slept past the time of *salatul fajr* and when he woke he waited for the sun to rise a little and then he ordered the *mu'dhdhin* to make the *adhan*. Then, the Prophet prayed the *fajr sunnah*, after which he ordered the *iqamah* to be made and prayed *salatul fajr*. It is apparent from this *hadith* that one is to make up the *sunnah* prayer before or after the sun rises, regardless of whether only *sunnah* prayer is missed or both *sunnah* and *fard* are missed, and whether there is a valid excuse or not. It may be made up by itself or with the obligatory dawn prayer.

The *Sunnah* Prayer Of *Zuhr*
It has been related that the *sunnah rak'at* at *zuhr* are four, six, or eight.

Reports concerning four *rak'at*: Ibn 'Umar said: "We observed and preserved from the Prophet ten *rak'at* [of *sunnah* prayers]: two before *zuhr* and two after it, two after *maghrib* in his house, two after *'isha* in his house and two *rak'at* before the *fajr*." This is related by al-Bukhari.

Al-Mughirah ibn Sulaiman reports that he heard Ibn 'Umar say: "The Prophet never left the two *rak'at* before *zuhr* and two *rak'at* after it, two *rak'at* after *maghrib*, two *rak'at* after *'isha* and two *rak'at* before *fajr*." This is related by Ahmad with a good chain.

---

[5]According to the principles of fiqh, if the Prophet kept silent about something, it meant he must have approved of it. Otherwise, he would have been obliged to speak out against it.

Reports concerning six *rak'at*: 'Abdullah ibn Shaqiq said: "I asked 'Aishah about the prayer of the Prophet and she said: 'He would pray four *rak'at* before *zuhr* and two after it.'" This is related by Ahmad, Muslim, and others.

Umm Habibah bint Abu Sufyan reports that the Messenger of Allah said: "Whoever prays twelve *rak'at* during the day and night will have a house built for him in paradise: four *rak'at* before *zuhr* and two after it, two *rak'at* after *maghrib*, two *rak'at* after *'isha*, and two *rak'at* before *fajr*." This is related by at-Tirmidhi who called it *hasan sahih*. Muslim reports it briefly.

Reports concerning eight *rak'at*: Umm Habibah reports that the Prophet said: "Whoever prays four *rak'at* before *zuhr* and four after it, Allah will forbid that his flesh be in the fire." This is related by Ahmad, Abu Dawud, an-Nasa'i, Ibn Majah, and at-Tirmidhi who calls it *sahih*.

It is related that Abu Ayyub al-Ansari would pray four *rak'at* before *zuhr*. The people said to him: "You made that prayer continue too long!" He said: "I saw the Messenger of Allah doing so. I asked him about it and he said: 'It is a time in which the doors of the heavens are opened and I wish that my good deeds be raised (to heaven) during it.'" This is related by Ahmad with a good chain.

The merits of four *rak'at* before *zuhr*: 'Aishah said: "The Prophet never left praying four *rak'at* before *zuhr* and two *rak'at* before *fajr* under any circumstances." This is related by Ahmad and al-Bukhari. It is also related from her that during those four *rak'at*, he would prolong the *qiyam* [the portion in which one recites the Qur'an] and perfect the *ruku'* and *sujud* therein.

There is no contradiction between the *hadith* of Ibn 'Umar, which states that the Prophet prayed two *rak'at* before *zuhr*, and other *ahadith* which state that the Prophet prayed four *rak'at* before *zuhr*. Ibn Hajar writes in *Fath al-Bari*: "It is better to take them as describing different circumstances, sometimes he prayed two *rak'at* and sometimes he prayed four *rak'at*. Some say that it may be construed that if he prayed them in the mosque, he prayed only two *rak'at*, and when he prayed in his house, he prayed four *rak'at*. On the other hand, it could imply that he prayed two *rak'at* in his house and then went to the mosque and prayed two *rak'at* there also. Ibn 'Umar only saw what he prayed in the mosque and not what he prayed in his house, while 'Aishah was aware of both of them. The first interpretation is strengthened by what Ahmad and Abu Dawud recorded from 'Aishah, namely, that the Prophet prayed four *rak'at* in his house before *zuhr* and then he went to the mosque."

Abu Ja'far at-Tabari says: "Most of the time he prayed four *rak'at* and occasionally he prayed two *rak'at*."

If one prays four *rak'at* before or after the noon prayers, it is preferred to pray them in two sets consisting of two *rak'at* each, although it is permissible to make them together with only one *taslim* at the end of the four *rak'at*, as the Prophet *sallallahu alehi wasallam* said: "The prayers of the night and day are (sets of) two [*rak'at*]." This was related by Abu Dawud with a *sahih* chain.

Making up the missed *sunnah* of *zuhr*: 'Aishah reports that if the Prophet missed the four *rak'at* before *zuhr*, he would pray them afterward. This is related by at-Tirmidhi who calls it *hasan ghareeb*. Ibn Majah records that she said: "If the Prophet missed the four *rak'at* before *zuhr*, he would pray them following the two *rak'at* after *zuhr*."

The preceding is concerned with making up the *sunnah* prayers that one is to pray before *zuhr*. Concerning making up the two *rak'at* after *zuhr*, we have the following reports as recorded by Ahmad.

Umm Salamah says: "The Prophet prayed *zuhr* and then he received some wealth and he sat to distribute it [and continued to do so] until the *mu'adhdhin* made the *adhan* for *'asr*. He prayed *'asr* and came to me, as it was my day, and he prayed two quick *rak'at*. I said: 'What are those two *rak'at*, O Messenger of Allah? Have you been ordered to perform them?' He said: 'No, they are the two *rak'at* that I perform after *zuhr* but I was busy distributing this wealth until the *adhan* was made for *'asr* and I hated to miss them.'" This is related by al-Bukhari, Muslim, and by Abu Dawud in somewhat different wording.

The *sunnah* of *maghrib*: It is *sunnah* to pray two *rak'at* after *maghrib*. Earlier we mentioned that Ibn 'Umar narrated that the Prophet would not miss them. As to their content, it is preferred to recite, after al-Fatihah: "Say: O Disbelievers," and "Say: He is Allah, the One," in the *sunnah* prayer after *salatul maghrib*.

Ibn Mas'ud says: "I cannot count how many times I heard the Messenger of Allah recite, in the two *rak'at* after *maghrib* and in the two *rak'at* before *fajr*. 'Say: O disbelievers,' and 'Say: He is Allah, the One.'" This is related by Ibn Majah[6] and at-Tirmidhi. The later grades it *hasan*.

It is preferred to pray this *sunnah* prayer in one's house. Mahmud ibn Labid reports that the Prophet *sallallahu alehi wasallam* prayed *maghrib* with the tribe of 'Abd al-Ashhal. After he made the *taslim*, he told them: "Perform these two *rak'at* in your houses." This is related by Ahmad,

---

[6]Actually, the *hadith* recorded by ibn Majah makes no mention of the words "after the *maghrib* prayer." (translator)

Abu Dawud, at-Tirmidhi, and an-Nasa'i. We have already mentioned that the Prophet prayed them in his house.

The **sunnah of 'Isha**: We have already mentioned the *ahadith* which record that the Prophet *sallallahu alehi wasallam* prayed two *rak'at* after *'isha.*

NONSTRESSED *SUNNAH* PRAYERS
(*AS-SUNAN GHAIR AL-MU'AKKADAH*)

We have been discussing the *sunnah* prayers which were stressed[7] by the Prophet and which he was careful not to miss. There are some other *sunnah* prayers (*al-sunan ar-ratibah*) which are commendable, but are not "stressed."

Two or four *rak'at* before *'asr*: Many *ahadith* have been related about this *sunnah* prayer and they all support each other.

Such *ahadith* include the following:

Ibn 'Umar reports that the Prophet said: "May Allah have mercy on a person who prays four *rak'at* before *'asr* prayer." This was related by Ahmad, Abu Dawud, at-Tirmidhi (who calls it *hasan*), Ibn Hibban, and Ibn Khuzaimah. The latter two hold it as *sahih*. 'Ali reports that the Prophet *sallallahu alehi wasallam* prayed four *rak'at* before *'asr* while separating every two sets of *rak'at* with salutations to the angels close to Allah, to the prophets, and to those who followed them – the believers and Muslims. This is related by Ahmad, an-Nasa'i, Ibn Majah, and at-Tirmidhi who grades it *hasan*.

As for praying only two *rak'at* at this time, this would fall under the generality of the Prophet's statement: "Between every *adhan* and *iqamah* there is a prayer."

Two *rak'at* before *maghrib*: Al-Bukhari records, from 'Abdullah ibn Mughaffal, that the Prophet said: "Pray before *maghrib*, pray before *maghrib*," and after saying it a third time, he said: "For whoever wishes to do so," not wanting the people to take it as a *sunnah*. Ibn Hibban records that the Prophet prayed two *rak'at* before *maghrib* prayer.

Muslim records that Ibn 'Abbas said: "We would pray two *rak'at* before *maghrib*, and the Prophet would see us but he would not order us to do so, nor would he prohibit us."

---

[7]"Non-stressed" *sunnah* are those actions which the Prophet *sallallahu alehi wasallam* did not do repeatedly or which others around him did and he did not object to.

Ibn Hajar says in *Fath al-Bari*: "All of the evidence points to the fact that it is preferred to say these two *rak'at* quickly like the two *rak'at* before the *salatul fajr*."

Two *rak'at* before *salatul 'isha*: 'Abdullah Ibn Mughaffal reports that the Prophet said: "Between every *adhan* and *iqamah* there is a prayer. Between every *adhan* and *iqamah* there is a prayer." And, after saying it a third time, he said: "For whoever wishes [to pray it]." This is related by the group. Ibn Hibban records from Ibn az-Zubair that the Prophet said: "There exists no obligatory prayer without there being, immediately preceding it, two *rak'at*."

Separating The Obligatory Prayer From The Supererogatory

It is preferred to make a separation between the *fard* and *nawafil* prayers after one finishes the *fard* prayer.

One of the companions of the Prophet *sallallahu alehi wasallam* reports that the Prophet prayed the afternoon prayer and right afterward a man stood up to pray. 'Umar saw him and told him: "Sit, the People of the Book were destroyed because they did not differentiate between their prayers." The Prophet said: "Well said, Ibn al-Khattab [i.e., 'Umar]." This is related by Ahmad with a *sahih* chain.

The *Witr* Prayer

Its excellence and justification: The *witr*[8] prayer is one that the Prophet *sallallahu alehi wasallam* practiced and which he encouraged others to practice. As such, praying witr comes under *as-sunnah al-mu'akkadah*.

'Ali says: "The *witr* prayer is not required like your obligatory prayers, but the Prophet would perform the *witr* prayer and say: 'O you people [followers] of the Qur'an, perform the *witr* prayer, for Allah is one and He loves the *witr*.'" This is related by Ahmad, an-Nasa'i, Abu Dawud, Ibn Majah, at-Tirmidhi who calls it *hasan*, and al-Hakim who grades it *sahih*.

The opinion of Abu Hanifah that the *witr* prayer is obligatory is a weak opinion. Ibn al-Mundhir says: "I don't know anyone who agrees with Abu Hanifah on this point."

---

[8]*Witr* in Arabic means "odd" and refers to the particular prayer described here.

Ahmad, Abu Dawud, An-Nasa'i, and Ibn Majah record that Al-Mukhdaji [a person of the Kinana tribe] heard from one of the Ansar, nicknamed Abu Muhammad, that the *witr* prayer is obligatory. He went to 'Ibadah ibn as-Samit and mentioned to him what Abu Muhammad had said. 'Ibadah observed: "Abu Muhammad is mistaken for I heard the Messenger of Allah say: 'Five prayers are ordained by Allah for his slaves. Whoever fulfills them properly without any shortcoming, he will have a pact with Allah that He will admit him into paradise. whoever does not do them, he will have no pact with Allah, and if He wills He may punish him and if He wills He may forgive him.'"

Also al-Bukhari and Muslim record from Talhah ibn 'Ubaidullah that the Prophet said: "Five prayers during the day and night have been prescribed by Allah." Hearing this a bedouin asked the Prophet: "Is there anything else upon me [in the way of prayer]?" The Prophet said: "No, unless you want to do more voluntarily."

Its time: All the scholars agree that the time for the *witr* prayer does not begin until after *salatul 'isha* and it continues until the time of *salatul fajr*.

Abu Tamim al-Jishani relates that 'Amr ibn al-'Aas was addressing the people during a Friday *Khutbah* and he said: "Abu Basra related to me that the Prophet said: 'Verily, Allah has added a prayer for you, and it is the *witr* prayer. Pray it between *salatul 'isha* and *salatul fajr*.'" Abu Tamim said: "Abu Dharr took me by my hand and we went in the mosque to Abu Basra and [Abu Dharr] said: 'Did you hear what 'Amr just said from the Messenger of Allah?' He answered: 'I heard it from the Messenger of Allah!'" This is related by Ahmad with a *sahih* chain.

Abu Mas'ud al-Ansari relates: "The Prophet *sallellahu alehi wasallam* would make the *witr* prayer in the first part of the night or the middle of it or the latter part of it." Ahmad has reported it with a sound chain.

'Abdullah ibn Abi Qais relates that he asked 'Aishah about the *witr* prayer of the Prophet *sallallahu alehi wasallam* and she said: "Sometimes he would make the *witr* prayer in the first part of the night and sometimes he would make the *witr* prayer in the latter portion of the night." Then 'Abdullah asked: "How was his recitation, audible or inaudible?" She replied: "He did both. Sometimes he would be inaudible and sometimes audible. Sometimes he would make *ghusl* and sleep and sometimes he would make ablution and sleep [i.e., when he was sexually defiled]." This is related by Abu Dawud, Ahmad, Muslim, and at-Tirmidhi. It is preferred to pray it early if one suspects that one will not wake during the latter portion of the night. It is, on the other hand, advisable to delay it if one believes that one will be able to wake up during the latter portion of the night.

If one suspects that one will not be able to perform the prayer in the latter portion of the night, it should be prayed during the early portion of the night (before sleeping).

Jabir reports that the Messenger of Allah said: "Whoever of you fears that he will not be able to wake during the latter portion [of the night], he should make the *witr* prayer during the early part [of the night]. And whoever of you believes that he will be able to wake during the latter portion of the night, he should make the *witr* prayer during that latter portion as it is the blessed time [the angels are attentive to the prayers in the last portion of the night]." This is related by Ahmad, Muslim, at-Tirmidhi, and Ibn Majah.

Jabir also narrates that the Messenger of Allah inquired of Abu Bakr: "When do you perform the *witr* prayer?" Abu Bakr replied: "In the early portion of the night after the night prayer" Then the Prophet said: "And you, O 'Umar?" He answered: "During the latter portion of the night." The Prophet said: "As for you, O Abu Bakr, you have taken the careful way. As for you, 'Umar, you have taken the way of hardship and firm will." This is related by Ahmad, Abu Dawud and al-Hakim who says it is *sahih* according to Muslim's criterion. However, the Prophet *sallallahu alehi wasallam* would pray the *witr* prayer near dawn time for it is the most blessed time, as mentioned previously.

'Aisha reports: "Out of the entire night, the Messenger of Allah would sometimes perform the *witr* prayer during the early portion; sometimes he would perform it during the middle portion; and sometimes in the latter portion of the night, just before dawn." This is related by the group.

Nevertheless, considering the possibility of losing *witr*, the Prophet advised some of his companions not to sleep until they had performed the *witr* prayer in order to be on the safe side.

Sa'd ibn Abi Waqqas would pray *salatul 'isha* in the Prophet's mosque and then would pray one *rak'ah* of *witr* without making any addition to it. The people said to him: "Abu Ishaq, do you make the *witr* with just one *rak'ah* without adding any (other *rak'ah*) to it?" He said: "Yes, for I heard the Messenger of Allah say: 'The one who does not sleep until he makes the *witr* prayer is prudent.'" This was related by Ahmad and its narrators are trustworthy.

Nature and number of rak'at: It is permissible to perform the *witr* by praying two *rak'at* [and concluding them] and then praying one *rak'ah* with a *tashahud* and *taslim*. Likewise,it is allowed to pray all the *rak'at* with two *tashahuds* and one *taslim*. One may pray a number of *rak'at*, one after another, without making any *tashahud*, save in the one before the last *rak'ah* in which case one makes the *tashahud* and then stands to perform the last *rak'ah* wherein one will make another *tashahud* and end the prayer with the *taslim*. One may also make only one *tashahud* and the *taslim*, in the last *rak'ah* of *witr*. All of that is permissible and can be traced to the Prophet.

Talking about the thirteen *rak'at* in *witr*, at-Tirmidhi says: "It has been related from the Prophet that he would perform the *witr* prayer with thirteen, nine, seven, five, three *rak'at* or one *rak'ah*."

On the other hand, Ishaq ibn Ibrahim holds: "The meaning of the statement that the Prophet prayed thirteen *rak'at* of *witr* is that during the night he would pray thirteen *rak'at* including the *witr* prayer, and so all of the night prayer came to be known as *witr*."

Ibn al-Qayyim's view is that "the clear, authentic *sunnah* is to pray the *witr* with five or seven connected *rak'at* as reported by Umm Salamah in her *hadith*. [She says] that the Prophet would perform the *witr* with five or seven *rak'at* without breaking them apart with *taslim* or any speech." This is related by Ahmad, an-Nasa'i, and Ibn Majah with a good chain.

As previously mentioned, al-Bukhari and Muslim quote 'Aishah saying that the Prophet would perform thirteen *rak'at* during the night and would make the *witr* prayer with five of them, and he would not 'sit' [during those five] except in the last *rak'ah* of them. In another *hadith*, 'Aishah reports that the Prophet *sallallahu alehi wasallam* would perform nine *rak'at* during the night and that he would not sit during them until the eighth *rak'ah* in which he would make remembrance of Allah, praising Him, and would make supplication. Then, he would stand without making the *taslim* and pray the ninth *rak'ah*, after which he would sit, make the *tashahud* and make the *taslim* in such a manner that we could hear him. Then, he would pray two *rak'at* after the *taslim* while sitting, and that would make eleven *rak'at*. When he became older and heavier, he would make the *witr* with seven *rak'at*, performing the (last) two *rak'at* like the first one. In another version from her, it is stated: "When he became older and bulkier, he would make the *witr* with seven *rak'at*, and he would not sit during them, save in the sixth and seventh *rak'ah* and he would not make the *taslim*, save in the seventh *rak'ah*." In yet another version, it is stated: "He would pray seven *rak'at* and would not sit, save in the last of them." This is related by the group.

All of the preceding *ahadith* are authentic and clear and there is no contradiction in them. As to the Prophet's statement: "The night prayer is in sets of two [*rak'at*]," it is not relevant here. This is an authentic *hadith*, and the statement that he observed *witr* with seven or five *rak'at* is equally true. Both statements confirm each other. The seven, five, nine, and one *rak'ah* constitute the *witr* prayer, for *witr* is the name given to the one *rak'ah* offered in conclusion of whatever is offered prior to it. And the *witr* of the five, seven and nine *rak'at* are all connected like the *maghrib* which is described as three connected *rak'at*. If one breaks apart the five or seven *rak'at* with two *taslim*, like in the eleven *rak'at*, it will all be called *witr* due to the last odd *rak'ah*. This is supported by the Prophet's statement: 'The night prayer is sets of two *rak'at*. If one fears the coming of the dawn, he should perform one *rak'ah*, thereby making all of them odd [*witr*].' Therefore, the Prophet's actions and statements are in agreement, each part confirming the other." The fact is that the Prophet was responding to a question about the night prayer when he said: "it is in pairs of two." He was not speaking about *witr*, for the man had asked him about night prayer, and not about the *witr*.

Recitation in the *witr*: It is permissible to recite after al-Fatihah any *surah* which one wishes to recite. 'Ali says: "There is not a part of the Qur'an that is obsolete, so make the *witr* prayer of whatever you wish from it." However, it is preferred to recite, in the first of the three *rak'at* of *witr*, al-A'la after reciting al-Fatihah. In the second *rak'ah*, it is preferred to recite al-Kafirun. In the third *rak'ah*, it is proper to recite the last three *surahs* of the Qur'an. This is narrated by Ahmad, Abu Dawud and Tirmidhi, who relate from 'Aishah, on sound authority saying: The Prophet *sallallahu alehi wasallam* would recite Ala'la in the first *rak'ah*, Al-Kafirun in the second and the last three surahs in the third *rak'ah*.

Al-Qunut in the *Witr*

It is part of *sunnah* to supplicate with *qunut*[9] in the *witr* prayer during the entire year. Ahmad, at-Tirmidhi, an-Nasa'i, Abu Dawud, Ibn Majah, and others record that al-Hassan ibn 'Ali said: "The Messenger of Allah taught me the [following] words to say in the *witr* prayer:

---

[9]*Qunut* means "being obedient" or "the act of standing." Here it refers to special supplications made in certain prayers during the standing posture. (translator)

'O Allah, guide me among those whom You have guided. Grant me safety among those whom You have granted safety. Take me into Your charge among those whom You have taken into Your charge. Bless me in what You have given me. Protect me from the evil that You have decreed, for You decree and nothing is decreed for You. And there is no humiliation for whom You take as a ward. Blessed and Exalted are You, our Lord.'"

اللهم اهدني فيمن هديت ، وعافني فيمن عافيت ، وتولني فيمن توليت ، وبارك لي فيما أعطيت وقني شر ما قضيت ، فإنك تقضي ولا يُقضى عليك ، وإنه لا يَذل من واليت ، ولا يَعز من عاديت ، تباركت ربنا وتعاليت ، وصلى الله على النبي محمد .

At-Tirmidhi grades this *hadith* as *hasan*, and says: "... nothing is known from the Prophet concerning *qunut* more authentic than that." Commenting on its status, an-Nawawi says that its chain is *sahih*. Ibn Hazm has some reservations about its soundness, but says: "This *hadith*, although it is not one that can be used as a proof, is all that we have from the Prophet, and a weak *hadith* is dearer to me than mere opinion." Ahmad says this is also the view of Abu Musa, Ibn Mas'ud, Ibn 'Abbas, al-Bara', Anas, al-Hassan al-Basri, 'Umar ibn 'Abdul'aziz, al-Thauri, Ibn al-Mubarak, and the Hanafi school. This, an-Nawawi says, gives credibility to the report.

Ash-Shaf'i and others are of the opinion that the *qunut* in the *witr* prayer should be made during the latter half of the month of Ramadan. This is based on what Abu Dawud records that, 'Umar ibn al-Khattab convoked the people in prayer, under the leadership of Ubayy ibn Ka'b, and they prayed together for twenty nights, and he did not make the *qunut* except for during the latter half of the month of Ramadan. It is moreover related that Muhammad ibn Nasr asked Sa'id ibn Jubair about the *qunut* in the *witr* prayer. Sa'id answered: "'Umar sent an army that suffered serious setback, which caused 'Umar to be alarmed, so, when it was the latter half of Ramadan, he made the *qunut* to supplicate for them."

How to perform the *qunut*: It is permissible to make the *qunut* before going into *ruku'* (bowing), or it may be recited when one stands up straight after the *ruku'*. Humaid says: "I asked Anas: 'Is the *qunut* before or after the *ruku'*?' He said: 'We would do it before or after.'" This was related by Ibn Majah and Muhammad ibn Nasr. In *Fath al-Bari*, Ibn Hajar comments that its chain is faultless.

If one makes the *qunut* before the *ruku'*, one should make the *takbir* and raise one's hands after the recital, and similarly make another *takbir* after the *qunut*, and then bow. This has been related from some companions. Some scholars hold that it is preferable to raise one's hands in supplication during the *qunut*, while others disagree.

As to wiping face with hands after the *qunut*, al-Baihaqi writes: "It is preferred not to do so and to confine one's self to what the early generations did. They raised their hands but did not wipe their faces during the prayer."

Supplications after the *witr*: It is preferred for a person to say after the *taslim*: "Glory be to the Master, the Holy," three times aloud, saying the third time: "Lord of the angels and the souls." Abu Dawud and an-Nasa'i record that Ubayy ibn Ka'b said: "The Prophet *sallallahu alehi wasallam* would recite al-A'la and al-Kafirun in the *witr* prayer. When he made the *taslim*, he would say:

'Glory be to the Master, the Holy,'

سبحان الملك القدوس .

three times, prolonging the third repetition and saying it aloud." This is the wording in which an-Nasa'i recorded it. Ad-Daraqutni has the addition: "And he would say,

'Lord of the angels and the spirits.'"

رب الملائكة والروح .

He would then make supplications and, according to what Ahmad, an-Nasa'i, Abu Dawud, Ibn Majah, and at-Tirmidhi record from 'Ali, he would say at the end of his *witr*:

"O Allah, I seek refuge in Your pleasure from your anger. And I seek refuge in Your granting well-being from Your punishment. And I seek refuge in You from You. I cannot reckon Your praise: You are as You have praised Yourself."

اللهم إنى أعوذ برضاك من سخطك ، وأعوذ بمعافاتك من عقوبتك ، وأعوذ بك منك ، لا أحصى ثناء عليك ؛ أنت كما أثنيت على نفسك .

Prohibition of two *witr* prayers in one night: Whoever has performed the *witr* prayer and then wishes to do some more, he may do so but he is not to repeat the *witr*.

Abu Dawud, an-Nasa'i, and at-Tirmidhi have recorded from 'Ali that he heard the Messenger of Allah say: "There are no two *witr* prayers in one night." At-Tirmidhi grades it *hasan*.

'Aishah relates that the Prophet would make the *taslim* in such a manner that we could hear him and then, he would pray two *rak'at* while sitting. This is related by Muslim.

Umm Salamah also narrates that he prayed two *rak'at* while sitting, after the *witr* prayer. This was related by Ahmad, Abu Dawud, at-Tirmidhi, and others.

Making up a missed *witr*: According to al-Baihaqi and al-Hakim, the majority of the scholars maintain that it is correct to make *qada'* for a missed *witr* prayer. Al-Hakim grades the following report by Abu Hurairah as *sahih* according to the criterion of al-Bukhari and Muslim.

Abu Hurairah reports that the Prophet said: "If the morning approaches, and you have yet to pray *witr*, you should pray the *witr* prayer." Abu Dawud records from Abu Sa'id al-Khudri that the Prophet said: "If one of you sleeps [past the time of] the *witr* prayer or he forgets it, he should pray it when he remembers it." Al-'Iraqi says that the chain of this hadith is *sahih*.

Ahmad and at-Tabarani record with a *hasan* chain that the Prophet *sallallahu alehi wasallam* would perform the *witr* prayer in the morning [if, for some reason, he had missed it during the night].

Generally speaking, there is a difference of opinion over what time it may be made up. The Hanafi school holds it should be performed during those times in which it is not forbidden to observe prayers. The followers of Shaf'i say that it may be made up during any time of the night or day, while according to Malik and Ahmad a missed *witr* prayer is to be made up for after the dawn.

Al-Qunut in the five prayers

It is legitimate to recite the *qunut* aloud in any of the five daily prayers at those times when Muslims are faced with calamities. Ibn 'Abbas relates that the Messenger of Allah *sallallahu alehi wasallam* made *qunut* consecutively for one month in the *zuhr*, *'asr*, *maghrib*, *'isha*, and *fajr* prayers. At the end of every prayer, after saying:

"Allah hears him who praises Him" سمـع الله لمن حمـده

in the last *rak'ah*, he would supplicate against Re'l, Dhakwan, and 'Usiyyah[10] of Banu Sulaim, and the people behind him would say 'Ameen'. This is related by Ahmad and by Abu Dawud adding that these three had killed the emissaries that the Prophet *sallallahu alehi wasallam*

---

[10]These are the clans who claimed to have embraced Islam and the Prophet sent to them seventy teachers whom they treacherously killed.

had sent to them. 'Ikrimah says: "That was the begining of the *qunut*."

Abu Hurairah reports that whenever the Prophet *sallallahu alehi wasallam* wanted to supplicate against or for someone, he would make *qunut* after going into *ruku'*. Sometimes, he would say: "Allah hears him who praises Him. Our Lord, to you is the praise. O Allah! Save al-Walid ibn al-Walid and Salamah ibn Hisham and 'Iyash ibn Abi Rabi'ah and the oppressed [and weak] believers. O Allah, put hardship and pressure on the tribe of Mudhar and give them years of famine like those during the time of Yusuf." He would say this aloud in some of the prayers. Also in the dawn prayer, he would say: "Oh Allah, curse so and so," cursing two tribes of Arabs until Allah revealed: "It is no concern at all of thee [Muhammad] whether He relent toward them or punish them, for they are evildoers."[11] This is related by Ahmad and al-Bukhari.

Al-Qunut in salatul fajr: It is not correct to make *qunut* in the dawn prayer except during times of calamity, in which case it may be made in any of the five daily prayers. Abu Malik al-Ashja'i said: "My father prayed behind the Prophet *sallallahu alehi wasallam* when he was sixteen years old, and he prayed behind Abu Bakr, 'Umar, and 'Uthman. I asked him, 'Did they make the *qunut*?' He said, 'No, son, it is something that has been innovated.'" This is related by Ahmad, an-Nasa'i, Ibn Majah, and at-Tirmidhi who calls it *sahih*. Anas said that the Prophet *sallallahu alehi wasallam* would not make the *qunut* in *fajr* unless he was supplicating for a people or supplicating against a people. This is related by Ibn Hibban, al-Khatib, and Ibn Khuzaimah who said it is *sahih*.[12]

It is also related that az-Zubair, Abu Bakr, 'Umar, and 'Uthman did not make the *qunut* in the dawn prayer. This is the opinion of the Hanafiyyah, the Hanbaliyyah, Ibn al-Mubarak, al-Thauri, and Ishaq. The followers of Shaf'i are of the opinion that the *qunut* is to be made after the *ruku'* of the second *rak'ah* in the obligatory dawn prayer. This opinion is based on the following two reports. Ibn Sireen narrates that Anas ibn Malik was asked: "Did the Prophet make the *qunut* in the dawn prayer?" He answered: "Yes." They asked him: "Before the *ruku'* or after it?" He replied: "After it." This is related by the group save at-Tirmidhi.

There is a report from Anas which says: "The Messenger of Allah *sallallahu alehi wasallam* did not stop making *qunut* during the dawn prayer until he left this world." This is related by Ahmad, al-Bazzar, ad-Daraqutni, al-Baihaqi, and al-Hakim who says it is *sahih*.

However, there remains some doubt concerning this evidence since the *qunut* which they asked Anas about, as is clear in the narrations of al-

---

[11]Qur'an 3:129
[12]Ibn Hibban is the only one who recorded the words, "in the dawn prayer."

Bukhari and Muslim, was the *qunut* during the time of calamities. Concerning the latter *hadith* (the one mentioned in support of their stand), in its chain of narrators there is Abu Ja'far ar-Razi who is not a credible source and, thus, one cannot build a case upon his *hadith*. How could it be that the Messenger of Allah never stopped performing this *qunut* until his death, and yet, the rightly guided caliphs did not perform it? It is even confirmed that Anas himself did not make the *qunut* in the dawn prayer! If we must accept this latter *hadith* as authentic, it would mean that the Prophet always made supplications and remembrance (*dhikr*), after the *ruku'*, until his death. This would also come under *qunut* and, in this sense, it would be more befitting. Still, this is one of the matters in which it is acceptable to have differences of opinion, and one may either do it or leave· it. The best guidance is that of Muhammad *sallallahu alehi wasllam*.

The Late Night Prayer
(*qiyam al-Layil*)

Its excellence and merit from the Qur'an: Allah ordered his Messenger to perform *salatul tahajjud*:[13]

"And some part of the night, awake for prayer, a largess for thee. It may be that thy Lord will raise thee to a praised position."[14]

﴿ومن الليل فتهجد به نافلة لك عسى أن يبعثك ربك مقاماً محموداً﴾

This order, although it was specifically directed to the Prophet, also refers to all the Muslims since the Prophet is their example and guide in all such matters.

Those who regularly perform the *tahajjud* prayers are the Righteous and are more deserving of Allah's bounty and mercy. Allah says: "Lo! Those who keep from evil will dwell amid gardens and watersprings, taking that which their Lord gives them. For, lo, they were doers of good. They used to sleep but little of the night and before the dawning of each day would seek forgiveness."[15]

Allah praised and complemented the deeds of those who perform the late-night prayers. "The slaves of the Beneficent are they who walk upon the earth in humbleness, and when the ignorant address them, they say: 'Peace' and they who spend the night prostrating before their Lord and

---

[13]A supererogatory prayer offered between 'isha and fajr, preferably in the last one third of the night.
[14]Qur'an 17:79
[15]Qur'an 51:15-18

standing" [al-Furqan: 63-64].

Allah bears witness to their belief in His signs. He says: "Only those believe in Our revelations who, when they are reminded of them, fall down prostrate and hymn the praise of their Lord and they are not scornful: who forsake their beds to cry unto their Lord in fear and hope and spend of what We have bestowed on them. No soul knows what is kept hidden for them of joy as a reward for what they used to do."[16]

Allah proclaims that those who do not possess these qualities cannot be treated as equal to those who possess them: "Is he who pays adoration in the watches of the night, prostrate and standing, aware of the Hereafter and hoping for the mercy of his Lord equal to a disbeliever? Say: 'Are those who know equal with those who know not?' But only men of understanding will pay heed."[17]

Ahadith regarding _Tahajjud_: The preceding section was primarily concerned with what Allah says about those who perform *salatul tahajjud*. There also exist a number of *ahadith* that reinforce the importance of *tahajjud*.

'Abdullah ibn as-Salam reports: "When the Prophet *sallallahu alehi wasallam* came to Medinah, the people gathered around him and I was one of them. I looked at his face and understood that it was not the face of a liar. The first words I heard him say were: 'O people, spread the salutations, feed the people, keep the ties of kinship, and pray during the night while the others sleep and you will enter paradise in peace.'" This is related by al-Hakim, Ibn Majah, and at-Tirmidhi who calls it *hasan sahih*.

Salman al-Farsi relates that the Prophet *sallallahu alehi wasallam* said: "Observe the night prayer, it was the practice of the rightous before you and it brings you closer to your Lord and it is penance for evil deeds and erases the sins and repells disease from the body."

Sahl ibn Sa'd reports: "Gabriel came to the Prophet *sallallahu alehi wasallam* and said: 'O Muhammad, live as long as you like, for you are to die. Do whatever deed you wish, for you are to be rewarded. Love whomever you wish, for you are to be parted. And know that the honor of the believer is in the night prayer and his glory is being free from want from the people.'"

Abu ad-Darda' reports that the Prophet said: "Three people are loved by Allah, and He laughs for them and He grants them glad tidings. [The first is] a man who fights behind a group that flees and does so with his own soul for Allah's sake, regardless of whether he is killed or he is aided by

---

[16]Qur'an 32:15-17
[17]Qur'an 39:9

Allah and made victorious. Allah says: 'Look to my slave there who is patient with his life for My sake.' [The second is] the one who has a beautiful wife and a soft bed and rises during the night. Allah says: 'He leaves his desires and remembers Me and if he wished he would sleep.' [The third] is a person who is traveling with a group and they pass the night awake and then sleep, but he still observes his prayer in hardship or ease."

Etiquettes of Late Night Prayer: The following acts are *sunnah* for one who wishes to perform the *tahajjud* prayers. Upon going to sleep, one should make the intention to perform the *tahajjud* prayers. Abu ad-Darda' relates that the Prophet *sallallahu alehi wasallam* said: "Whoever goes to his bed with the intention of getting up and praying during the night, and sleep overcomes him until the morning comes, he will have recorded for him what he had intended, and his sleep will be a charity for him from his Lord." This is related by an-Nasa'i and ibn Majah with a *sahih* chain. Upon waking, one should wipe one's face, use a toothstick, and look to the sky and make the supplication which has been reported from the Prophet *sallallahu alehi wasallam*:

"There is no God but Thee, Glory be to Thee, I seek forgiveness from You for my sins, and I ask for your mercy. O Allah, increase my knowledge and let my heart not swerve after You have guided me, and bestow mercy upon me from Thyself. All praise be to Allah who has given us back life after our death and unto Him is the resurrection."

لا إله إلا أنت سبحانك ، أستغفرك لذنبى وأسألك رحمتك ، اللهم زدنى علماً ولا تزغ قلبى بعد إذ هديتنى وهب لى من لدنك رحمة إنك أنت الوهاب . الحمد لله الذى أحيانا بعد ما أماتنا وإليه النشور .

Then, one should recite the last ten *'ayat* of al-'Imran, starting with, "Lo! In the creation of the heavens and the earth and [in] the difference of night and day are tokens (of His sovereignty) for men of understanding."[18] Then one should say,

"O Allah, to You belongs the praise. You are the Light of the heavens and the earth and what is therein. And to You belongs the praise. You are the truth and Your promise is true. And the meeting with You is true.

اللهم لك الحمد ، أنت نور السموات والأرض ومن فيهن ، ولك الحمد ، أنت قيم السموات والأرض ومن فيهن ، ولك الحمد ، أنت الحق ، ووعدك الحق ،

---

[18]Qur'an 3:190-200

And the paradise is true. And the Fire is true. And the prophets are true. And Muhammad is true. And the Hour is true. O Allah, to You have I submitted. And in You have I believed. And in You have I put my trust. And to You have I turned. And by You I argue. And to You do I turn for my decisions. Forgive me of my former and latter sins, and those done in private and those done in public. You are Allah, there is no God besides Thee."

، ولقاؤك حق ، والجنة حق ، والنار حق ،
والنبيون حق ، ومحمد حق ، والســاعـة
حق. اللهم لك أسلمت ، وبك آمنت ،
وعليك توكلت ، وإليك أنبت ، وبــك
خاصمت ، وإليك حاكمت ، فاغفر لى ما
قدمت وما أخرت ، ما أسررت وما أعلنت
، أنت الله لا إله إلا أنت.

One should begin *Qiyam al-Layil* with two quick *rak'at* and then one may pray whatever one wishes after that. 'Aishah says: "When the Prophet prayed during the late-night, he would begin his prayers with two quick *rak'at*." Both of these reports are related by Muslim.

One should wake up one's family. Abu Hurairah reports that the Prophet said: "May Allah bless the man who gets up during the night to pray and wakes up his wife and who, if she refuses to get up, sprinkles water on her face. And may Allah bless the woman who gets up during the night to pray and wakes up her husband and who, if he refuses sprinkles water on his face." The Prophet *sallallahu alehi wasallam* also said: "If a man wakes his wife and prays during the night or they pray two *rak'at* together, they will be recorded among those (men and women) who (constantly) make remembrance of Allah." This is related by Abu Dawud and others with a *sahih* chain.

Umm Salamah narrates that the Prophet *sallallahu alehi wasallam* got up during the night and said:

"Glory be to Allah. What trials are descended with the night. And what has descended of treasures. Who will waken the lady occupants of the rooms (i.e., his wives) for prayers; how many a well dressed in this world will be naked in the hereafter."
This is related by al-Bukhari.

سبحان الله ، ماذا أنزل الليلة من الفتنة ،
ماذا أنزل من الخزائن ، من يوقظ صواحب
الحجرات ، يارُب كاسية فى الدنيا عارية
يوم القيامة.

Al-Bukhari and Muslim record that the Messenger of Allah asked 'Ali and Fatimah: "Do you not pray [during the night]?" 'Ali said: "O Messenger of Allah, we are in Allah's hands. If He wishes to make us get up, we get up." The Prophet turned away when he said that. Then, they could hear him striking his thigh and saying: "Verily, man disputes a lot." This is related by al-Bukhari and Muslim.

One should stop praying and sleep if one becomes very sleepy. 'Aishah reports that the Messenger of Allah said: "When one of you gets up during the night for prayer and his Qur'anic recital becomes confused to the extent that he does not know what he says, he should lie down." This is related by Muslim.

Anas narrates that the Messenger of Allah entered the mosque and saw a rope stretching between two posts. He asked: "What is this?" The people told him that it was for Zainab [bint Jahsh] who, when she became tired or weary, held it (to keep standing for the prayer). The Prophet said: "Remove the rope. You should pray as long as you feel active, and when you get tired or weary, you should lie down to rest." This is related by al-Bukhari and Muslim.

One should not overburden one's self with the night prayer and should only pray it to the extent that is reasonable, and not leave that practice unless there is some great need to do so. 'Aishah reports that the Messenger of Allah said: "Do (good) deeds according to your capacity, for by Allah, Allah does not weary from giving rewards unless you get tired of doing good deeds." This is related by al-Bukhari and Muslim.

Al-Bukhari and Muslim also relate from 'Aishah that the Messenger of Allah was asked: "What is the most loved deed to Allah?" He answered: "One that is performed constantly even if it is a small deed." And Muslim recorded that 'Aishah said: "The Messenger of Allah was constant in his deeds, and if he did something, he would do it consistently."

'Abdullah ibn 'Umar reports that the Messenger of Allah said: "O 'Abdullah, do not become like so-and-so who used to make the *tahajjud* prayers and then he stopped praying it." This is related by al-Bukhari and Muslim.

Al-Bukhari and Muslim also record, on the authority of 'Abdullah ibn Mas'ud, that it was mentioned to the Prophet *sallallahu alehi wasallam* that a man slept until the morning. [Thereupon] he said: "Satan has urinated into the ears of that person." They also record from Salim ibn 'Abdullah ibn 'Umar, from his father, that the Messenger of Allah said to his father, "Abdullah would be a good man if he would pray the *tahajjud* prayers." Salim said: "After that, 'Abdullah would not sleep during the night save for a small amount at a time."

The recommended time for *tahajjud*: *Salatul Layil* may be performed in the early part of the night, the middle part of the night, or the latter part of the night, but after the obligatory *salatul 'isha*.

While describing the *salah* of the Prophet *sallallahu alehi wasallam*, Anas would say: "If we wanted to see him praying during the night, we could see him praying. If we wanted to see him sleeping during the night, we could see him sleeping. And sometimes he would fast for so many days that we thought he would not leave fasting throughout that month. And sometimes he would not fast (for so many days) that we thought he would not fast during that month." This is related by Ahmad, al-Bukhari, and an-Nasa'i.

Commenting on this subject, Ibn Hajar says: "There was no specific time in which the Prophet *sallallahu alehi wasallam* would perform his late night prayer; but he would do whatever was easiest for him."

Best time for *tahajjud*: It is best to delay this prayer to the last third portion of the night. Abu Hurairah reports that the Messenger of Allah said: "Our Lord descends to the lowest heaven during the last third of the night, inquiring: 'Who will call on Me so that I may respond to him? Who is asking something of Me so I may give it to him? Who is asking for My forgiveness so I may forgive him?'" This is related by the group.

'Amr ibn Abasah reports that he heard the Prophet say: "The closest that a slave comes to his Lord is during the middle of the latter portion of the night. If you can be among those who remember Allah, the Exalted One, at that time then do so." This is related by al-Hakim who grades it *sahih* according to Muslim's standards, and at-Tirmidhi calls it *hasan sahih*. An-Nasa'i and Ibn Khuzaimah also recorded it.

Abu Muslim asked Abu Dharr: "Which late-night prayer is the best?" He said: "I asked the Messenger of Allah the same that you asked me and he said, 'The (one done during) middle of the latter half of the night, and very few do it.'" This is related by Ahmad with a good chain.

'Abdullah ibn 'Amr reports that the Prophet said: "The most beloved fast to Allah is the fast of David. And the most beloved prayer to Allah is the prayer of David. He would sleep half of the night and then pray during the next third of the night and then sleep during the last sixth of the night. And he would fast one day and not fast the next." This is related by the group except at-Tirmidhi.

The number of *rak'at* to be performed during *tahajjud*: The *tahajjud* prayer does not entail a specific number of *rak'at* which must be performed nor is there any maximum limit which has to be performed. It would be fulfilled even if one just prayed one *rak'ah* of *witr* after the obligatory night prayer.

Samurah ibn Jundub says: "The Messenger of Allah ordered us to pray during the night, a little or a lot, and to make the last of the prayer the *witr* prayer." This is related by at-Tabarani and al-Bazzar.

Anas relates that the Messenger of Allah said: "Prayer in my mosque is equal to ten thousand prayers [elsewhere]. And prayer in the inviolable mosque is equivalent to one hundred thousand prayers [elsewhere]. And prayer in the battlefield is equivalent to one million prayers [elsewhere]. And what is more than all of that is two *rak'at* by a slave [of Allah] during the middle of the night." This is reported by Abu ash-Shaikh, Ibn Hibban in his work *ath-Thawab*, and al-Mundhiri, in his book *at-Targhib wat-Tarhib*, is silent about it.

Iyas ibn Mu'awiyyah al-Mazni reports that the Prophet *sallallahu alehi wasallam* said: "The night prayer should certainly be performed even if it is for the length of time that it takes one to milk a sheep. And whatever is after the obligatory *'isha* is of the *tahajjud.*" This is related by at-Tabarani, and all of its narrators are trustworthy save Muhammad ibn Ishaq.

Ibn 'Abbas relates: "I mentioned the *tahajjud* prayer and some of the people said that the Prophet *sallallahu alehi wasallam* said: 'It may be half of the night, a third of the night, a fourth of the night or a fraction of the time for milking a camel or a sheep.'"[19]

Ibn 'Abbas also narrates that the Prophet ordered them and encouraged them to make the *tahajjud* prayer to the extent that he said: "You should perform *salatul layil* even if it is just one *rak'ah.*" This is related by at-Tabarani in *al-Kabir* and *al-Awsat*.

It is preferable to pray eleven or thirteen *rak'at*. One may choose between praying them all together or to separate them. 'Aishah says: "The Messenger of Allah never prayed more than eleven *rak'at*, during Ramadan or otherwise. He would pray four *rak'at*, and don't ask about how excellent they were or how lengthy they were. Then, he would pray four *rak'at*, and don't ask about how excellent they were or how lengthy they were. Then, he would pray three *rak'at*. I asked: 'O Messenger of Allah, do you sleep before praying *witr*?' he replied: 'O 'Aishah, my eyes sleep but my heart does not sleep.'" This is recorded by al-Bukhari and Muslim who also record that al-Qasim ibn Muhammad said that he heard 'Aishah say: "The Messenger of Allah's prayer during the night would be ten *rak'at* and then he would make *witr* with one *rak'ah*."

Making qada' for the missed tahajjud: Muslim records that 'Aishah said: "If the Prophet *sallallahu alehi wasallam* missed the late-night prayers due to pain or anything else, he would pray twelve *rak'at* during the day."

'Umar reports that the Prophet *sallallahu alehi wasallam* said: "Whoever sleeps past his full portion [of the late-night prayers] or part of them, he

---

[19]According to Al-Mundhiri the Arabic term "*fawaq*" here means the time one takes in touching and pressing teats of a dromedary or a sheep etc., while milking them.

should pray between the dawn and noon prayers and it would be recorded for him as if he had prayed during the night." This is related by the group except for al-Bukhari.

THE SPECIAL PRAYERS DURING THE MONTH OF RAMADAN

The legality of the *Tarawih*: The specific prayers during the month of Ramadan, which are known as *tarawih*, are *sunnah* for both men and women, and they are to be performed after the obligatory *'isha* and before the performance of the *witr*. They should be prayed in sets of two *rak'at* each. It is allowed to pray them after *witr*; though, this is not the best thing to do. They may be performed until the end of the night.

Abu Hurairah reports that the Prophet *sallallahu alehi wasallam* would encourage people to perform the special prayers during Ramadan without commanding them as obligatory and he said: "Whoever prays during the nights of Ramadan [*tarawih*] with a firm belief and hoping for reward, all of his previous sins would be forgiven." This is related by the group.

'Aishah says: "The Prophet offered *salah* in the mosque and many people prayed with him. The next day he did the same and more people prayed with him. Then the people gathered on the third night but, the Prophet did not come out to them. In the morning, he said to them: 'Surely I saw what you did, and nothing prevented me from coming out to you, save that I feared that [*that prayer*] would be made obligatory upon you.' And that was during Ramadan." This is related by the group except for at-Tirmidhi.

The number of *rak'at* of *Tarawih*: 'Aishah reported that the Prophet *sallallahu alehi wasallam* would not pray more than eleven *rak'at* during Ramadan or otherwise. This is related by the group.

Ibn Khuzaimah and Ibn Hibban have recorded in their *sahihs* on the authority of Jabir that the Prophet prayed eight *rak'at* and the *witr* prayer with the companions. Then, the next day, the people waited for him but he did not come out to them.

Abu Ya'la and at-Tabarani record, with a *hasan* chain, from Jabir that Ubayy ibn Ka'b came to the Prophet *sallallahu alehi wasallam* and said: "O Messenger of Allah, I have done something last night," (i.e., during Ramadan). The Prophet said: 'And what was that, O Ubayy?' He said: The women in my house said, 'We don't recite Qur'an [well or much] so can we pray behind you?' I prayed eight *rak'at* and the *witr* prayer with them.

The Messenger of Allah *sallallahu alehi wasallam* was pleased with that and did not say anything."

This is the *sunnah* that has been related from the Messenger of Allah and nothing besides that is authentic. It is also true that during the time of 'Umar, 'Uthman, and 'Ali the people prayed twenty *rak'at*[20], and this is the opinion of the majority of the jurists of the Hanafi and Hanbali schools as well as that of Dawud.

At-Tirmidhi says: "Most of the people of knowledge follow what has been related from 'Umar and 'Ali and other companions of the Prophet, [i.e., that they prayed] twenty *rak'at*. And this is the opinion of al-Thauri, Ibn al-Mubarak, and ash-Shaf'i. And so I found the people of Makkah praying twenty *rak'at*."

Some of the scholars are of the opinion that the *sunnah* is eleven *rak'at*, including *witr*, and it is also preferred to pray the remainder [of the twenty *rak'at*].

Al-Kamal ibn al-Hamam says: "The evidence indicates that the *sunnah* of the twenty *rak'at* is what the Prophet *sallallahu alehi wasallam* himself did and then he stopped out of fear that it would become something obligatory (for his followers), therefore, the rest of the *rak'at* are only preferred. It is however, confirmed that he only prayed eleven *rak'at*, including the *witr*, as is stated in the two *sahihs*. According to the scholars, the *sunnah* is eight *rak'at* while it is preferred to pray twelve *rak'at*."

Praying *tarawih* in congregation: It is allowed to pray *tarawih* of the month of Ramadan in a congregation just as it is allowed to pray them on an individual basis. The majority of the scholars, however, prefer to pray them in congregation The Prophet *sallallahu alehi wasallam*, as stated earlier, prayed *tarawih* in congregation with the Muslims but he discontinued since he feared that it would be made obligatory.

'Umar was the one who convoked the Muslims to pray *tarawih* behind one imam. Abdurahman ibn Abdulqari reports: "One night during Ramadan, I went with 'Umar to the mosque and the people were praying in different groups. Some were praying by themselves and others were praying in small groups. 'Umar said: 'I think it would be better if I gathered them under one imam .' Then he did so and appointed Ubayy ibn Ka'b as the leader of the prayer. Then I went out with him on another night and all

---

[20]Malik is of the view that *tarawih* is thirty six *rak'at* without *witr*. Al-Zarqani says: And Ibn Hibban mentions that in the beginning *tarawih* prayer was eleven *rak'at*. As they prolonged recitation in them the people found it tiresome. So they shortened the recitation and increased the number of *rak'at*: they prayed twenty *rak'at* with moderate recitation. This did not include *witr*. Later on recitation was still further shortened and they prayed thirty six *rak'at* besides *witr*

the people were praying behind one imam and 'Umar said: 'What a good innovation (*bid'ah*) this is,' but, it is better to sleep and delay it until the latter portion of the night." The people (however) prayed it at the beginning of the night. This is related by al-Bukhari, Ibn Khuzaimah, al-Baihaqi, and others.

The recitation of the Qur'an in *tarawih*: There is no particular *sunnah* regarding the recitation during *salat at-tarawih*. It is related that some people of the early generations would pray with two hundred *'ayyahs* or so and the people would be leaning on staffs due to the protracted standing during the *salah*. They would not leave their prayers until shortly before dawn and some of them would rush their servants to prepare food for them fearing that dawn may break soon. They would recite al-Baqarah in eight *rak'at* and, if they would complete it in twelve *rak'at*, they would consider their prayers to have been very short.

Ibn Qudamah says: "Ahmad said: 'Recite of the Qur'an what is easy for the people and do not be hard upon them, especially during the short nights [i.e., during the summer].'"

[On the same subject], Al-Qadi says: 'It is not preferred to recite less than the entire Qur'an during the month: in this way, the people will be able to hear the whole Qur'an. Do not recite more than one reading of the Qur'an as this may be hard upon the people. [While reciting], consideration should be given to the condition of the people. If the people concur that they would prefer a long recital, that would be best.'

Likewise, Abu Dharr said: 'We prayed with the Prophet *sallallahu alehi wasallam* until we feared that we would miss the pre-dawn meal. And the imam would recite two hundred *'ayyahs*.'"

THE DUHA PRAYER (*SALATUL DUHA*)

Its excellence: Many *ahadith* describe the excellence of the *duha* prayer.

Abu Dharr reports that the Prophet *sallallahu aleihi wasallam* said: "Charity is required from every part of your body daily. Every saying of 'Glory be to Allah' is charity. Every saying of 'Praise be to Allah' is charity. Every saying of 'There is no God but Allah' is charity. Every saying of 'Allah is the Greatest' is charity. Ordering the good is charity. Eradicating the evil is charity. And what suffices for that (as a charity) are the two *rak'at* of *duha*." This is related by Ahmad, Muslim, and Abu Dawud.

Ahmad and Abu Dawud record from Buraidah that the Prophet *sallallahu alehi wasallam* said: "In a human (body) there are 360 joints and man must make a charity for each one." The people said: "Who can do that, O Messenger of Allah?" He responded: "One may cover the mucus that one finds in the mosque or remove something harmful from the road. If one could not do that, he could pray two rak'at of duha and that will be sufficient for him."

Talking of the legal import of these ahadith, ash-Shaukani says: "These two ahadith point to the greatness, excellence, and importance of the duha prayer, stressing its legality as its two rak'at suffice for 360 charities. Something like this should be performed regularly and persistently. The ahadith also establish the importance of saying 'Glory be to Allah', 'Praise be to Allah', and 'There is no God but Allah.' And [the importance of] ordering the good, eradicating the evil, removing the spittle, removing what is harmful from the path, and such other acts that will fulfill what is required of a person of daily charities."

An-Nawas ibn Sam'an relates that the Prophet sallallahu alehi wasallam said: "Allah said: 'Son of Adam, do not fail in performing four rak'at in the early day as it will be sufficient for the latter part of the day.'" This is related by al-Hakim and at-Tabarani and its narrators are trustworthy. Ahmad, at-Tirmidhi, Abu Dawud, and an-Nasa'i relate it on the authority of Na'im al-Ghatfani with a good chain. At-Tirmidhi's wording is: "Son of Adam, pray four rak'at for Me in the early day and it will be sufficient for you for the latter part of the day."

'Abdullah ibn 'Amr says: "The Messenger of Allah sent an expedition and they obtained lots of booty and returned quickly. The people talked about their quick victory, abundant booty, and quick return. At this the Messenger of Allah said: 'Shall I not guide you to a closer battle, a greater booty and a quicker return? Whoever makes wudu' and then goes to the mosque to pray duha, that is the closer battle, better booty, and quicker return.'" This is related by Ahmad and at-Tabarani. Abu Ya'la has something similar to it.

Abu Hurairah says: "My friend [the Messenger of Allah] advised me to do three things: fasting three days of every month, praying the duha prayer, and praying the witr prayer before I sleep." This is related by al-Bukhari and Muslim.

Anas says: "During a journey, I saw the Messenger of Allah pray eight rak'at in the early day. When he finished, he said: 'I prayed my prayer wishing and fearing. I asked my Lord for three things and He gave me two and withheld one. I asked Him not to put my ummah to trial by famine and He granted that request. And I asked that they would not be overtaken by their enemies and He granted that request. And I asked that they not be split into groups and parties and He refused that request.'" This is related by Ahmad, an-Nasa'i, al-Hakim, and ibn Khuzaimah who classifies it as sahih.

A Prized Prayer

Salatul duha is a prized prayer and whoever wishes to earn reward should pray it, while there is no blame upon the one who does not pray it.

Abu Sa'id reports: "The Prophet *sallallahu alehi wasallam* would pray *duha* until we thought he would never abandon it. And he would abandon it to the point that we thought he would no longer perform it." This is related by at-Tirmidhi who says it is *hasan*.

Recommended time for the *duha* prayer: The time for *duha* begins when the sun is about a spear's length above the horizon and it continues until the sun reaches its meridian. It is preferred to delay it until the sun has risen high and the day has become hot.

Zaid ibn Arqam relates: "The Messenger of Allah *sallallahu alehi wasallam* went to the people of Quba', and they were performing *duha*, and he said: 'The prayer of devotion should be observed when the young weaned camels feel the heat of the sun.'" This is related by Ahmad, Muslim, and at-Tirmidhi.

Its number of *rak'at*: The minimum number of *rak'ah* to be prayed is two, as was mentioned in the *hadith* of Abu Dharr. The most that the Prophet *sallallahu alehi wasallam* performed was eight *rak'at*, whereas, the most he mentioned was twelve *rak'at*. Some people, such as Abu Ja'far at-Tabari, al-Mulaimi, and ar-Ruwyani, who subscribes to the Shafi' school, say there is no maximum limit to the number of *rak'at* that one may perform for *duha*.

Al-'Iraqi says, in the commentary on *Sunan at-Tirmidhi*: "None of the companions or followers are known to have restricted it to twelve *rak'at*." As-Syuti agrees with it.

Sa'id ibn Mansur records that al-Hassan was asked: "Did the companions perform it?" He answered: "Yes...some of them would pray two *rak'at* and some of them would pray four *rak'at*. And some of them would continue until half the [early] day [had passed]."

Ibrahim an-Nakha'i reports that al-Aswad ibn Yazid was asked: "How many *rak'at* are to be prayed for *duha*?" He answered: "As many as you wish."

Umm Hani narrates that the Prophet *sallallahu alehi wasallam* prayed eight *rak'at* of *duha* and made the *taslim* after every two *rak'at*. This is related by Abu Dawud with a *sahih* chain.

'Aishah reports: "The Prophet *sallallahu alehi wasallam* would pray four *rak'at* for *duha* and would add to it whatever Allah willed." This is related by Ahmad, Muslim, and ibn Majah.

SALATUL ISTIKHARAH

It is a *sunnah* that, if one must choose between permissible alternatives, one may pray two non-obligatory *rak'at*, even if they are of the regular *sunnah* prayers or a prayer for entering the mosque, and so on, during any time of the day or night, and to recite therein whatever one wishes of the Qur'an after reciting al-Fatihah. Then one praises Allah and sends salutations to the Prophet *sallallahu alehi wasallam* and recites the following supplication which has been recorded by al-Bukhari in Jabir's narration: "The Prophet *sallallahu alehi wasallam* would teach us *al-istikhara* for all of our affairs as he would teach us a *surah* from the Qur'an. He said: 'If one of you is deliberating over an act, he should pray two non-obligatory *rak'at* and say:

"O Allah, I consult You as You are All-Knowing and I appeal to You to give me power as You are Omnipotent, I ask You for Your great favor, for You have power and I do not, and You know all of the hidden matters. O Allah! If you know that this matter (then he should mention it) is good for me in my religion, my livelihood, and for my life in the Hereafter, (or he said: 'for my present and future life,') then make it (easy) for me. And if you know that this matter is not good for me in my religion, my livelihood and my life in the Herafter, (or he said: 'for my present and future life,') then keep it away from me and take me away from it and choose what is good for me wherever it is and please me with it."

اللهم أستخــيرك بعلمــك وأستقــدرك بقدرتك وأسألك من فضلك العظيم فإنك تقدر ولا أقــدر ، وتعلم ولا أعلم وأنت علام الـغيوب . اللهم إن كنت تعلم أن هذا الأمر خير لى فى دينى ومعاشى وعاقبة أمــرى ، أو قال: عاجـل أمـرى وآجله فاقدره لى ويسره لى ثم بارك لى فيه . وإن كنت تعلم أن هذا الأمـر شر لى فى دينى ومعاشى وعاقبة أمرى ، أو قال: عاجل أمـرى وآجله فاصرفه عنى واصرفنى عنه واقدر لى الخير حيث كان ، ثم أرضنى به .

There is nothing authentic concerning something specific that is to be recited in the prayer nor is there any authentic report concerning how many times one should repeat it.

An-Nawawi holds that "after performing the *istikharah*, a person must do what he is wholeheartedly inclined to do and feels good about doing and should not insist on doing what he had desired to do before making the *istikharah*. And if his feelings change, he should leave what he had intended to do, otherwise he is not completely leaving the choice to Allah, and would not be honest in seeking aid from Allah's power and knowledge. Sincerity in seeking Allah's choice, means that one should completely leave what he himself had desired or determined."

SALATUL TASBIH

'Ikrimah reports from Ibn 'Abbas that the Messenger of Allah said to 'Abbas ibn 'Abdal-Mutalib: "O 'Abbas, O Uncle, shall I not give you, shall I not present to you, shall I not donate to you, shall I not tell you ten things which, if you do, Allah will forgive your first and last sins, past and present sins, intentional and unintentional sins, private and public sins? The ten actions are: pray four *rak'at*, reciting in every *rak'ah* al-Fatihah and a *surah*. And when you finish the Qur'anic recitation of the first *rak'ah*, say, while standing, *'Subhanallah, al-hamdulillah, wa la ilaha illallah, wa Allahu Akbar'* ['Glory be to Allah. All praise is due to Allah. There is no God except Allah. Allah is the greatest.'] fifteen times. Then make *ruku'*, and while you are in *ruku'*, say the same ten times; then stand, and say the same ten times. Then go down and make *sajdah*, and while you're in *sajdah*, say the same ten times. Then sit after the *sajdah*, and say the same ten times. Then make *sajdah*, and say the same ten times. Then sit after the second *sajdah*, and say the same another ten times. That is seventy-five [repetitions of the phrases] in each *rak'ah*. Do that in each of the four *rak'at*. If you can pray it once a day, do so. If you cannot, then once every Friday. If you cannot do that, then once a year. And if you cannot do that then once in your life." This is related by Abu Dawud, Ibn Majah, Ibn Khuzaimah in his *sahih*, and at-Tabarani. About this *hadith* al-Mundhiri says: "This *hadith* has been related through many chains and from a number of companions. The best of them is this one from 'Ikrimah. A group of scholars have graded it to be *sahih*, including al-Hafez Abu Bakr al-'Ajari, (al-Mundhiri's teachers), Abu Muhammad 'Abdurrahim al-Misri, and Abu al-Hassan al-Maqdisi." Ibn al-Mubarak says: "The *tasbih* prayer is a greatly desired act and it is desirable that one should punctually observe it and never neglect it.

THE PRAYER FOR NEED
(*Salatul Hajah*)

Ahmad has on sound authority reported from Abu Darda that the Prophet *Sallallahu Alehi wasallam* said: "He who makes *wudu*, and does it properly, then prays two *rak'at*, Allah will grant him whatever he may pray for, sooner or later."

THE PRAYER OF PENITENCE
(*Salatul Taubah*)

Abu Bakr reports: "I heard the Prophet *sallallahu alehi wasallam* saying: 'Allah forgives the man who commits a sin (then feels ashamed), purifies himself, offers a prayer[21] and seeks His forgiveness.' Then he recited the *'ayyah*: 'And those who, when they do an evil thing or wrong themselves, remember Allah and implore forgiveness for their sins – and who can forgive sins except Allah? – and will not knowingly repeat (the wrong) they did. The reward of such will be forgiveness from their Lord, and gardens underneath which rivers flow, wherein they will abide forever – a bountiful reward for workers.'" [al-'Imran: 135-136]. This is related by Abu Dawud, an-Nasa'i, Ibn Majah, al-Baihaqi, and at-Tirmidhi who calls it *hasan*.

At-Tabarani records in *al-Mu'jam al-Kabir*, with a *hasan* chain, from Abu ad-Darda' that the Prophet *sallallahu alehi wasallam* said: "Whoever makes *wudu'* and perfects the *wudu'* and then stands and prays two *rak'at* or four *rak'at*, obligatory or non-obligatory, and perfects therein his *ruku'* and *sujjud* and then asks for Allah's forgiveness, he will be forgiven."

THE PRAYER OF THE SOLAR AND LUNAR ECLIPSE
(*SALATUL KASUF*)

The scholars agree that the prayer of the eclipses is a *sunnah mu'ak-kadah*, a stressed one, which is to be performed by both men and women. It is best to pray it in congregation although the congregation is not a condition for it. The people are called to it by announcing *as-salatu jami'ah* "prayer in congregation." The majority of the scholars hold that it is to consist of two *rak'at* and that in every *rak'ah* one is to perform two bowings (*ruku'*) instead of the customary one.

'Aishah narrates: "There was a solar eclipse during the time of the Prophet *sallallahu alehi wasallam* and the Prophet went to the mosque, and he stood and made the *takbir*, and he put the people in rows behind him, and he made a lengthy recital during the *salah*. Next, he made the *takbir* and made a long *ruku'*, but it was not as long as the recital. Following

---

[21]According to a report recorded by Ibn Hibban, Al-Baihaqi, and Ibn Khuzaimah, a two *rak'at* prayer.

that, he raised his head, saying: 'Allah hears him who praises Him. And to You, our Lord, belongs the praise.' Afterward, he stood and made another long recital but it was shorter than the first one. Again, he made the *takbir* and made a *ruku'* that was shorter than the first one. Then, again he said: 'Allah hears him who praises Him. And to You, our Lord, belongs the praise.' After this, he prostrated. He did the same in the next *rak'ah* and finished four *ruku'* and four *sujjud*. The sun appeared again before he finished. Finally, he stood and addressed the people[22] and praised Allah as He deserves it and said: 'The sun and the moon are two signs from among Allah's signs and there is no eclipse due to someone's death or life. If you see them occurring, hurry to pray.'" This is related by al-Bukhari and Muslim.

Bukhari and Muslim also record that Ibn 'Abbas said: "There was a solar eclipse during the life time of the Prophet *sallallahu alehi wasallam* and he prayed with a long standing, similar to what it takes to recite al-Baqarah. Then, he made a long *ruku'*. After which, he stood and made another long recital but shorter than the first one. Again he went into *ruku'*, but for a shorter time than in the first one. Following this, he made *sajdah* [twice]. Next he made another long standing (*qiyam*) which was also not as long as the first. After that, he made another lengthy *ruku'* but it was not as long as the first one. Again, he made another long *qiyam* [and recital] but it was not as long as the first one. After which, he made another lengthy *ruku'* but it was not as long as the previous one. Following this, he went into *sajdah* [and so on]. When he had finished, the sun had appeared. He concluded his prayer and said: 'The sun and the moon are two signs from the signs of Allah, and there is no eclipse due to the death or life of anyone. If you see it, make remembrance of Allah.'" Grading these reports, Ibn Abdul Barr says: "These two *ahadith* are the most authentic reports on this topic."

Ibn al-Qayyim observes: "The authentic, clear, and prepondering *sunnah* concerning *salatul kasuf* is that the *ruku'* is to be repeated [twice] in every *rak'ah*. This is based on the *hadith* from 'Aishah, Ibn 'Abbas, Jabir, Ubayy ibn Ka'b, 'Abdullah ibn 'Amr ibn al-'Aas, and Abu Musa al-Ash'ari. They all report that the Prophet repeated the *ruku'* in one *rak'ah*. Those who mention the repeating of the *ruku'* are more in number, weightier, and closer to the Prophet *sallallahu alehi wasallam* than those who do not mention it." This is the opinion of Malik, ash-Shaf'i, and Ahmad.

---

[22]Ash-Shaf'i cites this as a proof that an address must be made with the eclipse prayer. Abu Hanifah and Malik say that there is no address with the prayer and the Prophet only addressed them to inform them that the eclipse had nothing to do with the death of the Prophet's son Ibrahim.

Abu Hanifah is of the opinion that *salatul Kasuf* consists of two *rak'at*, similar to *salatul 'id* and *jumu'ah*, based on the *hadith* of An-Nu'man ibn Bashir who says: "The Messenger of Allah *sallallahu alehi wasallam* prayed the *salatul kasuf* with us like one of your prayers. He went into *ruku'* and performed *sajdah*, praying two *rak'at* by two *rak'at*, and supplicated to Allah until the sun reappeared clearly again."

In the *hadith* from Qabsah al-Hillali, the Prophet said: "If you see that [i.e., an eclipse], pray as you pray the obligatory prayer." This is related by Ahmad and an-Nasa'i.

The reciting of *al-Fatihah* is obligatory in each *rak'ah*, and one may recite whatever one wishes to, after *Al-Fatihah*. It is allowed to make the recital audible or silent, but al-Bukhari says: "Audible recital is more proper."

The time for *al-kasuf* is from the beginning of the eclipse until the eclipse finishes. The prayer of the lunar eclipse is similar to that of the solar eclipse. Al-Hassan al-Basri reports: "There was a solar eclipse and Ibn 'Abbas, the governor of Basra, went out and prayed two *rak'at* with two *ruku'* in each *rak'ah*. Then, he mounted his mount and said: 'I prayed as I have seen the Prophet praying.'" This is related by ash-Shaf'i in his *Musnad*.

It is preferred to make the *takbir*, supplications, to give charity, and ask Allah for forgiveness during the eclipse. Al-Bukhari and Muslim record from 'Aishah that the Messenger of Allah said: "The sun and the moon are two signs from among Allah's signs and there is no eclipse due to the life or death of anyone. If you see that [an eclipse] supplicate to Allah, extol His greatness, give charity and pray." They also record from Abu Musa that there was a solar eclipse and the Prophet said: "If you see something of this nature, rush to the remembrance of Allah, supplicating Him and asking His forgiveness."

THE *ISTISQA'* PRAYER
(*SALATUL ISTISQA'*)

This prayer is taken recourse to when seeking rain from Allah during times of drought. It may be performed in one of the following manners:

(1) The imam prays, with the followers, two *rak'at* during any time except those times in which it is not desirable to pray. In the first *rak'ah*, the imam recites *al-A'la* after *al-Fatihah*. And in the second *rak'ah*, he reads *al-Ghashiyah* after *al-Fatihah*, and he delivers a *khutbah* before or after the *salah*. As soon as he finishes the *khutbah*, the people present should turn their outer garments around, each placing its left side on his

right side and its right side on his left, face the *qiblah*, supplicate Allah and raise their hands while doing so.

Ibn 'Abbas reports: "The Messenger of Allah went out [to make the *salatul istisqa'*] wearing old clothes, in a humble and lowly manner, and prayed two *rak'at* as he prayed the *'id*, but he did not give a similar *khutbah*." This is related by the five. At-Tirmidhi, Abu 'Awanah, and Ibn Hibban grade it *sahih*.

'Aishah says: "The people complained to the Messenger of Allah about lack of rain, so he gave orders for a pulpit, and when it was set up for him, he appointed a day for the people to gather. He came out on that day when the sun had just appeared and sat down on the pulpit. He extolled Allah's greatness and praised Him. Then he said: 'You have complained of drought in your areas and of delay in receiving rain at the beginning of its season, but you have been ordered by Allah to supplicate Him and He has promised that He would answer your prayers.' Then he said:

'All praise is for Allah, the Compassionate, the Merciful, the King of the Day of Judgment. There is no God but Allah Who does what He wishes. O Allah, there is no God except Thee. You are the Self-sufficient and we are the poor. Send down rain upon us and make it a source of strength for us and satisfaction for us.'

الحمد لله رب العالمين ، الرحمن الرحيم ، مالك يوم الدين ، لا إله إلا الله يفعل ما يريد : اللهم لا إله إلا أنت ، أنت الغنى ونحن الفقـراء ، أنـزل علينـا الغيث ، واجعل ما أنزلت علينا قوة وبلاغاً إلى حين .

He then raised his hands and kept raising them till the whiteness of his armpits could be seen.

After this, he turned his back to the people and inverted his cloak, keeping his hands raised. Finally, he faced the people, descended from the pulpit, and prayed two *rak'at*. At that time Allah produced a cloud, thunder, and lightning. And, by Allah's permission, it rained and before he reached the mosque there was flooding. When he saw how quickly the people were running for shelter, he laughed until his molar teeth could be seen. He said: 'I bear witness that Allah has power over all things and I am Allah's slave and Messenger.'" This is related by al-Hakim who classifies it to be *sahih* and by Abu Dawud who says: "This *hadith* is *ghareeb* and its chain is good."

It is furthermore related from 'Ibad ibn Tamim from his uncle 'Abdullah ibn Zaid al-Mazni that the Prophet *sallallahu alehi wasallam* went out to pray *salatul istisqa'* and prayed two *rak'at* reciting them aloud. This is related by the group. And Abu Hurairah says: "The Prophet of Allah went out one day to make *salatul ishtisqa'* and prayed two *rak'at* with us without any *adhan* or *iqamah*. Then, he addressed us and supplicated Allah and turned his face toward the *qiblah*, with his hands raised. Next, he reversed his cloak, placing its left side on his right side and its right side on his left side." This is related by Ahmad, Ibn Majah, and al-Baihaqi.

(2) The supplication for rain can also be made on the occasion of *salatul jumu'ah*. In this case, the imam makes supplications during *khutbatul jumu'ah* with the people of the congregation saying (Ameen).

Al-Bukhari and Muslim record from Shuraik on the authority of Anas that a man entered the mosque on Friday while the Prophet was addressing the people. The man said: "O Messenger of Allah, our wealth has been destroyed and we have no transport to the market place. Supplicate for us for rain." The Prophet raised his hands and said: "O Allah, give us rain. O Allah, give us rain. O Allah, give us rain." Anas said: "By Allah, at that time there were no clouds in the sky and there was no house or building between us and the mountain. From behind the mountain came a cloud looking like a shield. By the time it reached the middle of the sky, it burst and started to rain. By Allah, we did not see the sun for one week. Then, on the next Friday, a man entered the mosque from that (same) door while the Prophet was making the address. The man faced the Prophet and said: 'Our livestock is dead and the paths are unpassable. Ask Allah to make it stop.' The Prophet raised his hands and said: 'O Allah, around us and not upon us. O Allah, make it upon the hills, small mountains, bottom of the valleys, and plantations.' The rain stopped and we walked out in the sunshine."

(3) One may also make a supplication (for rain) without it being Friday and regardless of whether or not the prayer takes place inside or outside the mosque. Ibn Majah and Abu 'Awanah record that Ibn 'Abbas said: "A Bedouin came to the Messenger of Allah and said: 'O Messenger of Allah, I come to you from a people whose shepherds do not have any fodder and whose prize stallion cannot move its tail due to the [drought].' The Prophet mounted the pulpit, praised Allah and said: 'O Allah, give us saving rain which leads to something good and which is productive – a general heavy rain – now and not later.' Then, he descended from the pulpit. People came from every direction saying that it was raining." This is reported by Ibn Majah and Abu 'Awanah and its chain is sound, but Ibn Hajar is silent about it in his *Al-Talkhis*.

Shurahbil ibn as-Simt said to Ka'b ibn Murrah: "O Ka'b, relate to us something from the Messenger of Allah." Ka'b said: "When a man came and said to the Prophet of Allah, 'Seek rain for the tribe of Mudhar,' I heard the Prophet say: 'You are a bold man. You want me to seek rain for the tribe of Mudhar?' The man said: 'O Messenger of Allah, you have sought victory from Allah and He gave you victory. You supplicated Allah and He answered you.' The Messenger of Allah raised his hands and said:

'O Allah, give us a saving rain, good and productive, general and heavy, now and not later, beneficial and not harmful.' Allah responded to his supplication. It was not long before the people came complaining about the profusion of rain, and damage to their dwellings. The Messenger of Allah raised his hands and said: 'O Allah, around us and not upon us.' The clouds began dispersing left and right." This is related by Ahmad, Ibn Majah, al-Baihaqi, Ibn Shaibah and al-Hakim. The later grades this hadith as *hasan sahih* and holds that its chain meets the conditions of al-Bukhari and Muslim.

Ash-Sha'biy says: "'Umar went out to make *istisqa'* and he did no more than seeking Allah's forgiveness. The people said: 'We did not see you making *istisqa'*.' He said: 'I sought rain by what makes it descend (i.e., *istighfar* or seeking forgiveness of Allah), unlike those (Arabs of days of ignorance) who sought it by the stars of the sky.' Then, he recited the following two *'ayat*: 'Seek forgiveness of your Lord. Lo! He is Ever-Forgiving. He will let loose the sky for you in plenteous rain.'[23] and: 'Ask forgiveness of your Lord, and turn to Him (in repentance): He will send you the skies pouring abundant rain.'[24]" This is related by Abu Sa'id in his *Sunan*, 'Abdurrazzaq, al-Baihaqi, and Ibn abi Shaibah.

Some supplications for rain: The following are some of the supplications that have been transmitted.

Ash-Shaf'i states that it has been related from Salim ibn 'Abdullah, on the authority of his father that the Prophet would say for *istisqa'*:

"O Allah, give us a saving rain, productive, plentiful, general, continuous. O Allah, give us rain and do not make us among the despondent. O Allah, (Your) slaves, land, animals, and (Your) creation all are suffering and seek protection. And we do not complain except to You. O Allah, let our crops grow, and let the udders be refilled. Give us from the blessings of the sky and grow for us from the blessings of the earth. O Allah, remove from us the hardship, starvation, and barrenness and remove the affliction

اللهم اسقنا غيثاً مغيثاً مريعاً غدقاً مجلّلا عاماً ، طبقاً سحّاً ، دائماً ، اللهم اسقنا الغيث ، ولا تجعلنا من القانطين : اللهم إن بالعباد والبلاد ، والبهائم ، والخلق من اللأواء والجهد والضنك ما لا نشكوه إلا إليك . اللهم أنبت لنا الزرع ، وأدرّ لنا الضرع ، واسقنا من بركات السماء وأنبت لنا من بركات الأرض : اللهم ارفع عنا الجهد ، والجوع والعرى ، واكشف عنا من

---

[23]Qur'an 71:10
[24]Qur'an 11:52

from us as no one removes afflictions save Thee. O Allah, we seek Your forgiveness as You are the Forgiving, and send upon us plenteous rains."

البــلاء ما لا يكشفــه غيرك : اللهم إنـا نستغفرك إنك كنت غفاراً ، فأرسل السماء علينا مدراراً.

Ash-Shaf'i said: "I prefer that the imam would supplicate with that (prayer)."

Sa'd reported that for *istisqa'*, the Prophet would supplicate:

"O Allah, let us be covered with thick clouds that have abundant and beneficial rain, frequently making a light rain upon us and sprinkling upon us with lightning. O Allah, You are full of majesty, bounty and Honour."

اللهم جللُنا سحاباً كثيفاً ، قصيفاً دلوقاً ، ضحوكاً تمطرنا منه رذاذاً ، قطقطاً ، سجْلاً ، يا ذا الجلال والإكرام.

This is related by Abu 'Awanah in his *Sahih*.

'Amr ibn Shuaib relates from his father, on the authority of his grandfather, that for *istisqa'*, the Prophet would say:

"O Allah, provide water for Your slaves and Your cattle, display Your mercy and give life to Your dead lands."

اللهم اسق عبــادك وبهــائمك ، وانشر رحمتك ، واحي بلدك الميت.

This is related by Abu Dawud.

It is preferred for the one who is making this supplication to raise his hands with the back of his hands toward the sky. Muslim records from Anas that the Prophet would point with the back of his hands during *istisqa'*.

It is also preferred, upon seeing the rain, to say:

"O Allah, make it a beneficial rain"

اللهم صيّباً نافعاً.

and he should uncover part of his body to the rain. On the other hand, if one fears that there is too much rain, one should say:

"O Allah give us mercy and do not give us punishment, calamaties, destruction or flooding. O Allah, make it upon the woods, farms and trees. Make it around us and not upon us."

اللهم سُقيا رحمة ، ولا سُقيا عذاب ولا بلاء ولا هدم ولا غرق . الـلهـم على الـظراب ومنابت الشجر ، اللهم حوالينا ولا علينا.

All of this is authentic and confirmed from the Prophet *sallallahu alehi wasallam*.

The Prostration During the Qur'anic Recitation

Whoever recites an " 'ayyah of prostration (*sajdah*)" or hears an " 'ayyah of prostration" should preferably pronounce the *takbir* and prostrate and then make the *takbir* again and rise from the prostration. This is called "the prostration of recital." There is no *tashahud* or *taslim* with the *sajdah*. Naf'i relates that Ibn 'Umar said: "The Prophet would recite the Qur'an to us and when he came to an ' *'ayyah* of *sajdah*,' he would make the *takbir* and go into *sajdah* and we would make the *sajdah*." This is related by Abu Dawud, al-Baihaqi, and al-Hakim. The later holds it to be *sahih* according to al-Bukhari's and Muslim's criteria. Abu Dawud says: "Abdurrazzaq said: 'At-Thauri was amazed by that *hadith*.' He was amazed by it because it mentions the *takbir*." 'Abdullah ibn Mas'ud said: "If you read an *'ayyah* of *sajdah*', then make the *takbir* and prostrate. And when you raise your head, make the *takbir*."

Their excellence: Abu Hurairah narrates that the Prophet *sallallahu alehi wasallam* said: "If a son of Adam recites an *'ayyah* of prostration and prostrates, the Satan departs from him and cries: 'O woe, he was ordered to prostrate and he did, so for him is paradise. I was ordered to prostrate and I disobeyed, so for me is the Hell.'"

Ruling concerning them: The majority of the scholars say that prostrations for the " *'ayyat* of *sajdah*" are *sunnah* for the one who recites the *'ayyah* and for the one who hears it. This is based on what al-Bukhari recorded from 'Umar who recited *an-Nahl*[25] upon the *minbar* one Friday, until he came to the " *'ayyah* of *sajdah*," and he descended from the pulpit and prostrated along with the people. On the next Friday, he recited the same and when he came to the *'ayyah* of *sajdah*, he said: "O people, we have not been ordered to prostrate. Whoever does so has acted correctly, while, there is no sin upon one who does not do so." In another narration it is stated: "Allah has not forced upon us the *sajdah* but if one wishes to do so (he may make a prostration.)"

In addition, the group, except for Ibn Majah, records that Zaid ibn Thabit said: "I recited *an-Najm*[26] to the Prophet *sallallahu alehi wasallam* and he did not prostrate during it." Ad-Daraqutni records it and observes: "None of us prostrated during it."

Ibn Hajar al-Asqallani says that the strongest opinion is that he left it to show that it is permissible not to do it. Shaf'i holds a similar view. This opinion is supported by what is recorded by al-Bazzar and ad-Daraqutni from Abu Hurairah who says: "The Prophet *sallallahu alehi wasallam* recited *an-Najm* and prostrated and we prostrated with him." (In *Fath al-Bari*, Ibn Hajar holds that its narrators are trustworthy.) Ibn Mas'ud

---

[25]Qur'an 16:50
[26]Qur'an 53:62

moreover reported that the Prophet *sallallahu alehi wasallam* recited *an-Najm*[27] and prostrated, and all of the people with him prostrated, save one old man from the Quraish who simply lifted some pebbles or dirt to his forehead and said: "That is sufficient for me." Ibn Mas'ud said: "After [some time] I found that he was killed while still an unbeliever." This is recorded by al-Bukhari and Muslim.

The "'ayyat of prostration": There are fifteen places in the Qur'an at which one is to prostrate. 'Amr ibn al-'Aas relates that the Prophet *sallallahu alehi wasallam* recited fifteen *'ayyat* of prostration in the Qur'an, three coming from the *Mufassal* and two from *surah* al-Hajj. This is related by Abu Dawud, Ibn Majah, al-Hakim, and ad-Daraqutni. Al-Mundhiri and an-Nawawi say it is *hasan*. The fifteen *'ayyat* are:

1. "Lo! Those who are with thy Lord are not too proud to do Him service, but they praise Him and prostrate to Him" (al-A'raf: 206).

2. "And unto Allah falls prostrate whoever is in the heavens and the earth, willingly or unwillingly, as do their shadows in the morning and the evening hours" (ar-Ra'd: 15).

3. "And unto Allah does whatever is in the heavens and whatever is in the earth of living creatures make prostration, and the angels (also) and they are not proud" (an-Nahl: 49).

4. "Say: Believe therein or believe not, lo! Those who were given knowledge before it, when it is read unto them, they fall down prostrate on their faces, adoring" (al-Isra': 107).

5. "When the revelations of the Beneficent were recited unto them, they prostrated, adoring and weeping" (Maryam: 58).

6. "Haven't you seen that unto Allah prostrates whoever is in the heavens and whoever is in the earth, and the sun, and the moon, and the stars, and the hills, and the trees, and the beasts, and many of mankind, while there are many unto whom the doom is justly due. He whom Allah scorns, there is none to give him honor. Lo! Allah does what he wills" (al-Hajj: 18).

7. "O you who believe, bow down and prostrate yourselves, and worship your Lord and do good, that you may prosper" (al-Hajj: 77).

8. "And when it is said unto them: 'Prostrate unto the Beneficent,' they say: 'And what is the Beneficent? Are we to prostrate to whatever you bid us?' And it increases aversion in them" (al-Furqan: 60).

9. "So they prostrate not to Allah! [He] who brings forth the hidden in the heavens and the earth. And He knows what you hide and what you proclaim" (an-Naml: 25).

---

[27] Qur'an 53:62

10. "Only those who believe in Our revelations who, when they are reminded of them, fall down prostrate and hymn the praise of their Lord and who are not scornful" (as-Sajdah: 15).

11. "And David guessed that we had tried him, and he sought forgiveness of his Lord, and he bowed himself and fell down prostrate and repented" (Sad: 24).

12. "And of His portents are the night and the day and the sun and the moon. Prostrate not to the sun or the moon, but prostrate unto Allah who created them, if it is Him you worship" (Ha-Mim: 37).

13. "Rather prostrate before Allah and serve Him" (an-Najm: 62).

14. "And, when the Qur'an is recited unto them, they do not prostrate (unto Allah)" (al-Inshiqaq: 21).

15. "But prostrate yourself and draw near (unto Allah)" (al-'Alaq: 19).

The conditions for Prostration of Recital: The majority of the scholars lay down the same conditions and prerequisites for the prostration of recital as they do for the *salah*, with respect to purity, facing the *qiblah*, and covering the *'aurah*[28]. Ash-Shaukani says: "There is no *hadith* concerning prostrations of recital which proves that to prostrate one must be in a state of purity [free from major or minor defilements]. The people who were with him [the Prophet] prostrated with him and he did not order any of them to perform ablution, and it is hard to believe that they all were in a state of purity. Furthermore, the polytheists prostrated with him and they are impure, and their ablution would not be acceptable. Al-Bukhari relates from Ibn 'Umar that he would prostrate even when not free of minor impurities. Ibn Abi Shaibah recorded the same from him. As for the report from al-Baihaqi, (with a chain that Ibn Hajar calls *sahih*), which says: 'A man is not to prostrate unless he is in a state of purity.' These reports can be reconciled by Ibn Hajar's statement that this (either) refers to a major defilement or when an option is available, whereas in the first case it depends on (presence of defilement and) the need to wash. Similarly, there is no *hadith* which states that the clothes or place need to be pure. Concerning covering the *'aurah* and facing the *qiblah* if possible, there is no disagreement.

Ibn Hajar said in *Fath al-Bari*: "No one agrees with Ibn 'Umar that one may make the *sajdah* without being clean of minor impurities, save ash-Sha'biy. Ibn Abi Shaibah related it from him with a *sahih* chain. He also recorded from Abu 'Abdurrahman as-Salmi that he would recite an *'ayyah* of *sajdah* and then he would prostrate without ablution or facing the *qiblah* and while walking and just motioning only. Some among the Prophet's

---

[28]'Aurah: Refers to parts of body which a man or a woman must cover while in Prayer. (editor)

household agree with Ibn 'Umar.

Supplications during the prostration: Whoever makes this prostration may supplicate whatever he wishes. There is nothing authentic from the Prophet *sallallahu alehi wasallam* on this point except for the *hadith* from 'Aishah who said: "When the Prophet made the *sajdah* of the Qur'anic recital, he would say: 'I have prostrated my face to the One Who created it and brought forth its hearing and seeing by His might and power. Blessed be Allah, the best of Creators.'" This is related by the five, except Ibn Majah, and al-Hakim. At-Tirmidhi and Ibn as-Sakan grade it *sahih*. The later however adds that at the end the Prophet would say, three times, what he always said in his *sujjud*: "Glory be to my Lord, the Most High," that is, if he was making the *sujjud* of recital during a prayer.

Prostration of recital during the prayers: It is allowed for the imam or the one praying individually[29] to recite "*'ayyah* of *sajdah*" during the *salah*, even if the recital is audible (*jahriyyah*) or inaudible (*siriyyah*), and he should prostrate, during the *salah*, after reading such *'ayat*. Al-Bukhari and Muslim record from Abu Raf'i who said: "I prayed *salatul 'isha* with Abu Hurairah and he recited *Idhas-sama'u un-shaqqat* [al-Inshiqaq] and he prostrated during the prayer. I asked: 'O Abu Hurairah, what prostration is this?' he said: 'I made a prostration when reciting (this *surah*) behind Abu al-Qasim (Prophet), and since then I never stopped making a *sajdah* whenever I recite it.'" Al-Hakim relates, from Ibn 'Umar, with a sound chain that meets the criteria of al-Bukhari and Muslim, saying that the Prophet *sallallahu alehi wassalam* made a *sajdah* during the first *rak'ah* of the noon prayer and his companions were of the opinion that he had recited *surah* as-Sajdah.[30]

An-Nawawi says: "It is not disliked for the imam to recite *'ayat* of *sajdah*, according to our school, or for the one who prays individually. And it does not matter if the recital is audible or inaudible. And he should make *sajdah* after he recites them."

Malik holds: "In general it is disliked." Abu Hanifah's opinion is that: "It is disliked during the silent recitals but not during the audible recitals." The author of *al-Bahr* maintains: "According to our school, it is preferred to delay the *sajdah* until after he [the imam] makes the *taslim* in order not to confuse the people praying behind him."

---

[29]The one praying behind an imam must follow the imam. If the imam prostrates, even if the followers did not hear the verse of prostration, they must follow him. If the imam recites such a verse and does not prostrate, the others must not prostrate but they should just follow the imam. Similarly, if one in congregation recites a verse of prostration or hears someone else reciting such a verse, he should not prostrate during the prayer, as he must follow the imam, but he may perform the prostration after finishing the prayer.

[30]Qur'an 32:1-15

Combining a number of *sujjud*: One may combine a number of *sujjud* and make only one *sajdah* if one recites an "*'ayyah* of *sajdah*" over and over, or one hears it being recited over and over, provided one delays the *sajdah* until all the recitals are finished. Some say that if one prostrates after the first recital, it will be sufficient. Others hold that one should prostrate again since the cause for the prostration is reintroduced.

Performing *sajdah* after recital: The majority of the scholars are of the opinion that the *sajdah* is to be performed right after the recital or hearing of the *'ayyah*. Delaying such a *sajdah* does not rescind it. If an extended period of time lapses between recitation of an *'ayah* and the actual *sajdah*, one need not do it, for it does not have to be made up for.

The Prostration of Thankfulness
(*Sajdat ush-Shukr*)

The majority of the scholars say that it is preferred to make prostrations of thankfulness (*shukr*) when one receives a bounty or is rescued from some trial. Abu Bakr reports that, when the Prophet *sallallahu alehi wasallam* received something which pleased him or some glad tidings, he would make the *sajdah* in thanks to Allah. This is related by Abu Dawud, Ibn Majah, and at-Tirmidhi who says it is *hasan*.

And al-Baihaqi records, with a chain that meets al-Bukhari's conditions, that when 'Ali wrote to the Messenger of Allah, informing him that Hamadhan had embraced Islam, the Prophet prostrated, and when he raised his head, he said: "Peace be upon Hamadhan, peace be upon Hamadhan."

'Abdurrahman ibn 'Auf relates that the Messenger of Allah went out once and he followed him until he entered a grove of palm trees and prostrated. His prostration was so long that 'Abdurrahman feared that Allah had taken his soul. 'Abdurrahman came to look at him and he raised his head and said: "What is wrong, Abdurrahman?" Abdurrahman mentioned what had happened, and he said: "Gabriel *alehi as-salam* came to me and said: 'Shall I not give you glad tidings? Allah says to you, Whoever prays upon you, I pray upon him. Whoever salutes you, I salute him.' Therefore, I prostrated to Allah in thanks." This is related by Ahmad and by Al-Hakim who says: "It is *sahih* according to the criterion of al-Bukhari and Muslim. And I do not know anything more authentic than that."

Al-Bukhari records that Ka'b ibn Malik made a *sajdah* when he received the news that Allah had accepted his repentance. Ahmad records that 'Ali performed the *sajdah* when he heard the news that Dhul-Thudayyah of the Khawarij was killed. Also, as mentioned before, Sa'id ibn Mansur recorded that Abu Bakr made *sajdah* in thankfulness when Musailimah was killed.

The prostration of thankfulness is bound by the same requirements as the prostration in prayer, while some disagree as it is not a prayer. The author of *Fath al-'Alam* remarks: "This latter opinion is closer to being correct." Ash-Shaukani said: "There is nothing in the *hadith* to prove that ablution and purity of the clothes and place are required for *sajdat-ush-shukr*. And that is the opinion of Imam Yahya and Abu Talib. And these *ahadith* are silent about any *takbir* being made with the prostration. In *al-Bahr* it is stated that there is a *takbir*. Imam Yahya says: 'One is not to make the prostration of thankfulness during a prayer as it is not part of the prayer.'"

Prostrations of forgetfulness during the prayer

It is confirmed that the Prophet *sallallahu alehi wasallam* sometimes forgot something in the *salah*. It is also true that he said: "I am a human being and forget like you forget. If I forget, remind me." There are specific points concerning such prostrations and they are presented below.

How to perform these prostrations: The "prostrations of forgetfulness" (*sujjud us-sahu*) are two prostrations which a person makes before the *taslim*. All of this has been confirmed from the Prophet *sallallahu alehi wasallam*. In the *sahih*, it is recorded from Abu Sa'id al-Khudri that the Prophet said: "If one of you has some doubts during his *salah* and he does not re call (the number of *rak'at*) he has prayed, three or four, then he can put an end to his doubt by performing *salah* according to what he was certain of [the lesser amount] and then making two *sujjud* before the *taslim*." In the story of Dhul-Yadain, in the two *Sahihs*, we are told the Prophet *sallallahu alehi wassalam* made the prostrations after the *taslim*.

Ash-Shaukani says: "The best that is stated on this subject is that one must follow what the Prophet said or did, respecting the *sujjud* before or after the *taslim*. If one does something that necessitates *sujjud* before the *taslim*, one should make them before the *taslim*, and if one does something requiring *sujjud* after the *taslim*, then one should make them after the *taslim*. As for those acts of forgetfulness that are not related to any specific time either before or after the *taslim*, one may choose to make the prostrations before or after the *taslim* in cases of addition or reduction in the *salah*. This is based on what Muslim recorded in his *Sahih* from Ibn Mas'ud that the Prophet *sallallahu alehi wasallam* said: 'If one adds or decreases something from his *salah*, he should make two *sujjud*.'"

When to perform these prostrations: The *"sujjud us-sahu"* are to be performed in the following circumstances:

1. If a person makes the *taslim* before he actually completes the prayers. Ibn Sireen relates from Abu Hurairah who said: "The Prophet *sallallahu alehi wasallam* prayed either ̣ *zuhr* or *'asr salah* with us and he prayed only two *rak'at* and made the *taslim*. He got up and leaned against a piece of wood in the mosque as if he was angry. He put his right hand on his left and interlocked his fingers. Then, he placed his cheek on the back of his left hand. And some people left the mosque in a hurry. And they said: 'The prayer has been shortened?' Among the people were Abu Bakr and 'Umar, and they were shy to speak to him. One of the people, who was called Dhul-Yadain, said: 'O Messenger of Allah have you forgotten or has the prayer been shortened?' He answered: 'I have not forgotten and it has not been shortened.' Then he asked: 'Is it as Dhul-Yadain has said?' The people answered in the affirmative... At that, he led the people in what he had ommitted and made the *taslim*. After which he made the *takbir* and prostrated the way he usually prostrated or perhaps even longer. Next, he raised his head and made the *takbir*. Then, he made the *takbir* [again] and prostrated, like one of his customary *sujjud* or perhaps even longer, and finally, he raised his head." This is related by al-Bukhari and Muslim.

'Ata' relates that Ibn az-Zubair prayed *maghrib* and made the *taslim* after two *rak'at* and then he stood up and wanted to kiss the black stone, when the people tried to correct him he said: "What is the matter with you?" Then he prayed what he had left out and performed two *sujjud*. When this was mentioned to Ibn 'Abbas, he said that it was not far from the *sunnah* of the Prophet *sallallahu alehi wasallam*. This is related by Ahmad, al-Bazzar, and at-Tabarani.

2. In the case of an addition to the prayer. Ibn Mas'ud narrates that the Prophet prayed five *rak'at* and the people asked him: "Has there been an addition to the prayer?" He asked: "Why do you say that?" They replied: "You prayed five *rak'at*" Then he made two *sujjud* after he had made the *taslim*. This is related by the group. This *hadith* proves that the prayer of one who prays five *rak'at* out of forgetfulness, without sitting during the fourth *rak'ah*, is acceptable.

3. In the case of forgetting the first *tashahud* or one of the other *sunnah* acts of the prayer. Ibn Buhainah narrates that the Prophet stood after two *rak'at*. The people tried to correct him but he continued. When he finished his *salah*, he made two *sujjud* and made the *taslim*. This is related by the group.[31] This *hadith* shows that one who forgets the first sitting but is re-

---

[31]The followers are to prostrate with the imam when he makes a mistake. According to the Hanafi and the Shaf'i schools, the followers are to make prostrations due to the mistakes of the imam but not due to their own mistakes when the imam is not mistaken.

minded of it and he recalls it before he completely stands should return and sit, but if he is already completely standing, he should not sit down. This is supported by what Ahmad, Abu Dawud, and Ibn Majah recorded from al-Mughirah ibn Shu'bah, that the Prophet *sallallahu alehi wasallam* said: "If one of you stands after two *rak'at* and he has not completely stood, then he should sit. If he is already completely standing, he should not sit and he should make two *sujjud* of forgetfulness."

4. In the case of doubt over whether or not one performed some act of the prayer. 'Abdurrahman ibn 'Auf reported that he heard the Prophet say: "If one of you has some doubt during his *salah* and he does not know if he prayed one *rak'ah* or two, he should take it to have been just one. If he does not know if he prayed two *rak'at* or three, he should take it to have been just two. If he does not know if he prayed three *rak'at* or four, he should take it to have been just three. [In all such cases] at the end of his prayer, while sitting, he should make two *sujjud* before the *taslim*." This is related by Ahmad, Ibn Majah, and at-Tirmidhi. The latter grades it *sahih*.

In one narration, it is stated: "Whoever prays and has some doubt that he was short of the complete prayer, he should continue praying until he suspects that he has added something to the prayer [with respect to the number of *rak'at* that he has prayed]." Abu Sa'id al-Khudri narrated that the Prophet *sallallahu alehi wasallam* said: "If one of you has some doubts during his prayer and does not know if he prayed three or four [*rak'at*], then he should remove his doubt by praying according to the amount that he is certain he had performed and then make two *sujjud* before the *taslim*. If he had prayed five *rak'at*, the two *sujjud* would make it even. If he had prayed a complete four *rak'at* [when he had finished], they would be in defiance of the Satan." This is related by Ahmad and Muslim. These two *ahadith* prove what the majority of the scholars have said, namely, if one has some doubt concerning the number of *rak'at* one has prayed, one should act according to the amount that one is certain to have prayed (the lesser amount) and then make two *sujjud* before the *taslim*.

CONGREGATIONAL PRAYER
(SALATUL JAMA'AH)

Performing the prayers in congregation is a *sunnah mu'akkadah*.[32] Many *ahadith* discuss the superiority and excellence of prayers in congregation. Such *ahadith* include the following:

Ibn 'Umar reports that the Prophet *sallallahu alehi wasallam* said: "Prayer in congregation is superior to a prayer performed individually by twenty-seven degrees." This is related by al-Bukhari and Muslim.

Abu Hurairah reports that the Prophet *sallallahu alehi wasallam* said: "The prayer of a man in congregation is twenty-five times more superior (in reward) to his prayer in his house or market – and this is because he makes the *wudu'* and perfects it and goes to the mosque with the sole purpose of performing the *salah*. He does not take a step without being raised a degree and having one of his sins erased. When he prays, as long as he does not lose his *wudu*, the angels keep on praying [for him] 'O Allah, bless him. O Allah, have mercy on him.' And he is considered in *salah* as long as he is waiting for the *salah*." This is related by al-Bukhari and Muslim, and it is presented in al-Bukhari's wording.

Abu Hurairah also reports that a blind man said to the Prophet: "O Messenger of Allah, I have no guide to guide me to the mosque." He asked the Prophet *sallallahu alehi wasallam* for permission to pray in his house

---

[32]This is concerning obligatory prayers. As to the voluntary prayers, it is permissible to pray these in congregation, regardless of how large or small the congregation is. It has been confirmed that the Prophet *sallallahu alehi wasallam* prayed two *rak'at* of voluntary prayers with Anas on his right side ánd Umm Sulaim and Umm Haram behind him. And he did this on more than one occasion.

[49]

and the Prophet gave it to him. Then, when he turned to go, the Prophet called him and said: "Do you hear the call to prayer?" The blind man said "yes." The Prophet then said: "Then respond to it!" [by coming to the mosque.] This is related by Muslim.

Abu Hurairah also reports that the Prophet *sallallahu alehi wasallam* said: "By Him in whose hand is my soul! I have considered ordering a fire to be kindled and then ask someone to lead the people in *salah*. And then go to the men [who did not attend the prayer] and burn their houses over them." This is related by al-Bukhari and Muslim.

'Abdullah ibn Mas'ud says: "If anyone would like to meet Allah tomorrow as a Muslim, he should persevere in abserving these five prayers whenever the call for them is made, for Allah has chosen for your Prophet the way of right guidance. And the [five prayers in congregation] are part of this right guidance. If you were to pray them in your houses, as this man who stays behind in his house, you would be leaving a *sunnah* of your Prophet. If you leave the *sunnah* of your Prophet, you would go astray. Verily, I have seen a time when no one stayed away from them [the congregational prayers] except for the hypocrites who were well known for their hypocrisy. A man would be brought, supported by two people [due to his weakness] until he was placed in a row." This is related by Muslim.

Abu ad-Darda' reports that the Messenger of Allah *sallallahu alehi wasallam* said: "If there are three men in a village or desert and *salah* is not established among them, then the Satan takes mastery over them. So be with the congregation since the wolf devours the remote (stray) sheep." This is related by Abu Dawud with a *hasan* chain.

Women and congregational prayers: It is better for women to pray in their houses than to attend congregational prayers. However, they may go to the mosque and attend the congregational prayer if they avoid wearing or using any attractive or tempting adornment or perfume.

Ibn 'Umar reports that the Prophet *sallallahu alehi wasallam* said: "Do not prevent the women from going to the mosques, although their houses are better for them." Abu Hurairah relates that the Prophet said: "Do not keep the slave girls of Allah from the mosques of Allah. And they are to go out unperfumed." These two *ahadith* were related by Ahmad and Abu Dawud. Abu Hurairah also reports that the Prophet said: "Any woman who uses some scent should not be present with us during the night prayer." This is related by Muslim, Abu Dawud, and an-Nasa'i with a *hasan* chain.

As stated earlier, it is better for women to pray in their houses. Ahmad and at-Tabarani record that Umm Humaid as-Sa'diyah came to the Messenger of Allah and said: "O Messenger of Allah, I love to pray with you." The Prophet said: "I am aware of that, but your *salah* in your residence is better for you than your *salah* in your people's mosque. And your *salah* in your people's mosque is better than your *salah* in the [larger] congregational Mosque."

Praying at a larger and more distant mosque: It is preferable to pray in a mosque that is farther away and that has a larger congregation.

Muslim records from Abu Musa that the Prophet *sallallahu alehi wasallam* said: "The one who gets the greatest reward for a prayer is the one who walks the farthest distance." Muslim also records that Jabir said: "The area around the mosque became vacant and the tribe of Salamah wanted to move there. When this news reached the Messenger of Allah, he said: 'It has reached me that you want to move closer to the mosque?' They said: 'Yes, O Messenger of Allah, we desire that.' The Prophet said: 'O tribe of Salamah, your dwellings will record your steps.'" Al-Bukhari, Muslim, and others have recorded this on the authority of Abu Hurairah.

Ubayy ibn Ka'b reported that the Prophet *sallallahu alehi wasallam* said: "The *salah* of a man with another man is purer than the *salah* of a man by himself.[33] [In the same way,] his *salah* with two men is purer than his *salah* with only one man, and what is more, it is most dear to Allah." This is related by Ahmad, Abu Dawud, an-Nasa'i, Ibn Majah and Ibn Hibban. Ibn as-Sakin, al-'Uqaily and al-Hakim classify it as *sahih*.

Going to the mosque with calm and dignity: It is preferred for one to walk to the mosque with calm and dignity[34] and not in a hurry or rushing. This is because the person is considered to be in prayer when he is going to the *salah* (and also while he is waiting for it). Abu Qatadah says: "We were praying with the Prophet *sallallahu alehi wasallam* when we heard the clamoring of some men. When they had prayed, the Prophet inquired: 'What was the matter with you?' They answered: 'We were hurrying for the *salah*.' He said: 'Do not do that...when you come to the *salah* come in peace and calm, and pray what you can with congregation and complete what you have missed.'" This is related by al-Bukhari and Muslim.

Abu Hurairah narrates that the Prophet *sallallahu alehi wasallam* said: "When you hear the *iqamah*, proceed to the prayer with calm and dignity – and do not rush. Pray what you can (with congregation) and complete what you miss." This is related by the group except for at-Tirmidhi.

The imam should be "easy" on his followers: Abu Hurairah reports

---

[33]Purer means it brings more reward and more sins are expiated.
[34]An-Nawawi observes that "calm" refers to going in a peaceful, calm manner, while "dignity" refers to guarding one's eye sight, keeping the voice low.

that the Prophet said: "If one of you leads the people in prayer, he should be "easy," on them for among the people are the weak, sick, and aged. If one prays by himself, one may make it as long as one wishes." This is related by the group. It is narrated from Anas that the Prophet *sallallahu alehi wassalam* said: "Sometimes I enter prayer and I intend to prolong it, but then I hear a child crying, and I shorten my prayer thinking of the distress of the child's mother."

Al-Bukhari and Muslim record that Anas said: "I have not prayed behind anyone who prayed a lighter *salah* or a more complete prayer than that of the Prophet *sallallahu alehi wasallam*." Abu 'Umar ibn Abdul Barr said: The scholars agree that it is preferable for an imam to make the prayer light while preserving the minimum without which salah is incomplete and without leaving off any part of the *salah* or shortening part of it [not performing it properly]. The Prophet *sallallahu alehi wasallam* prohibited the pecking like a crow.[35] Once he saw a man who did not complete his *ruku'* and he told him: 'Go back and pray for you have not prayed.' And he said: 'Allah does not look to one who does not straighten his back during *ruku'* and *sujjud*.' I do not know of any difference of opinion among the scholars concerning the fact that it is preferred for an imam to be 'easy' on his followers while making the prayer properly. It is related that 'Umar said: 'Do not make people dislike Allah, by making the *salah* so long that it should become hard on those praying behind you.'"

The imam may prolong the first *rak'ah* to allow others to join: It is permitted for the imam to prolong the first *rak'ah* while waiting for others to join the congregation. In the same way, it is preferred for him to wait for people who are coming during the bowings and during the final sitting.

Abu Qatadah reports that the Prophet *sallallahu alehi wasallam* would prolong the first *rak'ah* and the people suspected that he did it to allow the late-comers to join the first *rak'ah*. Abu Sa'id says: "If the (congregational) *salah* was begun, one could go to al-Baqi', relieve himself, make *wudu'*, and return and find the Prophet still in the first *rak'ah* for he would prolong it (first *rak'ah*)." This is related by Ahmad, Muslim, Ibn Majah, and an-Nasa'i.

It is obligatory to follow the imam and forbidden to precede him:[36]

---

[35]To make the prostrations so quickly that it resembles the pecking of a crow.

[36]The scholars agree that to precede the imam in the opening *takbir* or in the *taslim* voids the prayer. There is a difference of opinion concerning preceding him in other acts of the prayer. According to Ahmad it would void the prayer. He said: "There is no prayer for one who preceds the imam." Obviously, it is disliked to make the actions at the same time as the imam.

Abu Hurairah reports that the Prophet *sallallahu alehi wasallam* said: "The imam is selected to be followed; therefore, do not differ with him. When he makes the *takbir*, make the *takbir*, when he goes into *ruku'*, make *ruku'*. When he says 'Allah hears him who praises Him,' say 'O Allah, our Lord, to You belongs the Praise.' When he goes into *sajdah*, make *sajdah*. If he prays sitting, then all should be sitting." This is related by the group. In the version by Ahmad and Abu Dawud, the wording is "the imam is to be followed. If he makes the *takbir*, make the *takbir*, and do not make the *takbir* until he does so. When he goes into *ruku'*, make *ruku'*, and do not perform *ruku'* until he does so. When he goes into *sajdah*, make *sajdah*, and do not make *sajdah* until he does so."

Abu Hurairah reports that the Prophet *sallallahu alehi wasallam* said: "Do you not fear that if you raise your head before the imam Allah may change your head into that of a donkey!" This is related by the group.

Anas reports that the Messenger of Allah *sallallahu alehi wasallam* said: "O people, I am your imam, so do not precede me in *ruku'* or in *sujjud* or in *qiyam* or in sitting or in finishing." This is related by Ahmad and Muslim.

Al-Bara' ibn 'Azib says: "We prayed with the Messenger of Allah and when he said 'Allah hears him who praises Him,' none of us would bend his back until the Messenger of Allah had put his forehead upon the ground." This is related by the group.

Consitution of a congregation: One person with the imam would constitute a congregation even if the other person is a child or a woman.

Ibn 'Abbas says: "I stayed with my Aunt Maimunah and the Prophet *sallallahu alehi wasallam* got up to pray during the night. I got up to pray with him and stood on his left and the Prophet took me by my hand and put me on his right side."[37]

Sa'id and Abu Hurairah both report that the Prophet *sallallahu alehi wasallam* said: "Whoever gets up during the night and wakes up his spouse and they pray two *rak'at* together, they both will be recorded among those (men and women) who remember Allah much." This is related by Abu Dawud. Abu Sa'id narrates that a man entered the Mosque, and the Prophet and his companions had already prayed. The Prophet *sallallahu alehi wasallam* said: "Who will give charity to him by praying with him?" So, a man from the people stood and prayed with him. This is related by Ahmad, Abu Dawud, and at-Tirmidhi who calls it *hasan*. Ibn Abi Shaibah

---

[37]This *hadith* shows that it is allowed for one to act as an imam although originally he had not intended to be an imam, (i.e., he was intending to pray by himself). This is also supported by the *hadith* of 'Aishah concerning the *tarawih* prayers. This rule applies to both obligatory and non-obligatory prayers.

relates that it was Abu Bakr who stood and prayed with the man. At-Tir-midhi uses this *hadith* as proof that a group can pray in congregation in a mosque in which the congregational prayer had already been made. He says that this is the opinion of Ahmad and Ishaq. Other scholars say that they should each pray individually and this is the opinion of Sufyan, Malik, Ibn al-Mubarak and ash-Shaf'i.[38]

An imam may change his place and become a follower: If the regular imam or appointed imam is not present, it is permissible to appoint some-one else to perform the duty of imam. If the regular imam appears during the prayers, the substitute imam may move back to the rows and allow the regular imam to take over. Al-Bukhari and Muslim record that Sahl ibn Sa'd said: "The Messenger of Allah *sallallahu alehi wasallam* went off to take care of the affairs of the tribe of 'Amr ibn 'Auf. The time for *salah* came and the mu'adhdhin went to Abu Bakr and said: 'Will you lead the people in *salah* and I shall make the *iqamah*?' Abu Bakr agreed. [While he was] leading the prayer, the Messenger of Allah appeared and joined the rows. The people clapped [their thighs with their hands] but Abu Bakr would not turn around during the prayer. When most of the people began clapping, he turned and saw the Prophet...[who] pointed to Abu Bakr to stay in his place. Abu Bakr raised his hands and praised Allah because of what the Prophet had told him. Then, Abu Bakr moved back until he joined the rows and the Prophet stepped forward [to lead]. After he had prayed, he went to Abu Bakr and said: O Abu Bakr, what prevented you from staying there when I told you to do so?' Abu Bakr said: 'It is not fit for the son of Abu Quhafah to lead the Prophet in prayer.' Then the Messenger of Allah said: 'Why did I see most of you clapping? If you find something in the prayer you should say *subhanallah*, for when you say it, it will attract his (i.e. imam's) attention and clapping [thighs with hands] is for the women.'"[39]

Catching up with imam or the congregation: Whoever joins a con-gregation, he should perform the opening *takbir* while standing and then move directly to the act that the congregation may be performing, for in-

---

[38]However, having different congregational prayers at the same place and time is absolutely forbidden and goes against the spirit of Islamic law.

[39]This *hadith* shows that it is permissible to move from one row to the next in the prayer, to praise Allah, to appoint another as the imam due to some necessity, for a person to be an imam during part of the prayer and a follower during part of the prayer, to raise the hands during the prayer for supplication or for praising Allah, to turn due to some necessity, to point to instruct another, for a less qualified person to lead a more qualified person in prayer, to perform minor actions during the prayer, and so on. (cf., Ash-Shaukani, *Nail al-Autar*).

stance, if the congregation is prostrating one should perform the opening *takbir* and then join it in the prostration. However, such a person is not considered as having performed the *rak'ah* unless he performs the *ruku'* (bowing), even if he just bows and puts his hands on his knees, when the imam is finishing his *ruku'*.

Abu Hurairah reports that the Messenger of Allah *sallallahu alehi wasallam* said: "If you come to the *salah* and we are in *sajdah*, then make *sajdah* with us but do not count it [as a *rak'ah*]. And whoever 'catches' the *ruku'*, he catches the *salah*." This is related by Abu Dawud, Ibn Khuzaimah in his *Sahih*, and by al-Hakim, who considers it *sahih*, in his *Al-Mustadrak*.

When it is permissible to not attend Congregation: Ibn 'Umar narrated that the Prophet ordered the *mu'adhdhin* to say: "Pray in your places," on a cold, stormy night during a journey. This is related by al-Bukhari and Muslim.

Jabir said: "We went on a journey with the Prophet and it rained upon us, so he said: 'Whoever wishes may pray in his stopping place.'" This is related by Ahmad, Muslim, Abu Dawud, and at-Tirmidhi.

Ibn 'Abbas said to the *mu'adhdhin*, on a rainy day: "When you say 'I bear witness that Muhammad is the Messenger of Allah,' do not say 'Come to the prayer,' but instead say 'Pray in your houses.'" The people didn't seem to like it, so he asked: "Are you surprised by that? One better than me did it [the Prophet]. The congregational prayer is a strict order but I hated that you should go out and walk in the mud and on slippery ground." This is related by al-Bukhari and Muslim. According to Muslim's version, this occurred on a Friday.

What applies in case of cold would also apply in cases of extreme heat, darkness, and fear of an oppressor. Ibn Batal writes: "The scholars are agreed on the permissibility of not attending the congregation due to heavy rain, darkness, wind, and so on."

Ibn 'Umar reports that the Prophet *sallallahu alehi wasallam* said: "If the food is presented to one of you, do not rush but fulfill your need of it even if the *salah* has begun." This is related by al-Bukhari.

'Aishah narrates that she heard the Prophet *sallallahu alehi wasallam* say: "There is no prayer when the meal is presented nor when one needs to answer the call of nature." This is related by Ahmad, Muslim, and Abu Dawud.

Abu ad-Darda' says: "It is a sign of the understanding of a person that he fulfills his needs first in order to make his prayer with a clear mind." This is related by al-Bukhari.

Who has the most right to be imam

The one who should be imam is the one who is the most versed in the Qur'an. If two or more are equal in this, then it is the one who has the most knowledge of the *sunnah*. If they are equal in that, then it is the one who performed the migration first. If they are equal in that, then it should be the eldest.

Abu Sa'id narrates that the Prophet said: "If you are three in number, then one of you should be the imam. And the one who has the most right to it is the one who is the most versed in the Qur'an." This is related by Ahmad, Muslim, and an-Nasa'i. The meaning of "most versed in the Qur'an" is the one who has more of the Qur'an memorized. This interpretation is based on the *hadith* from Amr ibn Salamah which says: "Your imam should be the one who is most versed in the Qur'an."

Ibn Mas'ud reports that the Prophet *sallallahu alehi wasallam* said: "The imam of a people should be the one who is the most versed in the Book of Allah. If they are equal in their recital, then the one who is most knowledgeable of the *sunnah*. If they are equal in the *sunnah*, then [it is] the one who migrated first. If they are equal in that, then [it is] the eldest. And no man should be an imam for another man if the other holds authority [i.e., a leader in any capacity or ruler of the Muslim people]. And one should not occupy his place of honor in his house without his permission." In another narration it is stated: "No man should be the imam for another while with the other's family or where the other is in authority." This is related by Ahmad and Muslim.

Sa'id ibn Mansur says: "A person should not be an imam for another where the other is in authority except with his permission." The meaning of this is that the one in authority, owner of a house, leader of a meeting, and so on, has more right than others to be the imam if he has not granted the permission to any of the others. Abu Hurairah reports that the Prophet *sallallahu alehi wasallam* said: "It is not allowed for a man who believes in Allah and the last day to be an imam for a people, except with their permission, nor may he specifically make supplications for himself without including them. If he does so, he is disloyal to them." This is related by Abu Dawud.

Whose imamate is acceptable: The imamate of all the following is acceptable: a discerning boy, a blind person, a standing person for those who are sitting, a sitting person for those who are standing, a person praying *fard* for people who are praying *nafl*, a person praying *nafl* for people who are praying *fard*. Likewise, a person who has performed ablution can be imam for people who have performed *tayammum*, as can be a person who has performed *tayammum* for people who have performed ablution, a traveler for the resident, a resident for the travelers, and a less qualified person for people who are more qualified.

'Amr ibn Salamah led his people in *salah* while he was six or seven years old. The Messenger of Allah *sallallahu alehi wasallam* twice appointed Ibn Umm Maktum, a blind man, to lead the people of Medinah in prayer. The Messenger of Allah, during his last illness, prayed behind Abu Bakr in a sitting position. And he prayed in his house in a sitting position while those behind him were standing. He pointed to them to sit and when he had finished the prayer he said: "The imam has been appointed to be followed. If he goes into *ruku'*, then make *ruku'*. When he raises his head, raise your head. If he prays sitting, then pray sitting behind him."

Mu'adh would pray *'isha* with the Prophet *sallallahu alehi wasallam* and then return to his people and lead them in the same prayer, it being *nafl* for him and *fard* for the others.

Muhjan ibn al-Adra' reports: "I came to the Messenger of Allah in the mosque and they prayed and I did not. He said to me: 'Why didn't you pray?' I said: 'O Messenger of Allah, I prayed in my place and then came here.' He then said: 'When you come [to the mosque], pray with them and make it supererogatory.'"

The Messenger of Allah saw a man praying by himself and said: "Who will give charity to this person by praying with him?" 'Amr ibn al-'Aas led others in prayer when he had made *tayammum* only and the Prophet approved of it.

The Prophet *sallallahu alehi wasallam*, after the conquest of Makkah, led the people in prayer by praying two *rak'at* (except for *maghrib*) and said: "O people of Makkah, stand and pray the last two *rak'at* as we are travelers."

If a traveler prays behind a resident, he must complete the whole four *rak'at* even if he only prayed part of a *rak'ah* behind the resident imam. Ibn 'Abbas was asked: "Why is the traveler to pray two *rak'at* if he prays by himself and four *rak'at* if he prays behind a resident?" He answered: "That is the *sunnah*." In another version, Musa ibn Salamah said to him: "If we pray with you, we pray four *rak'at* otherwise we pray two?" He told him: "That is the *sunnah* of Abu al-Qasim [the Prophet]." This is related by Ahmad.

Whose imamate is not acceptable: It is not allowed for one who has a health problem which does not allow him to remain in a state of purity to be an imam for others who do not have such a problem. This is the opinion of the majority of the scholars. According to the Maliki school, such a person's imamate will be valid, but it is disliked to make such a person the imam.

It is preferred to have a woman imam for women: 'Aishah used to lead the women in *salah* and stand with the women in the middle of the first row. Umm Salamah would also do so. The Prophet *sallallahu alehi wasallam* appointed Waraqah to go and make the *adhan* for her while he instructed her to lead the women of her household in the obligatory prayers.

A man leading a group of women in prayer: Abu Ya'la and at-Tabarani, in *al-Ausat*, record, with a *hasan* chain, that Ubayy ibn Ka'b came to the Messenger of Allah and said: "O Messenger of Allah, I did something last night." The Prophet asked: "What was that?" He said: "The women in my house said, 'You recite and we do not recite so lead us in *salah*.' So I prayed eight *rak'at* and *witr* (with them)." The Prophet remained silent, and Ka'b said: "We took his silence as a sign of his approval."

Evildoer or innovator forbidden to lead prayer: Al-Bukhari records that Ibn 'Umar prayed behind al-Hajjaj.[40] Muslim records that Abu Sa'id al-Khudri prayed *salatul 'id* behind Marwan.[41]

Ibn Mas'ud once prayed four *rak'at* of *fajr*, behind al-Walid ibn 'Uqbah ibn Abu Ma'it who used to drink wine, and 'Uthman ibn 'Affan had him flogged. The companions and their successors prayed behind Ibn 'Ubaid who was accused of propagating heresies. According to the scholars, anyone whose prayer is valid on an individual basis, his imamate is also valid for others. However, they dislike to pray behind an evildoer or innovator.

As-Sa'ib ibn Khilad relates that a man was leading the people in *salah* and he spat in the direction of the *qiblah*. The Messenger of Allah saw this and said: "Do not let him lead you in *salah*." After this, the man wanted to lead the people in *salah* but they prevented him and told him what the Prophet had said. The man went to the Prophet *sallallahu alehi wasallam*, to ask him about that, and the Prophet said: "Yes, [it is true] for you have offended Allah and His Messenger." This is related by Abu Dawud and Ibn Hibban. Abu Dawud and al-Mundhiri are silent about it.

Permission to leave the congregational prayer: If the imam makes the *salah* too long, it is permissible, under certain circumstances, to leave the *salah* with the intention of performing it individually. The following are examples of when this may be done: becoming ill, fearing that one's wealth may be lost or destroyed, missing one's companions or traveling group, being overcome by sleep, and so on. This is based on the following

---

[40]Al-Hajjaj, an Umayyad governor, was well-known for his ruthlessness, cruelty, and oppression.—J.Z.

[41]Marwan, another Ummayyad ruler, has been accused of evil deeds although he does not really compare to al-Hajjaj.—J.Z.

hadith related by Jabir: "Mu'adh would pray *'isha* with the Prophet *sallallahu alehi wasallam*, and then go and lead his people in *salah*. One night, the Prophet delayed *salatul 'isha* and Mu'adh prayed with him and then went to his people and led them in the night prayer by reciting al-Baqarah. One man left the *salah* and prayed by himself. The people said to him: 'O so and so, you have become a hypocrite.' He said: 'I have not become a hypocrite but I shall surely go to the Prophet and inform him of what has happened.' He told the Prophet what had happened and the Prophet said to Mu'adh: 'You put people to trials, Mu'adh! You put people to trials, Mu'adh. Recite such and such *surah*.'" This is related by the group.

Repeating a *salah* with a congregation: Yazid al-Aswad says: "We prayed dawn prayer (*fajr*) with the Messenger of Allah at Mina and two men came and stopped at their resting places. The prophet ordered for them to be brought and they came shaking with fear. The Prophet said to them: 'What prevented you from praying with the people? ...Are you two not Muslims?' They answered: 'Certainly we are, O Messenger of Allah, but we had prayed in our resting place.' The Prophet told them: 'If you pray in your resting places and then come upon an imam, pray with him, and it will be nafl for you.'" This is related by Ahmad and Abu Dawud. An-Nasa'i and at-Tirmidhi record it in these words: "If you pray in your resting places and then you come to a mosque with a congregation, pray with them, and it will be *nafl* for you." At-Tirmidhi calls it *hasan sahih* and Ibn as-Sakin says it is *sahih*.

This *hadith* shows that it is correct for one to repeat a *salah* as a *nafl* with a congregation even if he has already performed it, individually or with a congregation.

It is related that Hudhaifah repeated the *zuhr*, *'asr*, and *maghrib* prayers although he had prayed them in congregation. It is also related that Anas prayed *fajr* behind Abu Musa at the place where fruits are dried and then he went to the congregational mosque and repeated the *salah* behind al-Mughirah ibn Shu'bah. Nevertheless, this action contradicts authentic *hadith* of the Prophet *sallallahu alehi wasallam* in which he reportedly said: "Do not pray the same *salah* twice in one day." The apparent conflict has been resolved by Ibn 'Abdul-Barr who writes, "Ahmad and Ishaq agree that this refers to praying an obligatory *salah* and then, after a while, repeating it as the obligatory prayer. Now, as for the one who repeats the *salah* with a congregation with the intention that the second prayer is not a repeat of the obligatory *salah* but that it is simply a voluntary prayer, he obeys the Prophet's order of not making the same *salah* twice, as the first *salah* was obligatory and the second was *nafl*; hence, there is no repetition."

Imam's leaving the place after the *salah*: It is preferred for the imam to turn to the right or to the left after the *salah* and then to leave the place of prayer.

Qabaidah ibn Halb relates that his father said: "The Prophet would lead us in *salah* and then turn to both of his sides, to his right and to his left." This is related by Abu Dawud, Ibn Majah, and at-Tirmidhi. The latter calls it *hasan*. People who are informed on this subject act accordingly by turning to any side they wish. Both acts have been authenticated from the Prophet *sallallahu alehi wasallam*. 'Aishah says: "After the Prophet made the *taslim*, he would not sit except for the amount of time it takes to say:

'O Allah, You are the Peace, and from You comes the Peace. Blessed are You, Possessor of Majesty and Honor.'"

اللهم أنت السلام ومنك السلام تباركت يا ذا الجلال والإكرام .

This is related by Ahmad, Muslim, at-Tirmidhi, and Ibn Majah.

Ahmad and al-Bukhari record that Umm Salamah said: "Whenever the Messenger of Allah finished his prayers with the *taslim*, the women would get up and he would stay in his place for a while before getting up." She said: "I think, and Allah knows best, that he did that to allow the women to leave before the men [would stand to leave].

The imam or followers being elevated: It is disliked for the imam to be at a higher place than the followers.

Abu Mas'ud al-Ansari says: "The Prophet *sallallahu alehi wasallam* prohibited that the imam should stand on something higher than the people behind him." This is related by ad-Daraqutni, while al-Hafez is silent about it in *al-Talkhis*.

Hamam ibn al-Harith relates that Hudhaifah led the people in prayer in Mada'in (Iraq) and he stood on a bench. Abu Mas'ud pulled his shirt with a strong grip. When he finished his prayer Abu Mas'ud said: "Do you not know that this has been prohibited?" Hudhaifah said: "Certainly, I know it. I remembered it when you pulled me." This is related by Abu Dawud, ash-Shaf'i, and al-Baihaqi. Al-Hakim, Ibn Khuzaimah, and Ibn Hibban grade it *sahih*.

On the other hand, if the imam has some reason for being higher than the followers, the act is not disliked. Sahl ibn Sa'd as-Sa'ady says: "I saw the Prophet sitting upon the pulpit on the first day that it was set up. He made the opening *takbir* while he was upon it and then he performed *ruku'*. Afterward, he moved behind the pulpit and made *sajdah* at the foot of the pulpit. Then, he repeated the same. When he had finished, he turned to the people and said: "O people, I did that for you to follow me and to teach you my *salah*.'" This is related by Ahmad, al-Bukhari, and Muslim.

It is permissible for the followers to be at a higher place than the imam, for Sa'id ibn Mansur, ash-Shaf'i, al-Baihaqi, and al-Bukhari, in his comments, relate from Abu Hurairah that he prayed at the top of the mosque while following the imam. Anas used to pray in the room of Abu Naf'i to the right of the mosque and the room was his height's high and its door faced the mosque of Basrah and Anas would pray in it, following the imam. The companions did not say anything about it. This is related by Sa'id ibn Mansur in his *Sunan.*

Ash-Shaukani observes: "If the follower is extremely high above the imam, for example, three hundred lengths, and he could not know what action the imam is doing then it is prohibited by consensus whether he is in a mosque or somewhere else. If it is less than that, it is permitted on the principle that unless proved otherwise a thing is permissible. This basis is supported by the above mentioned act of Abu Hurairah to which no one objected."

Following the imam with a barrier in between: It is allowed for a follower to follow the imam, even if there is a barrier between them, as long as he or she can tell the imam's movements either by his sight or hearing.[42]

Al-Bukhari records: "Al-Hassan said: 'There is no problem if you pray and between you and him [the imam] there is a river.' Abu Majliz said: 'Follow the imam, even if between you and him there is a road or a wall, as long as you can hear the opening takbir.'" We have already mentioned the *hadith* in which the people prayed behind the Prophet *sallallahu alehi wasallam* while they were behind the room.

When imam leaves out an essential act of *salah*: A person's imamate is valid even if he leaves out one of the obligatory acts or prerequisites provided the followers complete them and the imam is not aware of the fact that he had left out an obligatory act or prerequisite.

Abu Hurairah reports that the Prophet said: "If the imam leads the prayer correctly, then both you and he will get the reward. If he is mistaken, you will get the reward and he the blame." This is related by Ahmad and al-Bukhari.

Sahl reports that he heard the Prophet *sallallahu alehi wasallam* say: "The imam is a warrantor. If he has done well, it is for him and them. If he has done wrong, it is upon him." This is related by Ibn Majah.

It has been authentically reported from 'Umar that he led the people in *salah* while he was sexually defiled and had forgotten that fact. He repeated his *salah* but those who had prayed behind him did not.

---

[42]It should be pointed out, however, that there is no prayer in following the imam over a radio. This carries the consensus of the scholars.

Appointing another to lead the rest of the salah: If the imam must leave during the salah due to some reason, for instance, he remembers that he is in need of making ablution or he loses his ablution during the salah, then he should appoint another to lead the remainder of the prayer.

'Amr ibn Maimun says: "I was standing and there was no one between me and 'Umar, the morning he was killed, except 'Abullah ibn 'Abbas. He had barely pronounced the takbir when he was stabbed and he said: 'The dog has bitten or killed me.' 'Umar bade 'Abdur Rahman ibn 'Auf to lead the salah and he led them in a short prayer." This is related by al-Bukhari.

Abu Razin reports: "'Ali was praying one day when his nose began to bleed. He took a man by the hand and put him in front of the congregation, and he left." This is related by Sa'id ibn Mansur.

Ahmad observes: "If the imam appoints another [it is acceptable] as 'Umar and 'Ali appointed another. If the people pray individually, [it is acceptable] as in the case of Mu'awiyyah when he was stabbed and the people prayed individually and completed their prayers."

When the people dislike their imam: Many ahadith have been related which warn against leading a congregation while one is disliked by them. Dislike here relates to one's religious conduct and is based on a valid reason.

Ibn 'Abbas relates that the Prophet said: "Three people's prayers will not rise above their head the length of a hand's span. [They are:] a man who leads a people in salah and they do not like him, a woman who has disobeyed her husband and he is displeased with her, and two brothers who are estranged." This is related by Ibn Majah. Al-'Iraqi says its chain is hasan.

'Abdullah ibn 'Amr relates that the Prophet sallallahu alehi wasallam said: "Allah does not accept prayers from three [types of] people: a man who leads a people and they dislike him, a man who attends the prayers after their time is finished, and a man who re-enslaves his freed slave." This is related by Abu Dawud and Ibn Majah.

Elaborating upon it, at-Tirmidhi says: "It is disliked that a man should lead a people in salah while they dislike him. If the imam is not a wrongdoer, then the sin is upon those who don't like him."

The Positioning Of The Imam And The Followers

It is preferred for one person to stand to the right of the imam and for a "group of two (or more)" to stand behind the imam.

Jabir reports: "The Prophet stood to pray and I came and stood on his left. He took me by my hand [and led me] around him until I stood on his right. Then, Jabir ibn Sakhr came and stood on the left of the Messenger of Allah *sallallahu alehi wasallam*. He took both of us by our hands and pushed us back until we stood behind him." This is related by Muslim and Abu Dawud.

If a woman is present with the group, then she is to stand in a row by herself behind the men and she is not to join them in their rows. If she did not stand in a separate row, her *salah* will still be valid according to the opinion of majority. Anas said: "An orphan and I prayed behind the Messenger of Allah in our house and my mother prayed behind us." In another version it is stated: "He put me and the orphan in a row behind him and the woman behind us." This is related by al-Bukhari and Muslim.

The position of the imam while leading the prayer: It is preferred for the imam to stand in the center of the rows and the people closest to him should be the people of intellect and understanding.

Abu Hurairah reports that the Prophet *sallallahu alehi wasallam* said: "Let the imam stand in the center, and close the gaps in the rows." This is related by Abu Dawud and both he and al-Mundhiri make no further comment on its authenticity.

Ibn Mas'ud reports that the Prophet *sallallahu alehi wasallam* said: "Let those who are prudent and sedate be near me, then those who are next to them, then those who are next to them, and beware of the tumult of the market place." This is related by Ahmad, Muslim, Abu Dawud, and at-Tirmidhi.

Anas said: "The Prophet loved that the emigrants (*muhajarin*) and helpers (*ansar*) stand next to him so that they would learn from him." This is related by Ahmad and Abu Dawud. The wisdom behind having such people close to the imam is that they can correct him if he makes a mistake and it is easy for the imam to appoint one of them in his place if he needs to leave.

The positioning of the young and the women: The Messenger of Allah placed the men in front of the young boys and the women behind the young boys.[43] This is related by Ahmad and Abu Dawud.

Abu Hurairah reported that the Messenger of Allah said: "The best rows for the men are the first rows and the worst rows for them are the last rows. The best rows for the women are the last rows and the worst for them are the front rows." The last rows are the best for the women because they are farther away from the men as against the first rows that are nearest to men's rows. This is related by the group except al-Bukhari.

---

[43]If there is just one boy, he should stand in the row of the men.

The prayer of an individual behind a row: If a person makes his opening *takbir* behind a row and then he enters the row and performs the *ruku'* with the imam, his *salah* will be valid.

Abu Bakra reports that he came to the *salah* while the Prophet was performing *ruku'* and Abu Bakra performed the *ruku'* before he entered the row. He mentioned this to the Prophet and he said: "May Allah increase your love for goodness, but do not repeat that act." This is related by Ahmad, al-Bukhari, Abu Dawud, and anNasa'i.

According to the majority, if a person prays behind the rows by himself, his *salah* will be valid but diliked. Ahmad, Ishaq, Ahmad, ibn Abu Laila, Waki', al-Hassan ibn Saleh, an-Nakha'i and Ibn al-Mundhir hold that if a person prays one complete *rak'ah* behind the rows, his *salah* will be invalid.

Wabsah relates that the Messenger of Allah saw a man praying behind the rows by himself and the Propeht ordered him to repeat his *salah*. This is related by the five save an-Nasa'i. In Ahmad's version, the Messenger of Allah was asked about a man who prays by himself behind the rows and he said: "He is to repeat his *salah*." At-Tirmidhi called this *hadith hasan* and Ahmad's chain is good.

'Ali ibn Shaiban relates that the Messenger of Allah saw a man praying behind the row and he waited for him and (when he finished) told him: "Go forward (and join the row) for the *salah* of a person standing alone behind the rows is not valid." This is related by Ahmad, Ibn Majah, and al-Baihaqi. Ahmad says it is *hasan*. Ibn Sayyid an-Nass said its narrators are well-known, trustworthy people.

The majority stick to the *hadith* of Abu Bakra who said that he preformed part of the prayer, behind the row, and the Prophet did not order him to repeat his *salah*. Repeating the *salah* signifies overzeal in practicing what is recommended and better.

Al-Kaman ibn al-Hamam said: "Our scholars are of the opinion that the *hadith* of Wabsah refers to what is preferred while the *hadith* of 'Ali ibn ash-Shaiban underlines failure to practice what is the best and, as such, they are in harmony with the *hadith* of Abi Bakra. It is clear, then, that it is not necessary to repeat the *salah* because such an act was not always ordered.

If someone comes to the row and does not find sufficient space or a gap to stand in the row, then, according to some, he should stand by himself and it is disliked that he should pull anyone back from the row. Others say that he should pull one, who is aware of the ruling, back from the row after they have performed the opening *takbir*, and it is preferred for the one who is pulled to join him."

Straightening the rows and filling the gaps: It is preferred for the imam to order the followers to straighten the rows and fill in any gaps before he starts the *salah*.

Anas relates: "The Prophet would turn his face to us before he began the *salah* and he would say: 'Be close together and straighten your rows.'" This is related by al-Bukhari and Muslim. He also reported that the Prophet would say: "Make your rows straight for the straightening of the rows is part of the completion of the *salah*."

An-Nu'man ibn Bashir says: "The Prophet would straighten us in our rows as one straightens an arrow, until he saw that we had learned from him. One day, he saw a person with his chest sticking out and he said: 'You had better straighten your rows or Allah will cause differences among you.'" This is related by the five. At-Tirmidhi says it is *sahih*.

Abu Umamah reports that the Prophet *sallallahu alehi wasallam* said: "Straighten your rows and put your shoulders close to each other and be gentle with each other and fill in the gaps for the Satan passes through what is between you like small sheep [are able to pass through gaps]." This is related by Ahmad and at-Tabarani with a chain that has no fault in it.

Anas reports that the Messenger of Allah said: "Complete the front row, then the ones after it, and if there is any incompletion, it should be in the last row." This is related by Abu Dawud, an-Nasa'i, and al-Baihaqi.

Ibn 'Umar says: "There is no step that carries a greater reward than the step a man takes to an empty gap in a row in order to fill it." This is related by al-Bazar with a *hasan* chain.

Ibn 'Umar also related that the Messenger of Allah said: "Whoever connects a row, Allah will join him. Whoever cuts off a row, Allah will cut him off." This is related by An-Nasa'i, al-Hakim, and Ibn Khuzaimah.

Jabir ibn Samrah says: "The Prophet *sallallahu alehi wasallam* came to us and said: 'Why don't you make the rows like the angels make their rows in the presence of their Lord?' We asked: 'O Messenger of Allah, how do the angels make their rows in the presence of their Lord?' He replied: 'They complete the first row and stand closely together, side by side, in the row.'" This is related by the group, save al-Bukhari and at-Tirmidhi.

Encouragement concerning being in the first row and on the right side: We have already mentioned the Prophet's words "If the people knew what [great blessings were] in the call to *salah* and in the first row the people would vie with one another to call the *adhan* and to be in the first row, and if they found no way to decide [who would be allowed to make the call to *salah* or to be in the first row] except by drawing lots, then they would draw lots."

Abu Sa'id al-Khudri reports that the Prophet noticed his companions going to the back rows, and he said: "Come close and follow me and let those behind follow you. People will continue going to the back until Allah will put them in the back." This is related by Muslim, an-Nasa'i, Abu Dawud, and Ibn Majah.

'Aishah reports that the Prophet *sallallahu alehi wasallam* said: "Allah and His angels send down blessings upon those who pray on the right side of the rows." This is related by Abu Dawud and Ibn Majah.

Ahmad and at-Tabarani record, with a *sahih* chain, from Abu Umamah that the Prophet said: "Allah and the angels send down blessings upon the first row." The people inquired: "O Messenger of Allah, and upon the second row?" The Prophet again said: "Allah and the angels send down blessings upon the first row." The people asked again: "O Messenger of Allah, and upon the second row?" Finally he said: "And upon the second row."

Repeating imam's words for others in the back rows: If some people cannot hear the imam, it is preferred for one to repeat in a loud voice the imam's words for the others to hear.[44] There is consensus among scholars that repeating aloud after the imams without there being any real need for it is an abhorent innovation.

---

[44]This obviously only applies to the *takbir*, "O Allah, Our Lord, and to You is the praise," and the *taslim* – that is, one is not to repeat the Qur'anic recital for others to hear it.—J.Z.

THE MOSQUES

The earth as a mosque: Allah the Exalted has conferred a special blessing upon this ummah – that is, the whole earth has been declared a mosque for it. Therefore, when the time for prayer comes, a Muslim may pray wherever he may be. Abu Dharr asked the Prophet, "What was the first mosque on the earth?" He said: "The Masjid al-Haram [in Makkah]." Abu Dharr asked: "which is the next oldest mosque?" The Prophet *sallallahu alehi wassalam* said: "The al-Aqsa Mosque." Abu Dharr asked: "How much time was there between [the building of the two]." The Prophet *sallallahu alehi wasallam* replied: "Forty years." Then, he said: "Wherever you may be, at the time of *salah*, you may pray for it [the earth] is all a mosque." This is related by the group.

The excellence of building mosques: 'Uthman reports that the Prophet *sallallahu alehi wasallam* said: "Whoever builds for Allah a mosque, seeking by it Allah's grace, Allah will build for him a house in paradise." This is related by al-Bukhari and Muslim.

Ibn 'Abbas reports that the Prophet *sallallahu alehi wasallam* said: "Whoever builds for Allah a mosque, even if it be tiny, like a bird's nest, Allah will build for him a house in paradise." This is related by Ahmad, Ibn Hibban, and al-Bazzar with a *sahih* chain.

Supplications while going to the mosque: It is *sunnah* to make supplications while going to the mosque. The following are examples of such supplications:

Umm Salamah reports: "When the Messenger of Allah left the house he would say:

'In the name of Allah, I put my trust in Allah. O Allah, I seek refuge in Thee lest I stray or be led astray or cause injustice or suffer injustice or do wrong or have wrong done to me!"

بسم الله توكلت على الله ، اللهم إني أعوذ بك أن أضل أو أُضل ، أو أَزِلّ أو أُزل ، أو أَظلم أو أُظلم ، أو أجهل أو يُجهل عليّ .

This is related by Abu Dawud, an-Nasa'i, Ibn Majah, and at-Tirmidhi, who calls it *sahih*.

Anas reports that the Messenger of Allah said: "Whoever says upon leaving from his house:

'In the name of Allah, I put my trust in Allah. There is no power or might except with Allah,'

بسم الله ، توكلت على الله ، ولا حول ولا قوة إلا بالله .

it will be said to him: 'That is sufficient for you...you are guided, defended, and protected and the devil will be driven away from you.'" This is related by Abu Dawud, an-Nasa'i, and at-Tirmidhi who calls it *hasan*.

Al-Bukhari and Muslim record from Ibn 'Abbas that the Prophet left for the mosque saying:

"O Allah, make light in my heart, and light in my vision, and light in my hearing, and light on my right, and light behind me, and light in my nerves, and light in my flesh, and light in my blood, and light in my hair and light in my skin."

اللهم اجعل فى قلبى نوراً ، وفى بصرى نوراً ، وفى سمعى نوراً ، وعن يمينى نوراً ، وخلفى نوراً ، وفى عصبى نوراً ، وفى لحمى نوراً ، وفى دمى نوراً ، وفى شعرى نوراً ، وفى بشرى نوراً .

In Muslim's version, we find the words:

"O Allah, make light in my heart and light on my tongue, and make light in my hearing, and light in my sight, and make light behind me, and light in front of me, and make light above me, and light below me . O Allah, give me light."

اللهم اجعل فى قلبى نوراً ، وفى لسانى نوراً ، واجعل فى سمعى نوراً ، وفى بصرى نوراً ، واجعل من خلفى نوراً ، ومن أمامى نوراً ، واجعل من فوقى نوراً ، ومن تحتى نوراً ، اللهم أعطنى نوراً .

Abu Sa'id al-Khudri reports that the Prophet said: "If a man leaves his house to go to the prayer and says, 'O Allah, I ask You by the right of the supplicant upon You and by the right of this walking – as I have not come out in an arrogant or unthankful manner or for show

اللهم إنى أسألك بحق السائلين عليك وبحق ممشاى هذا ، فإنى لم أخرج أشَراً ولا بطراً ولا رياء ولا سمعـة ، خرجت اتقاء

or for fame; I came out in fear of Your anger and desiring Your pleasure – I ask You to rescue me from the Fire and to forgive my sins as no one forgives sins, save You,'

سخطك ، وابتغاء مرضاتك ، أسألك أن تنقذنى من النار ، وأن تغفر لى ذنوبى إنه لا يغفر الذنوب إلا أنت .

Allah will assign for him seventy thousand angels to ask forgiveness for him and Allah turns His face to him until he finishes his prayer." This is related by Ahmad, Ibn Khuzaimah, and Ibn Majah. Al-Hafez said that it is *hasan*.

Supplications upon entering and leaving the mosques: It is a *sunnah* for one who wants to enter the mosque to enter with his right foot first and to say:

"I seek refuge in Allah, the Exalted, and by His honorable face, and in His everlasting authority, [away] from the outcast Satan. In the name of Allah! O Allah, shower blessings upon Muhammad. O Allah, forgive my sins for me and open for me the doors of Your mercy."

أعـوذ بالله العـظيم وبـوجهـه الكـريم ، وسلطانه القديم ، من الشيطان الرجيم . بسم الله : اللهم صل على محمد : اللهم اغفر لى ذنوبى وافتح لى أبواب رحمتك .

When one wants to leave the mosque he should step with his left foot first and say:

"In the name of Allah! O Allah, shower blessings upon Muhammad. O Allah, forgive my sins for me and open for me the doors of Your bounty. O Allah, protect me from the accursed Satan."

بسم الله : اللهم صل على محمد : اللهم اغفر لى ذنوبى وافتح لى أبواب فضلك : اللهم اعصمنى من الشيطان الرجيم .

The excellence of proceeding to the mosque to attend *salah*: Abu Hurairah reports that the Prophet *sallallahu alehi wasallam* said: "If anyone goes back and forth to the mosque [to attend the prayers], Allah will prepare for him a feast in paradise as often as he goes back and forth." This is related by Ahmad, al-Bukhari, and Muslim.

Abu Sa'id reports that the Prophet *sallallahu alehi wasallam* said: "If you see a man frequenting the mosque, then testify that he has faith. As Allah says, 'The attendants of Allah's mosque are those who believe in Allah and the last day [At-Taubah: 18].'" This is related by Ahmad, Ibn Majah, Ibn Khuzaimah, Ibn Hibban, and by at-Tirmidhi, who says it is *hasan*, and by al-Hakim who says it is *sahih*.

Muslim records, on the authority of Abu Hurairah, that the Messenger of Allah said: "If anyone purifies himself in his house, and then walks to one of the houses of Allah to fulfill one of the obligations laid down by Allah, then [each one] of his steps will erase one of his sins and the next will raise his degrees."

Abu ad-Darda' reports that the Messenger of Allah said: "The mosque is a house for every pious person, and Allah provides everyone whose house is the mosque with comfort, leisure, and a path to Allah's pleasure, to paradise." This is related by at-Tabarani and al-Bazzar with a *sahih* chain.

We have already mentioned the *hadith* which begins with words "Shall I not point out to you [an act] by which Allah erases sins and raises degrees...?"

The prayer of salutations to the mosque (*tahyyatul masjid*):
Abu Qatadah reports that the Messenger of Allah said: "When one of you comes to the mosque, he should pray two *rak'at* before he sits." This is related by the group.

Three most excellent mosques: Jabir reports that the Messenger of Allah said: "Prayer in the inviolable mosque [in Makkah] is like 100,000 prayers [elsewhere]. And prayers in my mosque [in Medinah] is like one thousand prayers [elsewhere]. And a prayer in Bait al-Maqdis [in Jerusalem] is like five hundred prayers [elsewhere]. This is related by al-Baihaqi, and as-Sayuti says it is *hasan*.

Ahmad records that the Messenger of Allah said: "Offering *salah* in my mosque is better than one thousand prayers elsewhere, save for those offered in the inviolable mosque. And *salah* in the inviolable mosque is better than *salah* in my mosque by one hundred prayers."

The Prophet said: "One should not undertake a journey, save to three mosques: the inviolable mosque [in Makkah], my mosque here [in Medinah], and Masjid al-Aqsa [in Jerusalem]." This is related by the group.

Embellishing the Mosques: Anas reports that the Messenger of Allah said: "The Hour will not come to pass until the people vie with each other in (building) the mosques." This is related by Ahmad, Abu Dawud, an-Nasa'i, Ibn Majah, and Ibn Hibban who calls it *sahih*. Ibn Khuzaimah's wording is: "A time will come when the people will vie with each other in (building) the mosques but very few will attend (the mosques)."

Ibn 'Abbas reports that the Messenger of Allah said: "I have not been ordered to build high and lofty mosques." Abu Dawud's version adds: "Ibn 'Abbas said: 'You will certainly embellish them as the Jews and Christians embellished [their places of worship].'" The preceding *hadith* was related by Abu Dawud and by Ibn Hibban who calls it *sahih*.

'Umar ordered mosques to be built and would say: "Protect the people from the rain. Beware of red and yellow decorations for they distract people." This is related by Ibn Khuzaimah in his *sahih* and by al-Bukhari in *mu'alaq*[45] form.

Keeping the mosques clean and scenting them: 'Aishah reports that the Prophet ordered that mosques be built in residential areas and that they be cleaned and perfumed. This is related by Ahmad, Abu Dawud, at-Tir-midhi, Ibn Majah, and Ibn Hibban with a good chain. Abu Dawud's word-ing is: "He ordered us to build the mosques in the residential areas, to build them well, and to purify them. 'Abdullah would burn incense when 'Umar would sit on the pulpit."

Anas reports that the Prophet *sallallahu alehi wasallam* said: "The re-wards of my *ummah* were placed before me, even for removing a speck of dust from the mosque." This is related by Abu Dawud, at-Tirmidhi, and Ibn Khuzaimah who calls it *sahih*.

Maintaining the Mosques: The Mosques are houses of worship and it is obligatory to keep them clean and free of filth and noxious smells.

Muslim records that the Prophet *sallallahu alehi wasallam* said: "These mosques are not meant for urine or filth but they are for the remembrance of Allah and the recital of the Qur'an.

Ahmad records, with a *sahih* chain, that the Prophet *sallallahu alehi wasallam* said: "If one of you expectorates, he should cover it lest it should besmear a believer's body or clothing and harm him."

Ahmad and al-Bukhari record from Abu Hurairah that the Messenger of Allah said: "When one of you stands to pray, he should not spit in front of him as he is facing Allah when he is in prayer. And he should not spit to his right as there is an angel on his right. So, he should spit to his left or under his feet and he should bury it."

Jabir reports that the Prophet *sallallahu alehi wasallam* said: "Whoever eats garlic, onion, or leek should not come close to our mosque for the angels are harmed by what harms the children of Adam." This is related by al-Bukhari and Muslim.

On Friday, 'Umar addressed the people saying: "O you people, you eat of two plants which I consider bad [onion and garlic] for I have seen the Prophet, when he perceived their smell from someone, he would order the man to go to al-Baqi'. Whoever eats them should suppress their odor by

---

[45]A report in which one or more authorities from the beginning is missing, and as a rule it is considered *sahih* when found in one of the authentic collections. (editor)

cooking them." This is related by Ahmad, Muslim, and an-Nasa'i.

Prohibition of announcing lost objects, trading or reciting poetry in the mosques: Abu Hurairah reports that the Messenger of Allah said: "If you hear a man announcing in the mosque about some object which he has lost tell him: 'May Allah not return it to you for the mosques are not built for that.'" This is related by Muslim.

Abu Hurairah also relates that the Prophet said: "If you see someone buying or selling in the mosque, say to him: 'May Allah not give you any profit in your trading.'" This is related by an-Nasa'i and at-Tirmidhi. The latter calls it *hasan*.

'Abdullah ibn 'Umar reports that the Peophet forbade buying and selling in the mosque, reciting poetry in it, or announcing lost items, and he especially prohibited making a circle [i.e., a meeting in a circle] before the Friday prayer. This is related by the five, and at-Tirmidhi calls it *sahih*.

The poetry which is prohibited is that which ridicules a Muslim, praises a wrongdoer or some lewdness, and so on. Concerning that which contains wisdom or praises of Islam or encouragement to piety, there is nothing wrong with it. Abu Hurairah reports that 'Umar passed by Hassan as he was reciting poetry in the mosque. 'Umar looked at him in a disapproving manner. Hassan said: "I used to recite when one better than you was present." He turned to Abu Hurairah and said: "I adjure you by Allah to state that you have heard the Messenger of Allah say: 'Respond for me [Hassan]. O Allah, support him with the Angel Gabriel.'" Abu Hurairah said: "Yes, [I heard it]." This is related by al-Bukhari and Muslim.

Begging in the mosque: Shaikh al-Islam Ibn Taimiyah says: "Begging is forbidden whether it is in the mosque or outside it, unless there is a real need for it. If necessary, one may beg in the mosque as long as one does not harm anyone and does not lie in begging, or disturb the people by stepping over them or with one's loudness, for instance, when the people are listening to the Friday *khutbah*, and one distracts them by one's voice.

Raising one's voice in the mosque: It is forbidden to raise one's voice in such a way that it disturbs others' prayers, even if it is done while reciting the Qur'an. Teaching or imparting knowledge (to others) is exempt from this prohibition.

Ibn 'Umar relates that the Prophet *sallallahu alehi wasallam* entered upon some people while they were praying and they were raising their voices in the Qur'anic recital. The Prophet said: "One who is praying is in a private conversation with his Lord so he should be mindful of whom he is conversing with. And you should not raise your voices against each other in [the recital of] the Qur'an." This is related by Ahmad with a *sahih* chain.

Abu Sa'id al-Khurdi reports that the Prophet was making seclusion (*i'tikaf*) in the mosque and he heard the people reciting aloud. He removed the covering and said: "Verily, each of you is in a private conversation with his Lord so you should not disturb each other. And you are not to raise your voices against each other in the recitation." This is related by Abu Dawud, an-Nasa'i, al-Baihaqi, and al-Hakim who grades it *sahih* according to the criteria of al-Bukhari and Muslim.

Talking in the mosque: An-Nawawi says: "It is permissible to engage in lawful conversation in the mosque and one may discuss worldly affairs and other things and even laugh, as long as it is about something permissible. This opinion is based on the *hadith* of Jabir ibn Samurah who said: 'The Prophet would not rise from his place of the morning prayer until the sun had risen, and when the sun rose, he would get up. And they would talk and laugh about [pre-Islamic] days of ignorance, and he would smile.'" This is related by Muslim.

Permission to eat, drink, or sleep in the mosque: Ibn 'Umar says: "During the time of the Messenger of Allah, we would sleep and take nap in the mosque, and at that time, we were young men."

An-Nawawi said: "It is confirmed that *ahl as-suffah*, 'Ali, Sufyan ibn Umayyah, and a number of the companions used to sleep in the mosque. Thumamah slept there before he embraced Islam. All of that was during the time of the Messenger of Allah." Ash-Shaf'i writes in *al-Umm*: "If a polythiest could sleep in a mosque, then definitely a Muslim can." In *al-Mukhtasar* it is said: "There is no harm in a polythiest staying in any mosque except the inviolable mosque [in Makkah]." 'Abdullah ibn al-Harith says: "During the time of the Messenger of Allah, we would eat meat and bread in the mosque." This is related by Ibn Majah with a *hasan* chain.

Clasping the hands or intertwining the fingers: It is disliked to clasp one's hands while going to the mosque or while waiting for the *salah* in the mosque, although it is perfectly permissible to do so at other times, even in the mosque. Ka'b relates that the Messenger of Allah said: "When one of you makes *wudu'*, perfects the *wudu'*, and leaves with the intention of going to the mosque, he should not intertwine his fingers as he is [considered to be] in *salah*." This is related by Ahmad, Abu Dawud, and at-Tirmidhi.

Abu Sa'id al-Khudri says: "I entered the mosque with the Messenger of Allah while a man was sitting in the middle of the mosque with his fingers intertwined. The Messenger of Allah motioned to him but the man did not notice or understand him. The Messenger of Allah turned and said: 'If one of you is in the mosque, he should not intertwine his fingers as intertwining of the fingers is from the Satan, and you are in the prayer while you are in the mosque until you leave it.'" This is related by Ahmad.

Salah **between walls and enclosures:** It is allowed for the imam or one who is offering salah by himself to pray between two walls or enclosures. Al-Bukhari and Muslim record from Ibn 'Umar that when the Prophet entered the Ka'bah, he prayed between two walls.

Sa'id ibn Jubair, Ibrahim at-Taimi, and Suwaid ibn Ghuflah led the people in *salah* while they were between two columns. It is disliked for the followers to pray between them if they have enough room because it cuts the row, but they may do so if they are constrained to it.

Anas says: "We were prohibited to offer *salah* between walls and we would keep others from it." This is related by al-Hakim who says it is *sahih*.

Mu'awiyyah ibn Qurrah relates that his father said: "We were prohibited to make rows between walls during the time of the Prophet and we kept others from it." This is related by Ibn Majah but one of its narrator is *majhul* (unknown as a trustworthy person). Sa'id ibn Mansur records in his *Sunan* that Ibn Mas'ud, Ibn 'Abbas, and Hudhaifah prohibited it. Ibn Sayyid an-Nass said: "There is no known difference among the companions [on this point]."

PLACES WHERE (OFFERING) PRAYER IS PROHIBITED

It is prohibited to make *salah* in the following places:

Graveyards: 'Aishah reports that the Prophet *sallallahu alehi wasallam* said: "Allah cursed the Jews and Christians [because] they took the graves of their prophets as mosques." This is related by al-Bukhari, Muslim, Ahmad, and an-Nasa'i.

Ahmad and Muslim record from Abu Marthad al-Ghanawi that the Prophet *sallallahu alehi wasallam* said: "Do not pray facing a grave and do not sit on one." They also record that Jundub ibn 'Abdullah al-Bajali heard the Prophet say, five days before he died: "The people before you took graves as mosques. I prohibit this to you."

'Aishah reports that Umm Salamah mentioned the churches she saw in

Abyssinia and the pictures they contained to the Messenger of Allah. The Prophet said to her: "These are the people who, when a pious servant or pious man among them dies, build a mosque [place of worship] upon their graves and put those pictures in it. They are the worst of the whole creation in the sight of Allah." This is related by al-Bukhari, Muslim, and an-Nasa'i.

The Prophet is also reported to have said: "Allah curses those who visit the graves and take them as mosques and light lamps over them." Many scholars take this prohibition to be one of dislike, regardless of whether the grave is in front of the imam or behind him. According to the *zahiri* school, this prohibition is one of complete forbiddance and as such, prayer at a grave site is not valid.[46] According to the Hanbali school, this applies only if there are three graves or more. If there is only one or two graves, then the prayer is valid although disliked if one prays facing a grave, otherwise it is not disliked.

Churches and synagogues: Abu Musa al-Ash'ari and 'Umar ibn 'Abdulaziz prayed in a church. Ash-Sh'abiy, 'Ata, and Ibn Sireen did not see anything wrong with praying in a church [if one happened to be in a church at the time of *salah*]. Al-Bukhari says: "Ibn 'Abbas would pray in churches [under unusual circumstances] except for those with statues or sculptures." The Muslims of Najran wrote to 'Umar saying that they found no place cleaner or better to pray in than a church. 'Umar wrote to them: "Sprinkle it with water and leaves and pray therein." According to the Hanafi and Shaf'i schools, it is disliked to pray in such places in general.

Dunghills, slaughterhouses, middle of the roads, resting places of the camels near watering holes, bathrooms and on the roof of the "house of Allah": Ibn 'Umar relates that the Prophet *sallallahu alehi wasallam* prohibited *salah* in seven places: "dunghills, slaughterhouses, graveyards, middle of the road, bathhouses, watering places where the camels drink and rest, and on the roof of the house of Allah [the Ka'bah in Makkah]." This is related by Ibn Majah, 'Abd ibn Humaid, and at-Tirmidhi who said its chain is not strong. The reason why it is prohibited to pray on dunghills and in slaughterhouses is the presence of impurities there. It is forbidden to pray at such places without any barrier, and if there is such a barrier one may pray, but it is disliked by the majority of the scholars, while Ahmad and other scholars of *zahiri* persuasion say it is prohibited. The reason why it is prohibited to pray in the resting places of the camels is the same as in the first two cases (i.e., the presence of impurities). The reason why

---

[46]This is apparently the correct opinion in the light of many authentic *ahadith*.

it is prohibited to pray at the middle of the roads is because there is usually a lot of commotion, which could take one's heart away from the *salah*. As for praying on the roof of the Ka'bah, this contradicts the order to offer *salah* facing it. For this reason, many are of the opinion that a *salah* performed on top of the Ka'bah is invalid. The Hanafi school holds that it is allowed, but disliked as it does not honor the Ka'bah. The reason it is disliked to pray in bath-houses is the presence of impurities there, according to the majority of the scholars. Ahmad, Abu Thaur, and the Zahiriyyah hold that a *salah* offered in the bath-house is not valid.

Prayer in the Ka'bah: Offering *salah* in the Ka'bah is valid regardless of whether it is an obligatory prayer or a supererogatory prayer. Ibn 'Umar reports: "The Messenger of Allah entered the house [the Ka'bah] with 'Usamah ibn Zaid, Bilal, and 'Uthman ibn Talhah and they closed the door behind themselves. When they opened the door, I was the first to come upon them and I asked Bilal: 'Did the Messenger of Allah pray [while he was inside]?' He said: 'Yes, between the two Yemeni pillars.'" This is related by Ahmad, al-Bukhari, and Muslim.

The *Sutrah* Or Partition In Front Of One Who Is Praying

Pray toward your *sutrah*: It is preferred for the one who is praying to place a *sutrah* (or some sort of partition) in front of him in order to keep others from passing in front of him and to keep his eyesight from going behind this partition.

Abu Sa'id reports that the Prophet *sallallahu alehi wasallam* said: "When one of you prays, he should pray toward his *sutrah* and he should be close to it." This is related by Abu Dawud and Ibn Majah.

Ibn 'Umar relates that "when the Prophet *sallallahu alehi wasallam* went out to pray *salatul 'id*, he asked for a spear and placed it in front of himself and he offered *salah* toward it and the people prayed behind him. And he would do that while he was traveling so that those in authority [for the affairs of the Muslims] would also do this." This is related by al-Bukhari, Muslim, and Abu Dawud.

The Hanafi and Maliki scholars are of the opinion that one should place a *sutrah* in front of him only if he fears that someone may pass in front of him; if he does not fear that someone will pass in front of him, it is not desirable for him to place a *sutrah* in front of himself. This opinion is based on the *hadith* of Ibn 'Abbas who said that the Prophet *sallallahu alehi wasallam* prayed in an open area and there was nothing in front of him. This is related by Ahmad and Abu Dawud. Al-Baihaqi related it and said: "It is supported by a report from al-Fadhl Ibn 'Abbas with a reliable chain of transmitters."

Requirements for a *sutrah* or partition: Anything which the person sets up in front of him will qualify as a *sutrah*, even if it is only the end of his bed. Sabrah ibn Mu'abid reports that the Messenger of Allah said: "When one of you prays, he should make a partition for his *salah*, even if it is an arrow." This is related by Ahmad and by al-Hakim who said it is *sahih* according to the criteria of Muslim. Al-Haithami observes: "Ahmad's narrators are sound."

Abu Hurairah relates that the Prophet said: "When one of you prays, he should place something in front of him. If he cannot find anything, he should prop up his staff [in front of him]. If he does not have a staff, he should draw a line [on the ground in front of him] then nothing that passes in front of him will harm him." This is related by Ahmad and Abu Dawud and Ibn Hibban. The later classifies it *sahih* as did Ahmad and Ibn al-Madini. Al-Baihaqi says: "There is no problem with that *hadith* regarding that ruling, Allah willing."

It is related that the Prophet *sallallahu alehi wasallam* prayed toward a column in his mosque, toward a tree, toward a bed upon which 'Aishah was lying, and toward his riding animal, and toward his saddle, and so on.

Talhah says: "We used to pray and the animals would pass in front of us. We mentioned that to the Prophet and he said: "If anything the size of a saddle is in front of you, nothing that passes beyond it would harm you." This is related by Ahmad, Muslim, Abu Dawud, Ibn Majah, and at-Tirmidhi who calls it *hasan sahih*.

The *sutrah* of the imam is *sutrah* of the followers: The *sutrah* of the imam is the *sutrah* of everyone behind him.

'Amr ibn Shu'aib relates from his father on the authority of his grand-father who said: "We were descending on a path near Makkah with the Messenger of Allah and the time for prayer came. The Prophet prayed toward a wall and we were behind him. A lamb tried to pass in front of him and he kept preventing the lamb from doing so until its stomach was up against the wall. Finally, it passed behind him." This is related by Ahmad and Abu Dawud.

Ibn 'Abbas says: "I was riding a donkey and was at the time on the threshold of maturity, and the Prophet was leading the people in *salah* at Mina. I passed in front of the row and let the animal graze, and then I joined the rows and no one objected to this." This is related by the group.

These *ahadith* prove that it is allowed to pass in front of people follow-ing the imam, and that the *sutrah* is required for the imam and the people praying individually.

Proximity of the *sutrah*: Al-Baghawi says: "The people of knowledge prefer that the *sutrah* be so close that there is only enough space to make the *sajdah*, and the same applies to the distance between the rows in the prayer."

In the *hadith* mentioned in the beginning of this section it is stated: "And he should be close to it."

Bilal reports that between the Prophet and the wall in front of him there was a distance of three arm spans. This is related by Ahmad and an-Nasa'i, and al-Bukhari has recorded something similar.

Sahl ibn Sa'd says: "Between the Messenger of Allah [and his *sutrah*] was enough space for a sheep to pass." This is related by al-Bukhari and Muslim.

Prohibition of passing in front of a praying person: It is forbidden to pass in front of a person who is praying (i.e., between him and his *sutrah*).

There are many *ahadith* which forbid passing between a person and his *sutrah*, and describe such an act as a major sin.

Busr ibn Sa'id says that Zaid ibn Khalid sent him to Abu Juhaim to ask him what he had heard from the Prophet *sallallahu alehi wasallam* concerning passing in front of someone who is praying. He said that the Messenger of Allah said: "If one knew [the sin] of passing in front of one who is praying, he would rather wait forty [...][47] than to pass in front of him." This is related by the group.

Zaid ibn Khalid relates that the Messenger of Allah said: "If the one who passes in front of one who is praying knew what was upon him [of sin], it would be better for him to stand [and wait] for forty autumns than to pass in front of him." This is related by al-Bazzar with a *sahih* chain.

Ibn al-Qayyim writes: "Ibn Hibban and others say that the prohibition mentioned in this *hadith* applies when one is praying with a *sutrah*. If one is praying without a *sutrah*, it is not forbidden to pass in front of him. As a proof, Abu Hatim [i.e., ibn Hibban] argues by the *hadith*, in his *sahih*, from al-Mutalib ibn Abi Wid'ah who said: 'I saw the Prophet, when he finished the circumambulation [of the Ka'bah], he went to the end of the circuit and he prayed two *rak'at* and there was nothing between him and the people who were circumambulating." Abu Hatim says: "This report proves that it is permissible to pass in front of a person who is praying but without a *sutrah*. In this lies a clear proof that the warning concerning

---

[47]The narrator did not recall if he said forty days or months or years.

passing in front of one who is praying refers only to one who is praying toward his *sutrah* and does not refer to one who does not have a *sutrah*." Abu Hatim explains that the Prophet's prayer was without anything between him and the people circumambulating the *ka'bah*. At the end of the hadith of al-Mutalib, he records: "I saw the Prophet of Allah offering *salah* facing the black stone and the men and women were passing in front of him and there was no *sutrah* between him and them. In *ar-Raudah an-Nadiyah*, it is stated that if one has no sutrah or is far away from the *sutrah*, then he is not to keep anyone from passing in front of him and it is not forbidden to pass in front of him although it is preferred not to do so.

Preventing someone from passing in front of a praying person: It is permissible to keep some one from passing in front of a person who is praying.

If a praying person has a *sutrah* in front of him, then it is allowed for him to prevent any human or animal from passing in front of him. If a person passes in front of him from beyond the *sutrah*, then the person in *salah* is neither to prevent the passer-by nor will he be harmed by him.

Abu Saleh as-Saman said: "I will narrate to you what I heard and saw from Abu Sa'id al-Khudri. One day I was with Abu Sa'id and he was offering *salah* on Friday facing something which concealed him from the people when a young man from the tribe of Mu'ait came and tried to pass in front of Abu Sa'id. He pushed him back. He tried again and Abu Sa'id struck him harder. The two scuffled. The man went to Marwan to complain. Abu Sa'id also went to Marwan. Marwan asked: 'What has happened between you and the son of your brother that caused him to complain?' Abu Sa'id said: 'I heard the Prophet *sallallahu alehi wasallam* say: 'If any of you prays toward a sutrah and someone tries to pass in front of you, then turn him away. If he refuses, use force for he is a devil.'" This is related by al-Bukhari and Muslim.

Passing of anything does not invalidate the prayer: The *salah* is not invalidated by anything (passing in front of the praying person).

'Ali, 'Uthman, ibn al-Musayyab, ash-Sh'abiy, Malik, ash-Shaf'i, Sufyan al-Thauri and the Hanafi scholars are of the opinion that the *salah* is not invalidated by anything which passes in front of a person. This is based on the *hadith* recorded by Abu Dawud from Abu al-Waddak who says: "A young person tried to pass in front of Abu Sa'id while he was praying. Abu Sa'id held him off and then the young man tried again. Abu Sa'id pushed him off. This happened three times and when [Abu Sa'id] finished [the prayer], he said: 'The *salah* is not invalidated by anything but the Messenger of Allah said: 'Repulse [the person who is trying to pass in front of you] to the best of your ability for he is a devil.'"

WHAT IS ALLOWED DURING THE PRAYER

The following acts are permissible during the prayer: Crying, moaning, or groaning, regardless of whether it is due to a fear of Allah or to any other reason (e.g., a moan due to some pain or injury that one cannot contain), is permissible. This is based on the Qur'anic verse: "When the revelations of the Merciful were recited unto them, they fell prostrating and adoring."[48] This verse is general and includes one who is praying.

'Abdullah ibn ash-Schikhir relates: "I saw the Messenger of Allah praying and his chest was 'buzzing', like the buzzing of a cooking pot, due to crying." This is related by Ahmad, Abu Dawud, an-Nasa'i, and at-Tirmidhi. The latter classifies it as *sahih*.

'Ali reports: "There was no horseman among us at the battle of Badr save al-Miqdad ibn al-Aswad. I saw that not one of us was standing save the Messenger of Allah who was praying under a tree and crying until the dawn." This is related by Ibn Hibban.

'Aishah relates the incident that occurred during the fatal illness of the Prophet *sallallahu alehi wasallam*. The Messenger of Allah said: "Order Abu Bakr to lead the people in prayer." 'Aishah responded: "O Messenger of Allah, Abu Bakr is a very soft-hearted man and he cannot control his tears, and if he recites the Qur'an, he cries." 'Aishah later admitted: "I said that only because I hated that the people should blame Abu Bakr for being the first to take the place of the Messenger of Allah." The Messenger of Allah said: "Order Abu Bakr to lead the people in *salah*. You women are like the companions of Yusuf." This is related by Ahmad, Abu Dawud, Ibn Hibban, and at-Tirmidhi who calls it *sahih*. The fact that the

---

[48]Qur'an 19:58

[81]

Prophet insisted that Abu Bakr lead the salah after he was informed that he would be overcome by weeping proves that it is permissible to cry while praying.

'Umar prayed fajr and recited Surah Yusuf,[49] and when he reached the verse "I expose my distress and anguish only unto Allah," he raised his voice in crying. This is related by al-Bukhari, Sa'id ibn Mansur, and ibn al-Mundhir. In 'Umar's raising his voice in crying is a refutation of those who say that crying invalidates the salah if it causes a sound from the mouth, regardless of whether it is due to the fear of Allah or not. They argue that sound from the mouth due to crying is like speaking, but this is not acceptable as crying and speaking are two different things.

Turning to a side due to some need: Ibn 'Abbas relates: "The Messenger of Allah would turn to his right and left but he would not turn his head to [see] behind him." This is related by Ahmad.

Abu Dawud records that when the Prophet sallallahu alehi wasallam prayed, "he looked toward a valley. because he had sent some horsemen to guard the valley."

Anas ibn Sireen says: "I saw Anas ibn Malik lift his eyes to something while he was praying." This is related by Ahmad.

Unneccessary turning during prayer: Turning to look at something without any genuine need is disliked, for it is against the etiqettes of humility while facing Allah in Prayer.

'Aishah says: "I asked the Messenger of Allah about turning in salah and he said: 'It is the portion that the Satan steals from the slave's prayer.'" This is related by Ahmad, al-Bukhari, an-Nasa'i, and Abu Dawud.

Abu ad-Darda' narrates from the Prophet: "O people, be careful about turning for there is no salah for the one who turns. If you must do it, do it in the voluntary prayers and not in the obligatory prayers." This is related by Ahmad.

Anas relates that the Messenger of Allah said to him: "Be careful about turning during the salah as turning in the salah is disastrous. If you must do it, then do it in the voluntary prayers but not in the obligatory prayers." This is related by at-Tirmidhi who calls it sahih.

In the hadith of al-Harith al-Ash'ari, the Prophet sallallahu alehi wasallam said: "Allah gave Yahya*, son of Zakariyah, five commands that he was to abide by and was to order the tribe of Isra'el to abide by..." One of them was, "Verily, Allah orders you to pray, and when you pray, do

---

[49]Qur'an 12:86
*John The Beptist, the forerunner of Jesus, peace be on them both.

not turn for Allah looks to the face of His slave in *salah* as long as he does not turn." This is related by Ahmad and an-Nasa'i.

Abu Dharr reported that the Prophet said: "Allah faces the slave while he is in the *salah* and keeps facing him as long as he does not turn. If [the slave] turns, [Allah] turns away from him." This is related by Ahmad and by Abu Dawud who said its chain of narrators (*isnad*) is *sahih*. The preceding *hadith* is concerned with turning the face during the *salah*. If one turns the whole (upper) body away from the *qiblah*, then the *salah* is invalidated, for not fulfilling the requirment of facing the *qiblah*. On this point, there is no difference of opinion.

Killing a snake, scorpion or other harmful animals: If killing these would only require a small action on the part of the person in *salah*, then there is no harm in doing it. Abu Hurairah reported that the Prophet *sallallahu alehi wasallam* said: "Kill the snake and the scorpion during the *salah*." This is related by Ahmad, at-Tirmidhi, Abu Dawud, an-Nasa'i, and Ibn Majah. The *hadith* is *hasan sahih*.

Taking a few steps due to some necessity: 'Aishah said: "The Messenger of Allah was offering *salah* in the house and the door was locked. I came and knocked on the door and he walked over to open it for me and then he returned to his place of prayer. The door was in the direction of the *qiblah*." This is related by Ahmad, Abu Dawud, an-Nasa'i, and at-Tirmidhi. The latter calls it *hasan*. It may be observed that in this *hadith*, he did not turn away from the *qiblah* either in opening the door, or in returning to his place. This is supported by what has been related that the Prophet would pray and if anyone knocked on the door, he would open the door provided the door was in the direction of the *qiblah* or on his right or on his left, but he would not turn his back to the *qiblah*. This is related by ad-Daraqutni.

Al-Azraq ibn Qais relates: "Abu Barzah Al-Aslami was at al-Ahwas, at the bank of a river, and he prayed while holding the reins of his horse. The horse started going back, and he (i.e.Abu Barzah) followed the horse. A man from the Khawarij said: 'O Allah, be rough on this man, see how he is doing his prayer.' When Abu Barzah finished his prayer, he said: 'I heard your statement. Certainly, I participated in six or seven or eight battles with the Prophet, and I am certainly aware of his leniency. Certainly, I would rather restrain my animal than let him run off loose as that would have caused me a great deal of trouble.' It was '*Asr* prayer that Abu Barzah offered, and he prayed two *rak'at*." This is related by Ahmad, al-Bukhari, and al-Baihaqi.

Concerning taking a lot of steps, Ibn Hajr says in *Fath al-Bari*: "The jurists are agreed that taking many steps invalidates an obligatory prayer.

They interpret the *hadith* of Abu Barzah as referring to taking just a few steps."

Carrying and holding a child during the *salah*: Abu Qatadah reports that the Prophet *sallallahu alehi wasallam* was offering *salah* and Umamah bint Zainab[50] was on his neck [shoulder]. When he performed *ruku'*, he put her down, and when he got up from his *sajdah*, he would place her back on his neck. 'Amr inquired during which *salah* this happened. Ibn Juraij said that it is related from Zaid ibn Abu 'Atab from 'Amr ibn Salim that this happened in the morning prayer. This is related by Ahmad, an-Nasa'i, and others. Al-Fakihani comments: "The purpose behind the action of the Prophet of carrying Umamah in the *salah* was to set an example before the Arabs who considered having daughters and carrying them around as something bad or shameful. The Prophet *sallallahu alehi wasallam* acted differently from them, and carried a girl on his neck in the prayer, and making something clear by example is much more effective than a mere precept."

'Abdullah ibn Shidad relates that his father said: "The Messenger of Allah came to us either during the noon or afternoon prayers and he was carrying Hassan or Hussain. The Prophet proceeded to the front and put him down and made the *takbir* for the *salah*. During the *salah*, he made a long *sajdah*. I raised my head and saw the child on the back of the Messenger of Allah while he was in *sajdah*. I returned to my *sajdah*. When the Messenger of Allah finished the *salah*, the people said to him: 'O Messenger of Allah, you prostrated during your *salah* so long that we suspected you were thinking about some matter or you were receiving some revelation.' He said: 'None of that happened but my son was resting and I hated to rush him until he had finished what he desired.'" This is related by Ahmad, an-Nasa'i, and al-Hakim.

An-Nawawi observes that this, according to the opinion of ash-Shaf'i and those who agree with him, points to the permissibility of carrying or holding a young child, male or female, or any pure animal during an obligatory prayer, and that it is permissible for both the imam and the followers. The companions of Malik say that the permissibility is only for voluntary prayers and not for obligatory prayers. This interpretation is incorrect as it is clear that the Prophet was leading one of the obligatory prayers, and as stated earlier it was the *fajr* prayer. Some followers of Malik claim that its permissibility has been abograted, while others say it was only permissible for the Prophet, and yet others hold that it was due to some necessity. All of this is wrong and to be rejected as there is no proof for any of it or any necessity. The authentic *hadith* clearly states that

---

[50]She was the daughter of Abul 'As Ibn al-Rabi'.

it is permissible and there is nothing in that ruling which contradicts any basic principle of the *shari'ah* as a human being is pure and what is in his/her abdomen is not relevant in this regard, as it remains within the stomach, its natural receptacle. Also, the clothing of a child is considered pure and the *shari'ah* is quite explicit on this point. Actions during the *salah* do not invalidate it if they are minor or few or dispersed. The fact that the Prophet *sallallahu alehi wasallam* did this is an exposition of its permissibility, and this argument is built upon the principle which we have mentioned before. This refutes what Abu Sulaiman al-Khattabi says, namely, that the Prophet did not carry the child intentionally but the child was holding onto the Prophet, and when he stood the child remained with him. He said: "Do not think that he held him again intentionally as that would be too much action and would distract the heart. If a curtain distracted him, how could [the child] not distract him?" This statement by al-Khattabi, may Allah have mercy on him, is incorrect and to be rejected. Among the things that refute it are the statements in *Sahih Muslim*, "when he stood, he carried him." And, "when he got up from his *sajdah*, he would return [the child to his place]." Further refutations are derived from a version other than *Sahih Muslim*, "He came to us while carrying Umamah and prayed..." Concerning the ruling about the curtain, it distracts the heart without there being any benefit to it. Concerning carrying Umamah, we are not convinced that it distracts the heart, and even if it does, it is allowed due to its benefit and the principles that we have mentioned. The source of that preoccupation is that benefit, which differs from the incident concerning the curtain. Thus, the correct position is that the *hadith* is a clear exposition that it is permissible to carry a child in *salah* and this will continue to be part of the Islamic law until the Day of Judgment. And Allah knows best.

Returning a Greeting by a motion: The one in *salah* who is greeted or spoken to may reply to the one who greets or speaks to him by making some motion.

Jabir said: "The Messenger of Allah sent me somewhere while he was going to the tribe of Mustaliq. I came to him and he was praying while on the back of his camel. [When] I spoke to him, he and Zubair motioned with their hands. I heard him reciting and saw him gesturing with his head. When he finished, he said: 'What have you done about the thing I sent you for? Nothing kept me from talking to you save that I was in *salah*.'" This is related by Ahmad and Muslim.

'Abdullah ibn 'Umar narrates that Suhaib said: "I passed by the Messenger of Allah while he was offering salah. I greeted him and he responded to me by only signaling." 'Abdullah said: "The only thing that I know is that he said he signaled to him with his finger." This is related by Ahmad and by at-Tirmidhi. The latter calls it *sahih*.

'Abdullah ibn 'Umar says: "I asked Suhaib: 'How did the Messenger of Allah respond to the people when they greeted him while he was praying?' He said: 'He would signal to them with his hand.'" This is related by Ahmad, at-Tirmidhi, Abu Dawud, an-Nasa'i, and Ibn Majah.

Anas says that the Prophet would signal while offering *salah*. This is related by Ahmad, Abu Dawud, and Ibn Khuzaimah and its *isnad* is *sahih*.

The same applies to signaling with one's finger or hand or by nodding the head. All of these actions have been related from the Prophet *sallallahu alehi wasallam*.

Saying *Subhanallah* and clapping: It is allowed for men to say *subhanallah* and for women to clap if there is some need to do so (such as alerting the imam to a mistake or informing someone that he or she may enter the room or to warn a blind person, and so on). Sahl ibn Sa'd as-Sa'di relates that the Prophet said: "If someone is faced with something during the *salah*, he should say '*subhanallah*.' Clapping is for the women and saying *subhanallah* is for the men." This is related by Ahmad, Abu Dawud, and an-Nasa'i.

Correcting the imam's mistake: If the imam forgets a verse, it is permissible for a follower to remind him of it, regardless of whether the recitation is a part of the obligatory recitation or not. Ibn 'Umar reports that the Messenger of Allah prayed and had some confusion in his recitation. When he finished, he said to 'Umar: "Were you present with us [during the prayer]?" He replied: "Yes." So, the Prophet *sallallahu alehi wasallam* asked him: "What prevented you from correcting me?" This is related by Abu Dawud and others and its narrators are trustworthy.

Praising Allah when one sneezes or recalls to mind a blessing: Rifa'ah ibn Rafi' relates: "I prayed behind the Messenger of Allah, and I sneezed and said, 'Praise be to Allah, a great deal of praise, beautiful and blessed, as our Lord loves and is pleased with.' [Afterward,] the Messenger of Allah asked: 'Who spoke during the *salah*?' No one said anything. He asked again, and no one said anything. He asked again, and I said: 'It was I, O Messenger of Allah!' He then said: 'By the One in whose hand is Muhammad's soul, thirty some odd angels raced to get that phrase to raise it [to the Lord].'" This is related by an-Nasa'i and at-Tirmidhi, and by al-Bukhari with a different wording.

Prostrating upon one's clothing or headdress due to some excuse: Ibn 'Abbas reports that the Messenger of Allah prayed in one garment and covered his face with a portion of it to avoid the heat or coldness of the ground. This is related by Ahmad with a *sahih isnad* (chain). It is disliked if it is done without any genuine reason.

A summary of other acts which are permissible during the prayer:
Ibn al-Qayyim has summarized some of the acts which are permissible during the *salah* and which the Prophet *sallallahu alehi wasallam* used to perform at times. He writes:

The Prophet would pray and 'Aishah would be lying between him and the *qiblah*. When he performed *sajdah*, he would signal to her with his hand and she would pull back her leg and when he would stand she would stretch out her leg again. The Prophet was praying and the Satan came to him to disturb his *salah* and the Prophet choked until his saliva came upon his hand. And the Prophet would pray upon the pulpit, making *ruku'* there, but when the time came to perform *sajdah*, he would descend, moving backward, and prostrate upon the ground, and then return to the pulpit. He once prayed toward a wall and an animal tried to pass between him and the wall. The Prophet prevented the animal from passing to the extent that its stomach was against the wall. Once while he was praying, two girls from the tribe of 'Abd al-Muttalib were fighting behind him and he separated them with his arms while he was praying. Ahmad's version says that they grabbed unto his knees and he separated them without leaving the *salah*. On another occasion, when he was praying, a boy came to him and he motioned to him to move back, and he moved back. Then a girl tried to pass in front of him, he beckoned her to move back, but the girl passed, and when he finished, he said: "They are more determined." Ahmad recorded it and it is also in the *Sunan*. He would also puff out air while praying. The *hadith* which states: " Puffing out is speech" cannot be traced to the Messenger of Allah, but Sa'id related it in his *Sunan* from Ibn 'Abbas as one of Ibn 'Abbas' statements – if it is authentic. The Prophet would cry during his *salah* and would also clear his throat while praying. 'Ali ibn Abi Talib said: "I had a certain time at which I would visit the Messenger of Allah. When I came to him, he would permit me to enter. If I found him praying, he would clear his throat and I would enter. If he was free, he would give me permission to enter." This is recorded by an-Nasa'i and Ahmad. Ahmad's version says: "I could enter upon the Prophet during the day or night. If I came to him while he was praying, he would clear his throat [as a sign that I may enter]. This was related by Ahmad who used to act by

it and he was not of the opinion that clearing one's throat invalidated the *salah*. Sometimes the Prophet would pray barefoot
and sometimes while wearing shoes. This is what 'Abdullah
ibn 'Umar said and he ordered people to pray with shoes on
in order to differ from the Jews. Sometimes he would pray in
one garment and sometimes in two garments and [this latter]
was the majority of the cases.

Reciting from a copy of the Qur'an: Dhakwan, the protege of
'Aishah, would lead her in prayer during Ramadan while reciting from a
copy of the Qur'an. This is related by Malik. Ash-Shaf'i's opinion is that
it is allowable. An-Nawawi holds: "If one sometimes turns pages during
a *salah*, it does not invalidate it. If he looks at something that is written
which is not the Qur'an and he reads it to himself, it does not invalidate
the *salah*, even if it is done for a long period of time, nevertheless, it is
a hated act." Ash-Shaf'i has made a statement about it in *al-Imla'*.

**Occupying the heart with something other than the affairs of the
prayer:** Abu Hurairah reports that the Prophet *sallallahu alehi wasallam*
said: "When the call to prayer is made, the Satan takes to his heels... and
when it is finished, he returns. He flees again when the *iqamah* is made
and when it is finished, he returns until he comes between the man and
his thoughts, saying: 'Remember this and remember that,' which he had
not recalled, until the person does not know how much he has prayed,
[i.e.,] three or four *rak'at*. Then, he makes two prostrations while sitting."
This is reported by al-Bukhari and Muslim.

Al-Bukhari also records that 'Umar said: "I arrange the troops [in my
mind] during the *salah*." Although it is true that such a *salah* is valid and
sufficient, it is a must for the person in prayer to keep his mind and heart
attuned to the *salah* and his Lord and to keep his thoughts on the meaning
of the Qur'anic verses and the significance of the different acts of the *salah*
since a person has for him only that portion of the *salah* which he is fully
aware of [while performing it].

Au Dawud, an-Nasa'i, and Ibn Hibban record from 'Ammar ibn Yasir
that he heard the Messenger of Allah say: "A man may complete the *salah*
and only have recorded for himself one-tenth or one-ninth or one-eighth
or one-seventh or one-fifth or one-fourth or one third or one-half."

Al-Bazzar records from Ibn 'Abbas that the Messenger of Allah said:
"Allah, the Glorious, said: 'I accept the *salah* of one who humbles himself
during it to My Greatness; and who does not perform the *salah* just for
show; and who does not spend the night in disobedience to Me; and who
spends the day remembering Me; and who is merciful to the poor, the
wayfarer and the widows; and who is merciful to one who is suffering

from an infliction. He has a light like the light of the sun. I protect him by My Glory and the angels guard over him. I give him light in darkness and sobriety in the presence of ignorance. And his similitude in My creation is like al-Firdaus in Paradise.'"

Abu Dawud records from Zaid ibn Khalid that the Messenger of Allah said: "Whoever makes ablution and perfects it and then prays two *rak'at*, without being unheedful during them, forgiven for him will be his previous sins." Muslim records that 'Uthman ibn Abi al-'Aas said: "O Messenger of Allah, the Satan comes between me and my prayers and my recitation, confusing me therein!" The Prophet said: "That Satan is called Khanzab. If he affects you seek refuge in Allah from him and 'spit out' on your left side three times."

Muslim records from Abu Hurairah that the Messenger of Allah said: "Allah, the Glorious, said: 'I have divided the *salah* [i.e., al-Fatihah] into two halves, between Me and My slave, and my slave shall receive what he asks for.' When the slave says 'All praise is due to Allah, the Lord of the Worlds,' Allah, the Exalted, says 'My slave has praised Me.' When he says 'The Compassionate, the Merciful,' Allah, the Exalted, says 'My slave has lauded Me.' When he says 'Master of the Day of Judgment.' Allah, the Exalted says 'My servant has glorified Me and entrusted his affairs to Me.' And when he says 'It is Thee we worship and from Thee that we seek aid,' Allah, the Exalted, says 'This is between Me and My slave. And for My slave is what he asks.' And when he says 'Guide us to the straight path, the path of those whom you have blessed and not of those with whom you are angry nor of those who have gone astray.' Allah says 'That is for My slave and My slave shall get what he asks for.'"

ACTIONS WHICH ARE DISLIKED DURING THE PRAYERS (*Makruhat us-Salah*)

It is disliked for anyone to leave any of the *sunnah* acts described earlier. The following acts are also disliked:

Fidgeting with one's clothing or one's body is disliked unless there is some need to do so: Ma'yaqib says: "I asked the Prophet about dusting [away] the pebbles during the *salah*, and the Prophet said: 'Do not dust [away] the pebbles while you are praying, but if you must do it, then do it only once in order to level the pebbles.'" This is related by the group.

Abu Dharr reports that the Prophet said: "When one of you stands for the *salah*, mercy is facing him. Therefore, he should not wipe away the pebbles." This is related by Ahmad, at-Tirmidhi, Abu Dawud, an-Nasa'i, and Ibn Majah.

Umm Salamah reports that there was a boy called Yassar who would puff out some air during the *salah*. The Messenger of Allah said to him: "May Allah fill your face with dust!" This is related by Ahmad with a good chain.

Placing one's hands on hips during the prayer: Abu Hurairah relates: "The Messenger of Allah prohibited putting one's hands on one's hips during the *salah*." This is related by Abu Dawud.

Raising one's sight to the sky or upwards: Abu Hurairah reports that the Messenger of Allah said: "Those who raise their sight to the sky during the prayer should stop doing so or their sight may be taken away." This is related by Ahmad, Muslim, and an-Nasa'i.

Looking at something which distracts attention: 'Aishah reports that the Messenger of Allah prayed in a cloak which had some designs on it. He said: "These designs have distracted me. Take [this cloak] to Abu Jahm [i.e., the person who gave it to the Prophet] and bring me a plain cloak." This is related by al-Bukhari and Muslim.

Al-Bukhari records that Anas said: "'Aishah had a curtain to cover [the doorway of] her house. The Prophet said to her: 'Remove your curtain for its pictures always distract me during my prayers.'" This *hadith* proves that looking at some writing or design does not invalidate the *salah*.

Closing one's eyes: Some say that this act is disliked while others hold that it is allowed, though disliked. Those *ahadith* which state it is disliked are not authentic.

Ibn al-Qayyim said: "The correct position is: if keeping one's eyes open does not affect one's attention, then it is preferred to keep them open; however, if there is something in front of the person, such as some ornament or decoration, which could affect his attention, then it is, in no way, disliked to close his eyes. In fact, under such circumstances, to say it is preferred to close one's eyes is more consistent with the principles and goals of the *shar'iah* than to say that it is disliked."

Motioning with both hands while making the salutations [i.e., the *taslim*]: Jabir ibn Samurah said: "We prayed behind the Prophet and he said: 'What is wrong with them that they make salutation with their hands as if they were the tails of horses? It is enough for you to place your hand on your thigh and say, *as salam 'alaikum, as salam 'alaikum!*'" This is related by an-Nasa'i and others.

Covering the mouth and letting one's garment down until it touches the ground: Abu Hurairah said: "The Messenger of Allah prohibited *as-sadl* in the *salah* and prohibited a man to cover his mouth." This is related by the five and by al-Hakim who says that it is *sahih* according to Muslim's conditions. Al-Khattabi explains: "*As-sadl* is to lower one's garment until it reaches the ground." Al-Kamal ibn al-Hamam adds: "This also applies to wearing a cloak without putting one's arms through its sleeves."

Performing the *salah* while the food has been served: 'Aishah reports that the Prophet said: "If dinner is served and the prayer is ready, start with the dinner [first]." This is related by Ahmad and Muslim.

Naf'i reports that the food would be served for Ibn 'Umar while the *iqamah* was being made, but he would not come to the *salah* until he finished his meal although he could hear the reciting of the imam. This is related by al-Bukhari.

Al-Khattabi says: "The Prophet ordered that one should begin with one's meal in order to satisfy his need. In this way, he will come to the *salah* in calm and his desire or hunger will not disturb the completion or perfection of his *ruku'* and *sajjud* and the rest of the acts of the *salah*."

Praying when one needs to anwer the call of nature and other things that may distract a person: Thauban reports that the Messenger of Allah said: "There are three acts which are not allowed: For a person to lead a people in prayer and then make supplications for himself without including them, for then he would be dishonest to them; to look inside a house without obtaining permission, for if he does so (it is as if) he has already entered it (without permission); and to offer prayer while he needs to answer the call of nature until he relieves himself." This is related by Ahmad, Abu Dawud, and at-Tirmidhi who calls it *hasan*.

'Aishah reported that she heard the Messenger of Allah say: "No one should pray when the food is served nor when one needs to answer the call of nature." This is related by Ahmad, Muslim, and Abu Dawud.

Praying when one is overcome by sleep: 'Aishah reports that the Messenger of Allah said: "When one of you becomes drowsy in *salah*, he should lie down until he is fresh again; otherwise, he will not know if he is asking forgiveness or vilifying himself." This is related by the group.

Abu Hurairah reports that the Messenger of Allah said: "When one of you gets up at night for *salah* and his tongue falters in reciting the Qur'an and he is not certain about what he is reciting, he should sleep." This is related by Ahmad and Muslim.

Praying at a fixed place in the mosque [except in the case of the imam]: 'Abdurrahman ibn Shabl said: "The Prophet prohibited pecking like a crow [i.e., while prostrating], imitating a lion's manner of sitting, and a man to pick a special place in the mosque [to pray] like a camel has his own place [to sit]." This is related by Ahmad, ibn Khuzaimah, ibn Hibban, and by al-Hakaim who calls it *sahih*.

ACTIONS WHICH INVALIDATE THE *SALAH*

The following actions would cause the *salah* to be nullified and the person to lose the reward of the *salah*:

Intentionally eating or drinking: Ibn al-Mundhir says: "The people of knowledge agree that if one intentionally eats or drinks during a *fard salah*, he is to repeat the *salah*. The same is the case with *nawafil* according to the majority of scholars as what invalidates an obligatory (*fard*) prayer also invalidates a voluntary (*nafl*) prayer."

Speaking intentionally about something unrelated to the *salah*: Intentionally speaking during the *salah*, if it is not beneficial to the *salah*, invalidates the *salah*.

Zaid ibn Arqam relates: "We used to talk while we were in *salah* and a person would speak to the person next to him until the verse was revealed: 'And stand before Allah in devout obedience*,' and we were then commanded to observe silence during the *salah*." This is related by the group.

Ibn Mas'ud reports: "We used to greet the Messenger of Allah while he was in *salah* and he would respond to our greeting. When we returned from Abyssinia, we greeted him [during prayer] but he did not respond to our salutation. We said to him: 'O Messenger of Allah, we used to greet you while you were in *salah* and you used to respond to us!' He then said: 'Prayer demands one's complete attention.'" This is related by al-Bukhari and Muslim.

---

*Qur'an 2:238

If one is ignorant of this ruling or speaks due to the fact that he has forgotten this ruling, his *salah* will still be valid. Mu'awiyyah ibn al-Hakam said: "I was praying behind the Messenger of Allah and someone in the congregation sneezed. I said [to him]: 'May Allah have mercy upon you.' The people then stared at me, showing their disapproval of my act. I said: 'Woe to me, why do you stare at me so?' They started to strike their hands on their thighs and when I saw that they wanted me to become silent, I was angered but said nothing. When the Messenger of Allah finished the prayer – and may my father and mother be ransomed for him, I found no teacher better than him either before or after him – he did not scold, beat, or revile me but he simply said: 'Talking to others is not seemly during the *salah*, for the *salah* is for glorifying Allah, extolling His Greatness, and reciting the Qur'an.'" This is related by Ahmad, Muslim, Abu Dawud, and an-Nasa'i. Mu'awiyyah ibn al-Hakam spoke out of ig-norance of this ruling and the Prophet *sallallahu alehi wasallam* did not order him to repeat his *salah*.

Talking [if it is a reminder as to the incompleteness of the *salah*], does not nullify the *salah* as can be seen in the following *hadith*. Abu Hurairah says: "The Messenger of Allah led us in either the noon or after-noon prayers and he made the *taslim* after praying just two *rak'at*. Dhul Yadain said to the Prophet: 'O Messenger of Allah, has the *salah* been shortened or have you forgotten [part of it]?' The Prophet *sallallahu alehi wassalam* said: 'It has not been shortened, nor did I forget any part of it." He said: 'Yes, O Messenger of Allah, you did forget.' Thereupon the Prophet asked (the people): 'Is Dhul Yadain correct in what he says?' The people said: 'He is correct, you offered only two *rak'at*.' Then, the Prophet prayed the two remaining *rak'at* and made the *taslim*, said the *takbir* and performed the *sajdah*, sat and made the *takbir* and performed the *sajdah* again, and finally said the *takbir* and sat again." This is related by al-Bukhari and Muslim.

The Maliki school allows talking during the prayer if it is done for any good of the *salah* as long as it does not become a common practice and (is done) only when saying *subhanallah* fails to alert the imam to correct his mistake. Al-Auza'i's comments are: "Whoever intentionally speaks dur-ing the *salah*, seeking some benefit to the *salah*, does not invalidate his *salah*." He said that if a person recites aloud in the *'asr* and someone be-hind him says: "It is the *'asr*," (i.e., the recital is not to be aloud) then the latter person would not invalidate his *salah*.

Intentionally making many motions: The scholars differ over what exactly constitutes a few motions and what constitutes many motions. Some say that one makes many motions when, if seen from behind, one would be certain that he was not performing *salah*, and anything less than that amount is considered only a few motions. Some say that it is any act or string of actions which would make others believe that the person is not praying.

An-Nawawi says: "If a person performs a lot of actions that are not part of the *salah*, he invalidates his *salah*, and, on this point, there is no difference of opinion. If the acts are few, then they do not invalidate the *salah* and, on this point, there also is no difference of opinion. This is the exact position. However, there does exist a difference of opinion over what exactly constitutes a few actions and many actions, [and there exist] four opinions on this point..." He says that the fourth opinion is the correct and most popular opinion. The fourth opinion is that the exact definitions of too much and too little are determined by generally accepted standards. One is not harmed in his *salah* by common acts such as nodding in reply to a salutation, taking off one's shoes, raising the headdress and putting it back in place, putting on or taking off a light garment, carrying or holding a small child, preventing someone from passing in front of the person in prayer, covering one's spittle in one's clothing and similar other actions. As for the other acts, those which are considered to constitute many actions (e.g., taking many consecutive steps, performing actions repeatedly) they invalidate the prayer. An-Nawawi also says: "The scholars are in agreement that many actions invalidate the prayer if they are performed consecutively [i.e., one after another]. If one separates the actions, for instance, taking a step and then stopping for a while, then taking another step or two, and then another two steps, after a pause (though a short one) between them, then the *salah* will not be harmed, even if he (in this manner should take a hundred or more steps. There is no difference of opinion on this point. As for light actions," he continues, "such as, moving one's finger in glorifying Allah or in itching, and so forth., these do not invalidate the prayer according to the well-known, authentic opinion, even when they are done repeatedly and consecutively, but they are disliked." Ash-Shaf'i, in a statement concerning it, says: "Even if one counts the verses on one's fingers, it would not invalidate one's *salah*, but it is best to avoid [such an act]."

Intentionally leaving out an essential act or condition of the prayer without any valid excuse for doing so: Al-Bukhari and Muslim record that the Prophet *sallallahu alehi wasallam* told a bedouin who had not performed his *salah* well: "Return and pray for you have not prayed." (This *hadith* was mentioned earlier.)

Ibn Rushd writes: "There is an agreement that if one prays and he is not in a state of purity, it is obligatory for him to repeat the prayer, [that is true if the act was done] intentionally or out of forgetfulness. Similarly,

one who prays without facing the *qiblah*, intentionally or due to forgetfulness, [must repeat the *salah*]. In general, if any of the conditions for
the correctness of the salah are absent, it becomes obligatory to repeat the
salah."

Smiling or laughing during the *salah*: Ibn al-Mundhir records that
there is a consensus of opinion that laughing (during the *salah*) invalidates
the prayer. An-Nawawi says: "This is the case if one laughs aloud, and
produces sound. Most of the scholars say that there is no problem with
smiling. If one is overcome by laughter and cannot control it, his *salah*
will not become invalid if it is of minor nature. If it is a hearty laughter,
it will invalidate the *salah*. Custom would determine whether it is a major
or a minor laughter."

MAKING (*Qada'*) FOR MISSED *SALAH*

The scholars agree that it is obligatory for one who has forgotten the *salah* or slept through its time to make up the missed [*qada'*] prayer. This opinion is based on the *hadith* of the Prophet mentioned earlier: "There is no negligence while one is asleep but forgetfulness occurs when one is awake. If one of you forgets the prayer or sleeps through its time, then he should perform the *salah* when he recalls it." If one falls unconscious, then he need not repeat the *salah*, unless he regains his consciousness with enough time to purify himself and perform the *salah* within its proper time.

'Abdurrazaq relates from Naf'i that Ibn 'Umar once fell sick and became unconscious and missed the prayer. When he regained his consciousness, he did not make up the missed prayer.

Ibn Juraij reports from Ibn Tawus on the authority of his father that if a sick person becomes unconscious, he is not to make up the prayers he missed.

Mu'ammar relates: "I asked az-Zuhri about one who becomes unconscious, and he said that he is not to make up the *salah* he missed."

Hamad ibn Salamah relates from Yunus ibn 'Ubaid that both al-Hassan al-Basri and Muhammad ibn Sireen said that a person who falls unconscious is not to make up the prayers he may miss.

Concerning missing a *salah* intentionally, the majority of the scholars say that it is a sin and the missed *salah* must be made up for. Ibn Taimaiyyah says:

> In law, there is no way for one who leaves a *salah* intentionally to make its *qada'*. He may however, resort to increasing his voluntary and supererogatory acts. Ibn Hazm has

[99]

thoroughly discussed this question. The following is a summary
of what he says on this subject:

Concerning one who leaves a *salah* intentionally until its
time expires, he will never be able to make up for that *salah*.
Such a person should turn to Allah and ask His forgivness and
increase his good deeds and *nawafil* in order to increase his
weight [of good] on the Day of Resurrection. Abu Hanifah,
Malik, and ash-Shaf'i say that he can make up the prayer after
its time has expired, and Malik and Abu Hanifa even say that
if a person intentionally misses a prayer or a few prayers, then
he is to make up those prayers before he prays the present
salah, even if he has missed all five prayers and should, while
making them up, miss the present *salah*. They say that if he
missed more than five prayers, he is to begin by praying the
salah whose time is present [and then he is to make up the
prayers he missed]. The proof for our position [i.e, the position
of Ibn Hazm] is found in the words of Allah, the Exalted:
"Woe unto the worshippers who are heedless of their
prayers,"[51] and:

"And then there succeeded them a later generation who
wasted the prayers and followed their own lusts, but they will
meet with destruction."[52] If one who intentionally misses a
salah could make it up later, then why is it mentioned with
affliction or transgression? Of course, there is no affliction or
transgression on one who delays the *salah*. But the case of one
who procrastinates until the last portion of its permissible time
expires is quite different. Allah, the Exalted, has appointed certain times for the *fard salah*; both the beginning time and the
ending time for the *salah* have been established, and there is
no difference between praying a *salah* before its time and praying it after its proper time elapses because, in both cases the
salah is not performed within its prescribed time. This is not
to draw an analogy between one and the other but it is applying
the same rule to them as they both must be performed within
the limits set by Allah. Allah, the Exalted, says: "Whoever
transgresses the limits set by Allah has verily wronged his own
soul!"[53] The principle of making *qada'* must be established by
the proper sources of Islamic law. Legislating [in *shari'ah*] is
not permissible, save by Allah's authority as evidenced by His

---

[51]Qur'an 107:5
[52]Qur'an 19:59
[53]Qur'an 65:1

His Prophet. We ask those people who say that one may make *qada'* for a *salah* which he misses intentionally: "Tell us about this *salah* that you want him to perfom, is it the same *salah* that Allah ordered him to perform or is it a different one?" If they say it is the same one, then we may say to them: "Then one who misses it intentionally is not guilty of being disobedient [to Allah, the Exalted], as he has done what Allah had ordered him to do, and there is no sin upon him according to your statement and likewise there should be no blame upon one who intentionally delays a *salah* until its time expires, but that is not an acceptable position for any Muslim." If they say that it is not the *salah* which Allah ordered, we may say: "You have told the truth," and this is a sufficient confession from them. Then, we may ask them: "Is one who intentionally leaves the *salah* until its time expires being obedient or disobedient to Allah?" If they say obedient, they will be differing from the consensus of the Muslims and the Qur'an and the confirmed *sunnah*. If they say he is being disobedient, they are speaking the truth and it is not valid that an act of disobedience should replace an act of obedience. Also, Allah, the Exalted, has set specific limits, through the tongue of His Messenger, for the times of the *salah*. Each *salah* has a specific beginning time, and no one may perform the salah before that time, and each prayer has a specific ending time, and no one may perform the *salah* after that time. No one of this *ummah* will dispute that point. However, if one is allowed to pray after the time set by the Messenger of Allah, then setting an ending time for the *salah* has no meaning to it. Such an opinion is nonsense and may Allah, the Exalted, keep us from it. Every action is connected with a certain time and it is not valid outside of that time; if it was valid outside of that time, what would be the purpose of that time being specifically singled out for that act? [The logic of this argument] is clear and Allah, the Almighty, is our Supporter.

Ibn Hazm discusses this point at great length, and adds: "If making up a *salah* is obligatory for one who has left a *salah*, even after its time has expired, why is it that Allah and His Messenger have chosen not to mention that fact as (surely) they did not forget it: "And your Lord is not forgetful!"[54] Any law that is not based on the Qur'an or the *sunnah* is not valid. It

---

[54]Qur'an 19:64

has been authentically reported that the Prophet said: "Whoever
misses the *'asr salah*, it is as if he has lost his family and his
property." It is correct to say that if one "misses"[55] something,
he cannot make it up, for if he makes it up or could make it
up, the act would not be "missed." The entire Muslim *ummah*
is in agreement with the statement and ruling that if the time
of the *salah* has elapsed, then the *salah* is "over" [i.e., "*qada*"
in Arabic], but if one can make it up, the statement that the
salah is "over" becomes false and untrue; therefore, there is no
way that it could ever be made up. The people who agree with
us on this include 'Umar ibn al-Khattab, his son 'Abdullah,
Sa'd ibn Abi Waqas, Salman al-Farsi, ibn Mas'ud, al-Qasim
ibn Muhammad ibn Abu Bakr, Budail al-'Uqaili, Muhammad
ibn Sireen, Mutraf ibn 'Abdullah, 'Umar ibn 'Abdulaziz, and
others. Allah has left no excuse, for anyone required to perform the *salah*, to delay the *salah* from its proper time for any
reason whatsoever, not even during times of fighting, fear, extreme illness, or travelling. Allah says: "And when you are
among them and arrange them for *salah*, let only one party be
with you"[56] And: "But if you are in danger, then walking or
riding."[57] Allah, the Exalted, does not permit even the extremely sick person to delay the *salah*. In fact, such a person
has been ordered to pray sitting, if he cannot pray standing,
and if he cannot pray sitting, then he may pray on his side.
Also, if one cannot make ablution with water, he may make
tayammum; and if he cannot find soil to make *tayammum*, he
may still pray. Whence has the permission been obtained that
one may intentionally leave the *salah* until its time is finished
and who has ordered that it be performed after its time and
how is it that the belated *salah* would be sufficient? None of
this is derived from the Qur'an, *Sunnah*, *Qiyas* (analogical
reasoning), and so forth.

Ibn Hazm further says: "Concerning our statement that the
one who intentionally leaves a *salah* until its time expires is to
repent to Allah, the Exalted, ask for His forgiveness, pray an
increased number of *nawafil*, and do good deeds. This statement is based on Allah's words: "Then there succeeded them
a generation who missed prayers and followed after lusts. But
they will meet destruction save him who repents and believes

[55]Qur'an 19:64
[56]Qur'an 4:102
[57]Qur'an 2:239

and does right. Such will enter the garden and will not be wronged,"[58] and: "...those who, when they do an evil thing or wrong themselves, remember Allah and implore forgiveness for their sins – who forgives sins, save Allah – and will not knowingly repeat the wrong they did,"[59] and: "Whoever does an atom's weight of good shall see it and whoever does an atom's weight of evil shall see it,"[60] and: "...We set a just balance for the day of resurrection so no soul shall be wronged."[61]

This [Muslim] *ummah* is in agreement, and there are texts that state that voluntary acts are a type of good deeds and Allah knows how much they are really worth. It necessarily follows that a number of voluntary works may be equivalent in merit to an obligatory deed and may even amount to a greater merit. Furthermore, Allah has informed us that He does not waste the action of any person[62] and that the good deeds erase the evil ones.[63]

THE PRAYER OF A PERSON WHO IS ILL
(*Salatul Mariḍ*)

Whoever has some excuse due to illness and cannot stand during the *fard salah* is allowed to pray sitting. If he cannot pray in a sitting posture, he may pray while on his side by making gestures. In such a case, his gestures for *sajdah* should be lower than those for his *ruku'*. This principle is based on Allah's words: "...And celebrate Allah's praises, standing, sitting, and lying on your sides."[64]

'Imran ibn Hussain says: "I had piles [hemorrhoids], so I asked the Prophet about the prayer and he said: 'Offer the *salah* while standing and if you cannot do so, pray while sitting, and if you can't do that, then make *salah* while lying on your side.'" This is related by the group, except for Muslim. An-Nasa'i adds: "And if you cannot offer *salah* while lying on your side, then do it while lying on your back. Allah does not burden a soul, save with what it can bear."

Jabir reports: "The Messenger of Allah visited a sick person and found him praying on a cushion. The Prophet pushed it aside and said: "Pray on

---

[58]Qur'an 19:59-60
[59]Qur'an 3:135
[60]Qur'an 99:7-8
[61]Qur'an 21:47
[62]Qur'an 3:195
[63]Qur'an 11:114
[64]Qur'an 4:103

the ground if you can, and if you cannot, then pray by making gestures, and make your *sajdah* lower than your *ruku'*.'" This is related by al-Baihaqi.

What is meant by inability is that the person if he prays [in the regular way], will suffer hardship, or his disease will aggravate, or his recovery would be hampered, or he will swoon if he prays in the customary manner. One should sit cross-legged while praying in a sitting position.

'Aishah narrates that she saw the Prophet *sallallahu alehi wasallam* sitting cross-legged while praying. This is related by an-Nasa'i and al-Hakim says it is *sahih*.

It is also permissible to sit in the manner that one sits while performing the *tashahud*. One who can offer the *salah* neither sitting nor standing is to lie down on his side, and if he cannot do that, he is to lie down on his back with his legs toward the *qiblah* according to his state of health. Ibn al-Mundhir prefers this opinion. On this point, there is a weak *hadith* reported by 'Ali which states that the Prophet said: "The sick person is to pray standing if he is able. If he cannot do so, he should pray sitting. If he is not able to make the *sajdah*, he should nod with his head and make the nod of his *sajjud* lower than that of his *ruku'*. If he cannot pray in a sitting posture, he should pray while lying down on his right side facing the *qiblah*. If one cannot pray on his right side, he should pray while lying on his back with his legs stretched out toward the *qiblah*." This is related by ad-Daraqutni. Some scholars maintain that one can pray in whatever manner is easy for him. It is apparent from the *hadith* that if one can only nod while lying on his back, then nothing else is obligatory upon him.

THE PRAYER DURING TIMES OF FEAR OR DANGER
(*Salatul Khauf*)

The scholars are all in agreement about the legality of "fear prayer" (*salatul Khauf*). The Qur'an says: "When You (O Prophet) are with them, and stand to lead them in prayer, let one party of them stand up (in prayer) with you, taking their arms with them. When they finish prostrations, let them take their position in the rear. And let the other party come up which has not yet prayed – and let them pray with you, taking all precautions, and bearing arms: the unbelievers wish if you were negligent of your arms and your baggage, to assault you in a single rush. But there is no blame on you if you put away your arms because of the inconvenience of rain or because you are ill; but take (every) precaution for yourselves. For the unbelievers Allah has prepared humiliating punishment.[65]

On this subject Imam Ahmad says: "There are six or seven confirmed *ahadith* about '*salatul khauf*,' and whichever way one performs it, it will be valid."

Ibn al-Qayyim says: "Basically, there are six ways to pray *salatal khauf*, although some say there are more than (six ways of praying it). Whenever they notice any difference in the narration of an incident, they discribe it as a difference [in the manner of prayer] thus coming to seventeen ways. This might be due to different acts of the Prophet or simply to differences in the narrations." Al-Hafiz says: "This is the true position and its explanation is given below.

Different ways of offering *salatul Khauf*:

1. If the enemy is not in the direction of the *qiblah*, then the imam should lead a group in the performance of one *rak'ah* after which he should wait until they complete the second *rak'ah* by themselves, and then, they should go and face the enemy. And the second group should come and the imam would lead them in *salah* while he is performing his second *rak'ah*. He should again wait for them to complete another *rak'ah* by themselves before leading them in the salutations.

Saleh ibn Khawat relates from Saleh ibn Abu Khaithimah that a group lined up with the Prophet *sallallahu alehi wasallam* while another group faced the enemy. He prayed one *rak'ah* with the group that was with him and remained standing while they finished the *salah* and left and faced the enemy. The second group came and prayed the remaining *rak'ah* with him, then he stayed sitting until they had completed their prayers individually, after which he led them in making the *taslim*. This is related by the group, except for Ibn Majah.

2. If the enemy is not in the direction of the *qiblah*, then, the imam prays one *rak'ah* with one group of the army while the other group faces the enemy, after which the two groups exchange places, and the imam prays one *rak'ah* with the second group. The members of each group will complete one *rak'ah* of their prayers on their own.

Ibn 'Umar says: "The Messenger of Allah prayed one *rak'ah* with one group while the other group faced the enemy, [At that point, those who had prayed] took the place of their companions facing the enemy and the second group came and prayed one *rak'ah* with the Prophet and then he made the *taslim*. Then each group made (the remaining) one *rak'ah*." This is related by al-Bukhari, Muslim, and Ahmad. It is apparent that the second group completed their *salah* after the imam made the *taslim* without discontinuing their *salah* (i.e., for them, it was two continuous *rak'at*), and

---

[65]Qur'an 4:102

the first group did not complete their *salah* until the second group had completed their *salah* and went back to face the enemy. Ibn Mas'ud says: "Then, he made the *taslim* and they stood up to finish the second *rak'ah* individually and, then they made their *taslim.*"

3. The imam prays two *rak'at* with each group, the first two *rak'at* being his *fard salah* and the latter two being *nafl*. It is allowed for one who is making a *nafl* to lead others in *salah* who are praying *fard*. Jabir reports that the Prophet prayed two *rak'at* with one group of his companions and then another two *rak'at* with another group and then he made the *taslim*. This is related by ash-Shaf'i and an-Nasa'i.

Abu Dawud, Ahmad, and an-Nasa'i record that he said: "The Prophet prayed the *salatul Khauf* with us, and he prayed two *rak'at* with some of his companions, and then the others came and took their places and he prayed two *rak'at* with them, and he made the *taslim*. So, the Prophet prayed four *rak'at* and the people prayed two *rak'at* each."

Ahmad, al-Bukhari, and Muslim record that he said: "We were with the Prophet during the campaign of Dhat al-Riqa and the *salah* was made, and he prayed two *rak'at* with one group and then they withdrew, and he led the other group in two *rak'at*. The Prophet prayed four *rak'at* and the people prayed two *rak'at.*"

4. If the enemy is in the direction of the *qiblah*, then the imam leads both of the groups in *salah* at the same time and they share in guarding against the enemy, and they follow the imam in every one of his actions until he performs *sajdah*, in which case one group will make the *sajdah* with him and the other will wait until they are finished and then perform their own *sujjud*. After the first *rak'ah* is finished, the people in front will move to the back and those in the back will move to the front.

Jabir said: "I prayed *salatul khauf* (fear prayer) with the Prophet. He arranged us in two rows behind him. The enemy was between us and the *qiblah*. The Prophet *sallallahu alehi wasallam* made the *takbir* and we all made the *takbir*. He performed the *ruku'* and we all made the *ruku'*. Then, he raised his head from the *ruku'* and we all raised our heads from the *ruku'*. Next he went down for *sajdah* as well as the row closest to him, while the back row stood facing the enemy until the Prophet and the first row had completed their prostrations, after which the back row made *sajdah* and then stood [after completing their *sajjud*]. Following this, those in the back row moved to the front while those in the front row moved to the back. The Prophet performed the *ruku'* and we all made *ruku'*. Then, he raised his head and we raised our heads from *ruku*. Afterward, he made the *sajdah* and the row that was previously in the back during the first *rak'ah* prostrated with him while the [new] back row stood facing the enemy. When the Prophet and the [new] front row had completed their *sujjud*, the [new] back row made the *sujjud*. Finally, the Prophet made the *taslim* and we all made the *taslim*. This is related by Ahmad, Muslim, an-Nasa'i, Ibn Majah, and al-Baihaqi.

5. Both of the groups begin the prayer with the imam, and then one group would guard against the enemy while the other group would pray one *rak'ah* with the imam, after which they would face the enemy while the other group would come and pray one *rak'ah* by themselves (individually) while the imam is standing. Then, they would join him in what is the imam's and their second *rak'ah*. At that point, the group which had gone to face the enemy would come and pray one *rak'ah* (their second) individually while the others would be sitting (in *salah* waiting for them to sit in their second *rak'ah*), after which the imam would make the *taslim* and both groups would make the *taslim* together [behind the imam].

Abu Huraira reports: "I prayed *salatul khauf* with the Messenger of Allah during the year of the Battle of Najd. He stood to pray *'asr* and one group stood with him while the other group was faced the enemy with their backs toward the *qiblah*. When he made the *takbir*, all the people made the *takbir* – that is, those with him and those facing the enemy. Then, he performed one *rak'ah* and the group with him also performed their *ruku'* and *sujjud* with him while the others were still facing the enemy. Next, the group which was with the Prophet went to face the enemy while the other group came and prayed one *rak'ah* and the Prophet kept standing [in prayer] as he was. Then, he performed the *ruku'* and the new group performed the *ruku'* with him and he performed the *sajdah* and they performed the *sajdah* with him. After this, the group which had gone to face the enemy came and prayed one *rak'ah* while the Prophet and those with him were sitting [in prayer]. Finally, the Prophet made *taslim* and both groups made the *taslim* with him. The Prophet prayed two *rak'at* and both groups prayed two *rak'at*." This is related by Ahmad, Abu Dawud, and an-Nasa'i.

6. Each group prays only one *rak'ah* with the imam and the imam prays a total of two *rak'at* whereas each group prays one. Ibn 'Abbas reports that the Prophet prayed at Dhi-qard, and he arranged the people into two rows, one row behind him and one row guarding against the enemy. The group behind him prayed one *rak'ah* (with him) and then left the place to the other group. The other group then came and prayed one *rak'ah* (with the Prophet), and [neither group] made up a *rak'ah*. This is related by an-Nasa'i and Ibn Hibban. Ibn 'Abbas also says: "Allah made the prayer obligatory on your Prophet [in the following manner]: four *rak'at* while resident, two while traveling, and only one during times of fear." This is related by Ahmad, Muslim, Abu Dawud, and an-Nasa'i.

How to pray *maghrib* during times of fear: The sunset prayer is not to be shortened and there is no *hadith* which states how it is to be prayed during times of fear. Therefore, the scholars differ over how it is to be performed. The Hanafi and Maliki schools say that the imam is to pray two *rak'at* with the first group and then one *rak'ah* with the second group. Ash-Shaf'i and Ahmad say it is permissible for the imam to pray one *rak'ah* with the first group and then two *rak'at* with the second group as it has been related that 'Ali performed it in that manner.

Prayer during times of extreme fear: If the fear [of the enemy] is great or fighting is taking place, each person is to pray individually to the best of his ability – that is, standing or riding, facing the *qiblah* or not facing the *qiblah*, making gestures for the *ruku'* and *sajjud* – whatever he can do. He should make the gesture for his *sajjud* lower than that for his *ruku'*. He is excused from any of the acts of *salah* which he is unable to perform.

Ibn 'Umar relates: "The Prophet described *salatul khauf* and said: 'If the danger is greater than that, then [pray] standing or riding.'"

In *Sahih al-Bukhari*, the wording is: "If the danger is greater than that, then pray while standing on your feet or riding, facing the *qiblah* or not facing the *qiblah*." In Muslim's version, Ibn 'Umar is reported to have said: "If the danger is greater than that, then pray standing or riding and by making gestures."

The prayer of attacker or the attacked: If one is attacking the enemy and fears that he will miss the time of *salah*, he may pray by making gestures even if he is moving in a direction other than that of the *qiblah*. The case of the one who is being attacked is the same as the one who is attacking. The same is the case for anyone whose enemy prevents him from making the *ruku'* or the *sajdah* or a person who fears for himself or his family or his wealth from an enemy or a thief or a wild animal; in all such cases, the person may [if necessary] pray by making gestures and facing any direction. Al-'Iraqi writes: "The same applies to anyone who is fleeing from a flood or fire and has no other option open to him. The same is true for one who is in straitened conditions and is in debt and cannot pay it and he fears that his debtor might catch him and imprison him while not believing his claim. This applies also to one who fears a punishment of *qisas* and hopes that by his absence the prosecuting party's anger will abate and they will forgive him."

'Abdullah ibn Unais reports: "The Messenger of Allah sent me to Khalid ibn Sufyan al-Hadhili, who was close to 'Arafat, and said: 'Go and kill him.' I saw him and the time of the afternoon prayer came and I said [to myself]: 'I fear that something between him and me will cause me to delay the *salah*, so I left walking and offered the *salah* by making gestures. When I came close to him, he said to me: 'Who are you?' I said: 'A man from among the Arabs. It has reached me that you are gathering the people against this man [i.e, the Prophet] so I came to you for that reason.' He said: 'I am doing that.' I walked with him for a while until I could strike him dead with my sword." This is related by Ahmad and Abu Dawud. Al-Hafiz says its chain is *hasan*.

THE PRAYER OF A TRAVELER

Shortening the prayers that consist of four *rak'at*: Allah says in the Qur'an: "And when you go forth in the land there is no sin upon you, if you shorten your prayer when you fear the disbelievers may attack you."[66] This concession is not limited to situations of danger.

Ya'la ibn Umaiyyah said: "I said to 'Umar ibn al-Khattab: 'Explain to me why the people shorten the *salah* when Allah says, 'And when you go forth...[the preceding verse] and those days are gone now!' 'Umar said: 'I wondered about that too and I mentioned that to the Prophet and he said: "This is a charity that Allah, the Exalted, has bestowed upon you, so accept His charity.'" This is related by the group.

At-Tabari records that Abu Munib al-Jarshi mentioned this verse to Ibn 'Umar and said: "We are safe now and are not in fear, should we, then, shorten the salah?" He answered him: "You have indeed in the Messenger of Allah a beautiful pattern (of conduct)."[67]

The issue was also referred to 'Aishah and she said: "The *salah* was made fard in Makkah in sets of two *rak'at*. When the Prophet *sallallahu alehi wasallam* came to Medinah, two *rak'at* were added to each *salah* except the *maghrib salah* because it is the *witr* of the daytime, and the dawn prayer due to its lengthy Qur'anic recital. But if one travels, he performs the original prayer [i.e., only two *rak'at*]." This is related by Ahmad, al-Baihaqi, Ibn Hibban, and Ibn Khuzaimah. Its narrators are trustworthy.

Ibn al-Qayyim says: "The Prophet would pray only two *rak'at* for those prayers which consisted of four, whenever he traveled until he returned to Medinah. And it is not confirmed that he ever prayed four *rak'at* [while traveling], and none of the imams differ on this point, although they do differ about the ruling of shortening the *salah*."

'Umar, 'Ali, Ibn Mas'ud, ibn 'Abbas, ibn 'Umar, Jabir and the Hanafi scholars say that it is *fard*. The Maliki school holds that it is *sunnah*

---

[66]Qur'an 4:101
[67]Qur'an 33:21

mu'akadah (the stressed one); it is even more emphasized than the congregational *salah*. If the traveler cannot find another traveler to lead him in the *salah*, he may pray by himself as it is disliked that he should follow one who is a resident [i.e., and pray four *rak'at*] according to the Maliki school. The Hanbali school holds that it is preferred for the person to shorten the prayer rather than to pray the complete *salah*. The Shaf'i school has a similar opinion, if the person has traveled a sufficient distance.

The distance one must travel before shortening one's prayer: The conclusion from the Qur'anic verse is that any traveling, be it long or short, which falls within the linguistic definition of the word "travel" would suffice to shorten one's *salah*, to combine them and to break the fast. There is nothing in the *sunnah* which confines this general term to any particular meaning. Ibn al-Mundhir and others have mentioned more than twenty reports on this point. Here we shall mention some of the more important reports.

Ahmad, Muslim, Abu Dawud, and al-Baihaqi record that Yahya ibn Yazid said: "I asked Anas ibn Malik about shortening the prayer, and he said: 'The Messenger of Allah would pray two *rak'at* if he had traveled a distance of three miles or *farsakh*.'" Ibn Hajar writes in *Fath al-Bari*: "This is the most authentic *hadith* which states and clarifies [that question]." The conflict between mile and *farsakh* is made clear in Abu Sa'id al-Khudri's statement: "If the Prophet traveled a distance of one *farsakh*, he would shorten his prayer." This was related by Sa'id ibn Mansur in his *Sunan* and by al-Hafiz ibn Hajar in *at-Talkhis*, and he implicitly accepted it by not making any further comments about it. It is well-known that a *farsakh* equals three miles and, therefore, Abu Sa'id's *hadith* removes the confusion which arises from Anas' *hadith* when he says that the shortest distance, due to which the Prophet shortened his prayer, was three miles. One *farsakh* is equivalent to 5,541 meters while one mile equals 1,748 meters. The shortest distance which has been mentioned with respect to the shortening of *salah* is one mile. This was recorded by Ibn abi Shaibah, with a *sahih* chain, on the authority of Ibn 'Umar. Ibn Hazm follows this report, and argues that if the distance is less than one mile, one is not to shorten the *salah*, the Messenger of Allah went to the graveyard of al-Baqi' to bury the dead and (similarly) he went off to answer the call of nature and did not shorten his *salah*.

Concerning what some jurists say, namely, that the journey must be at least two days long or as some say three days, Imam Abu al-Qasim al-Kharqi's refutation of their opinion is sufficient for us. In *al-Mughni* he says:

> 'I do not find any proof for what those scholars say. The statements of the (*sahabah*) companions are contradictory, and they

are not a (conclusive) proof if they differ. Something has been related from Ibn 'Umar and Ibn 'Abbas which differs from what these scholars use as proof. Even if that were not the case, their statements do not constitute a proof when a statement or action of the Prophet himself exists. Even if their statements were accepted, we would not be able to follow the distance they mentioned due to the following two reasons. One, they differ from the *sunnah* that has been related from the Prophet and from the clear meaning of the Qur'an, as the clear meaning of the verse allows one to shorten one's *salah* if one makes any journey upon the earth. Allah says: "If you journey on the earth, there is no blame upon you if you shorten your prayer." The condition of there being fear has been deleted as can be seen in the *hadith* we recorded from Ya'la ibn Umayyah, and what remains is the clear meaning of the verse which covers every type of journey. The Prophet said: "The traveler may wipe over his socks for a period of three days." This shows the length of time that one may wipe over the socks and it cannot be used as a proof for the question we are discussing here. One could argue that traveling is less than a three-day journey on the basis of the *hadith*: "It is not allowed for any woman who believes in Allah and the last day to travel a journey of one day, save in the presence of a male relative." Two, the question of the distance to be traveled is one that may only be answered by some sort of revelation from Allah, the Exalted [the Qur'an or *Sunnah*]; it is not the type of issue which one may address on the basis of personal reasoning, nor is there any way to derive an analogy. The proofs which exist support the opinion that shortening the *salah* is permissible for every traveler, unless there is some consensus to the contrary."

Similar to that is the traveling by planes, trains, and so forth, or a trip that is in obedience to Allah, the Exalted, or otherwise. If there is someone whose occupation requires him to always be traveling, for instance, a pilot, a ship captain, truck driver, and so on, then he is permitted to shorten his *salah* or break his fast as he is truly traveling.

Whence one may shorten one's *salah*: The majority of the scholars are of the opinion that it is permissible to shorten one's *salah* when one leaves one's residence and is outside of one's city, and that is a condition, and he is not to resume his regular *salah* until he reaches the first houses of his city.

Ibn al-Mundhir says: "I do not know of the Prophet shortening his *salah* during any of his travels until after he had left Medinah."

Anas relates: "I prayed four *rak'at* at Dhul-Halifah." This is related by the group. Some of the early scholars say that if one makes the intention to travel, he may shorten his *salah* even if he is in his house.

When the traveler is to pray the complete *salah*: A traveler may shorten his *salah* as long as he is on a journey. Likewise if he stays in some place for business or some other affair, then he may shorten his *salah* as long as he is there, even for years. If the person intends to stay in a place for a certain amount of time then, according to Ibn al-Qayyim, he remains a traveler, regardless of whether he plans to stay there for a long or short time, as long as he does not plan to stay [i.e., reside and not return] in the place that he has traveled to. The scholars differ on this point. Summing up and giving his own opinion, Ibn al-Qayyim says: "The Messenger of Allah stayed in Tabuk for twenty days and during that time he shortened his *salah* and he did not say that one may not shorten his *salah* if he stays longer than that, although there is agreement that he did stay there for that period of time."

In *Sahih al-Bukhari*, it is recorded that Ibn 'Abbas said: "The Prophet stayed, during some of his journeys, for nineteen day and he prayed only two *rak'at*. If we stayed in a place for nineteen days, we would not pray the complete *salah*. However, if we stayed longer than that, we would perform the whole *salah*." Ahmad states that ibn 'Abbas was referring to the Prophet's stay in Makkah at the time of its conquest when he said: "The Messenger of Allah stayed in Makkah for eighteen days during the time of the conquest as he had to go to Hunain and was not planning to stay there." This is his interpretation of Ibn 'Abbas' statement. Others say that Ibn 'Abbas was referring to the Prophet's stay in Tabuk as Jabir ibn 'Abdullah said: "The Messenger of Allah stayed in Tabuk for twenty days and performed *qasr salah*." Imam Ahmad related this in his *Musnad*. Al-Miswar ibn Makhramah reports: "We stayed with Sa'd in some of the cities of ash-Sham [Syria] for forty days, and Sa'd would perform *qasr* while we would offer the whole *salah*." Naf'i relates: "Ibn 'Umar was in Azerbaijan for six months, as there was snow blocking the pass, and he would pray two *rak'at*." Hafs ibn 'Ubaidullah says: "Anas ibn Malik stayed in ash-Sham for two years and he prayed the *salah* of a traveler." Anas relates: "The companions of the Prophet stayed in Ram Hurmuz for seven months and they shortened their *salah*." Al-Hassan reports: "I stayed with 'Abdurrahman ibn Samurah for two years in Kabul, and he shortened his *salah* but he did not combine the *salah*." Ibrahim says: "We resided in Rai for a year or more and in Sijistan for two years…[and we prayed *qasr*].

This is the guidance of the Prophet and his companions, and this is the correct position.

Concerning other opinions which people follow Imam Ahmad say: "If a person intends to stay for four days, he has to offer the whole *salah* and he may offer *qasr* if his intention is for less than that. This is based on an interpretation of the reports from the Prophet and his companions [i.e., they never intended to stay for longer than that and would always say: 'We will leave tomarrow,' and so on]. This interpretation is obviously suspect. The Prophet conquered Makkah and stayed there to establish Islam, eradicate polytheism, and to guide the Arabs. It definitely goes, without saying, that such an objective does take more than a day or two to complete. Similarly, his stay in Tabuk was in preparation for the impending war and he knew that this might take longer than just four days. In the same way, Ibn 'Umar's stay in Azerbaijan for six months, and his praying *qasr* during the entire time was with the knowledge that it takes more than two or three days for such snow to melt and the pass to become traversable. The same is the case with Anas' stay of two years in ash-Sham and his praying *qasr* and the companions' stay in Ram Hurmuz for seven months while shortening their prayers. It is well known that activities like theirs, such as *jihad* and guarding, took more than four days." The followers of Ahmad maintain: "If one is staying in a place for the purpose of *jihad* or due to imprisonment or sickness, then one may shorten one's *salah* regardless of whether the person thinks that such a situation may last for a short time or a long time." This is correct but there is no proof that such conditions have been stipulated in the Qur'an, *Sunnah*, *ijma'* (consensus), or practice of the Prophet's companions. They argued that such conditions are based on what is needed for the person to fulfill his need while remaining a traveler, and that is what is less than four days. His response to them was: 'From where do you derive those conditions, while the Prophet *sallallahu alehi wasallam* stayed for more than four days, shortening his *salah*, in Makkah and Tabuk, and he did not mention to anyone anything about it and he never told them that he never intended to stay for more than four days, even though he knew that the people would [strictly] follow his actions concerning the *salah*. They surely followed him in his shortening of the *salah*, and he did not object to their praying *qasr* if they were to stay for more than four nights. This should be made clear as it is very important. Similarly, the companions (*as-sahabah*) followed him in that and he did not say anything [in objection] to those who prayed with him."

Malik and ash-Shaf'i say: "If one intends to stay for more than four days, he should perform the whole *salah*, and if he intends to stay for less than that, he is to offer *qasr*."

Abu Hanifah holds: "If one intends to stay for fifteen days, he should do the *qasr*. If he intends to stay for less than that, he should not shorten the *salah*." This is also the opinion of al-Laith ibn Sa'd, and it has also been related from three companions: 'Umar, ibn 'Umar, and Ibn 'Abbas.

Sa'id ibn al-Musayyab is of the opinion that: "If you stay for four days, you pray four *rak'at*." A statement similar to that of Abu Hanifah's has also been related from him. 'Ali ibn Abi Talib says that if one stays for ten days, he is to perform the whole *salah*, and the same has been related from Ibn 'Abbas.

Al-Hassan says: "One who does not get to his destination or (city of residence) may shorten *salah*."

'Aishah says: "One who does not put down his provision is to shorten the *salah*."

The four imams agree that if one has some need to take care of and always has the intention of leaving the next day, then he may shorten his *salah* for as long as he is in that state. However, according to one statement of ash-Shaf'i, he may do so only for seventeen or eighteen days and he is not to shorten his *salah* after that time. Ibn al-Mundhir states in his *Ishraf*: "The people of knowledge are in agreement that a traveler may perform *qasr* as long as he does not intend to stay in a place, even though he stays there for years."

Nawafil during travel: The majority of the scholars are of the opinion that it is not disliked to perform *nawafil* during the state in which one is shortening his *salah*. On this point, there is no difference between regular *sunnah* prayers and other *nawafil*.

Al-Bukhari and Muslim record that the Prophet made the *ghusl* in the house of Umm Hani on the day of the conquest of Makkah and then he prayed eight *rak'at*.

Ibn 'Umar reports that the Prophet prayed while riding in whatever direction he was facing and nodding his head [i.e., for the movements of the *salah*].

Al-Hassan relates: "The companions of the Prophet while on a journey performed supererogatory prayers before and after the *fard salah*."

Ibn 'Umar and others are of the opinion that there are no *nawafil*, before or after the *fard salah*, except for during the middle of the night. He saw some people praying after the *salah* and said: "If I were to pray, I would have performed the whole *salah* [as obviously that would have taken preference]. O nephew, I accompanied the Messenger of Allah [on journeys] and he never prayed more than two *rak'at* until Allah took his soul. And I accompanied Abu Bakr and he did not pray more than two *rak'at*." He also mentioned the name of 'Umar and 'Uthman, then he recited the verse: "Ye have indeed in the messenger of Allah a beautiful pattern (of conduct)."[68] This is related by al-Bukhari.

Ibn Qudamah combines what al-Hassan and what Ibn 'Umar say by con-

---

[68]Qur'an 33:21

cluding that al-Hassan's report points to the fact that there is no harm in praying *nawafil* while traveling, whereas Ibn 'Umar's report points to the fact that there is no harm in not praying such *nawafil*.

Traveling on a Friday: There is no harm in traveling on a Friday if it is not during the time of the *salah*.

'Umar heard a man say: "If today was not Friday, I would have left." 'Umar said: "Leave. Friday does not keep one from traveling."

Abu 'Ubaidah traveled on Friday and he did not wait for the *salah*.

Az-Zuhri wanted to travel before noon on Friday and the people mentioned something to him, and he said: "The Prophet traveled on Friday."

COMBINING TWO PRAYERS

It is allowed for a person to combine the *zuhr* and *'asr salah*, either during the time of the earlier or the later *salah*, or the *maghrib* and *'isha* prayers[69] if he is in one of the following circumstances:

Combining the *salah* at 'Arafa and al-Muzdalifah: The scholars are in agreement that one is to combine the *zuhr* and *'asr* prayer during the time of the *zuhr* prayer, at 'Arafa [during the performance of the pilgrimage], and the *maghrib* and *'isha* prayers during the time of the *'isha* at muzdalifah, following the example of the Prophet.

Combining the *salah* during traveling: Most of the people of knowledge are of the opinion that it is permissible to combine two prayers during the time of either one of them while traveling, regardless of whether the person is actually on the road or has stopped at a place for some time.

Mu'adh reports that while the Prophet was at Tabuk and the sun had passed the meridian, the Prophet *sallallahu alehi wasallam* combined the *zuhr* and *'asr* prayers before he started his journey. If he started his journey before the sun passed its meridian, he would delay the *zuhr* prayer until the time when he stoppped for the *'asr* prayer. He would do likewise for the *maghrib* prayer. If the sun set before he began his journey, he would combine the *maghrib* and *'isha* prayers [at that time]. If he began a journey before the sun had set, he would then combine them at the time of *'isha*. This is related by Abu Dawud and at-Tirmidhi who call it *hasan*.

Kuraib reported that Ibn 'Abbas said: "Shall I not inform you of the *salah* of the Prophet *sallallahu alehi wasallam* during a journey?" We said:

---

[69]The scholars agree that these, *zuhr* and *'asr* or *Maghrib* and *'isha*, are the only combinations which are permissible.

"Certainly." He said: "If the sun passed its meridian while he stopped, he would combine the *zuhr* and *'asr* prayers before remounting [i.e., moving on]. If the sun had not passed its meridian while he had stopped [i.e., before breaking camp], he would travel until the time of the *'asr* prayer and then he would combine the *zuhr* and *'asr* prayers. If the sun set while he had stopped, he would combine the *magrib* and *'isha* prayers. If that did not occur while he had stopped, he would ride until the *'isha* time and then combine them." This is related by Ahmad.

Ash-Shaf'i has something similar in his *Musnad*, namely that when he [the Prophet] set out to travel before the sun passed its meridian, he delayed the *zuhr* prayer and combine it with the *'asr* during the time of the *'asr salah*. Al-Baihaqi recorded it with a good chain and he says: "To combine the two prayers due to traveling is something that is well-known and was practiced by the companions of the Prophet *sallallahu alehi wasallam* and those who followed them."

Imam Malik records in *al-Muwatta'* from Mu'adh that the Prophet *sallallahu alehi wasallam* delayed his *salah* one day during the battle of Tabuk and then went and prayed the *zuhr* and *'asr* prayers together. Then he returned and went back again and said the *maghrib* and *'isha* prayers together.

Commenting on this report, ash-Shaf'i says: "His statement, 'then he returned and left again,' only refers to a situation where the Prophet was staying in a certain place [i.e., he was not traveling from one site to another]."

Ibn Qudamah mentions the preceding *hadith* and writes in *al-Mughni*: "Ibn 'Abdul-Barr said: 'That *hadith* is sahih and its chain is confirmed. The people who are familiar with the life history of the Prophet say that the battle of Tabuk took place in the ninth year of the *hijrah*. This *hadith* is a clear proof and the strongest evidence against those who claim that one can only combine the prayers while one is actually moving from one site to another as the Prophet was settled and was not traveling since the Prophet was staying in his tent and would come out and combine two prayers and then return to his tent. Muslim recorded this *hadith* in his *Sahih* and stated: 'He would pray the *zuhr* and *'asr* together and the *maghrib* and *'isha* together. One must follow this *hadith* as it is confirmed [to be authentic] and it is a clear statement on this rule and there is nothing which contradicts it. The permission to combine the *salah* is a concession for anyone who is traveling but it is by no means confined to just those times when the person is actually on the road [i.e., traveling from one place to another]. The same is the case for shortening the *salah* and for wiping over the socks, but it is best to delay it.'"

Having the intention to combine is not a condition for combining or shortening the *salah*. Ibn Taimiyyah holds: "That is the position of the majority of the scholars. When the Prophet combined the *salah* with his companions or shortened the *salah* with them, he never ordered any of them to make the intention for combining or shortening the *salah*. In fact, when he left Medinah for Makkah, he prayed two *rak'at* without combining the *salah*, and then he prayed the *zuhr* prayer at 'Arafa without telling the people that he intended to pray the *'asr* right afterward, next he prayed the *'asr* with them and they did not have the intention to combine their prayers, and in that combination he prayed the latter *salah* early. When he went from Medinah, he led the people in the *'asr salah* at Dhul-Halifah and he did not order them to make the intention to shorten the *salah*."

Concerning offering the two combined prayers right after each other, Ibn Taimiyyah writes: "The correct opinion is that it is not a necessary condition to do so under any circumstances, neither during the time of the first *salah* nor during the time of the latter *salah*. There is no such limit in the *shari'ah* and doing so would defeat the purpose of the concession [i.e., permission to combine the two *salah*]." Ash-Shaf'i says: "It is quite permissible for a person to pray the *maghrib* in his house with the intention of combining the prayers and then go to the mosque to pray the *'isha*." A similar statement has been related from Ahmad.

Combining two prayers during rain: Al-Athram records in his *Sunnan* that Abu Salamah ibn 'Abdurrahman said: "It is a *sunnah* to combine the *maghrib* and *'isha* prayers when it is raining." Al-Bukhari records that the Prophet *sallallahu alehi wasallam* combined the *maghrib* and *'isha* prayers on a rainy night.

A summary of the opinions of the different schools of fiqh on this point follows:

The Shaf'i school says that it is allowed for the resident to combine the *zuhr* and *'asr* or the *maghrib* and *'isha*, praying each pair in the time of the earlier *salah* only, given that it is raining when one begins the earlier prayer and it is still raining by the time one begins the second prayer.

According to the Maliki school, it is allowed to combine the *maghrib* and *'isha* in the mosque at the time of the *maghrib* due to rain or expected rain, if there is mud and darkness along the way, or if there is a lot of mud and it prevents the people from wearing their shoes. Nevertheless, he dislikes that the *zuhr* and *'asr* should be combined due to rain.

According to the Hanbali school, it is only allowed to combine the *maghrib* and *'isha* in the time of the former or the latter due to snow, ice, mud, severe cold, or rain which soaks the clothes. This concession is allowed only for one who prays with a congregation in the mosque and who comes from a distance over which he could be harmed by the rain. However, for one who prays in a congregation in his house or whose path to the mosque is covered or protected, or for one whose house is right next to the mosque, it is not allowed to combine the *salah*.

Combining the two prayers due to some illness or other excuse: Ahmad, Qadi Hussain, al-Khattabi, and al-Mutawali of the Shaf'i school are of the opinion that it is allowed to combine two prayers, either during the time of the earlier or later *salah*, due to illness as it is a greater hardship than rain. An-Nawawi says: "This is a strong opinion based on [sound] evidence." In *al-Mughni* it is stated: "The illness which permits one to combine the prayers is the one which would otherwise cause hardship and more weakness [if he prayed each *salah* separately]."

The Hanbali school is the most accommodating as it allows one to combine the prayers, at the time of the early or later *salah*, for one who is ill as well as for the woman who is breast-feeding and will face hardship in cleaning her dress for every *salah*, for the woman who is plagued by a prolonged flow of blood, for the person who cannot control his urine, and for one who cannot purify himself or herself, and for the one who fears for his life, property, or family.

Ibn Taimiyyah says: "Among the opinions the most accommodating on this question is that of the Hanbali school which allows one to combine the prayers if he is busy (since an-Nasa'i has related something to that effect from the Prophet *sallallahu alehi wasallam*) and they also say that the cook and baker, and so forth., may also combine their prayers if they fear their wealth (i.e., their investment or what they are working on) will otherwise be ruined."

Combining two prayers due to some pressing need: Imam an-Nawawi writes in his commentary on *Sahih Muslim*: "The majority of the scholars are of the opinion that it is allowed for the resident to combine the prayers due to some pressing need. This is the statement of Ibn Sireen and Ashhab from the companions of Malik, and al-Khattabi records it from al-Qifal and ash-Shaf'i and from Abu Ishaq al-Maruzi, and from a number of *aṣ-hāb al-ahadith*, and it is the conclusion of Ibn al-Mundhir. This is supported by the statement of ibn 'Abbas: 'The Prophet combined his *salah* because he did not want to put his *ummah* to hardship, and not because of illness or any other reason.'" The *hadith* from Ibn 'Abbas, mentioned previously, has been recorded by Imam Muslim who states: "The Messenger of Allah combined the *zuhr* and '*asr* and then the *maghrib* and '*isha* in Medinah without there being any danger or rain." Ibn 'Abbas was asked: "What did he desire by that action?" He replied: "He did not want any hardship for his *ummah*." Al-Bukhari and Muslim record from him that the Prophet prayed seven *rak'at* and eight *rak'at*, i.e., the *zuhr* and '*asr* together and the *maghrib* and *'isha* together, in Medinah. Muslim also records from 'Abdullah ibn Shaqiq that 'Abdullah ibn 'Abbas addressed the people one day after the *'asr salah* until well after the sun had set and the stars began to appear. The people said to him: "The prayer, the prayer." A man from the tribe of Taim continuously repeated: "The prayer, the prayer." Ibn 'Abbas said: "Are you teaching me the *sunnah*? May you have no mother." Then he said: "I saw the Messenger of Allah combine the *zuhr* and *'asr* and the *maghrib* and *'isha*." 'Abdullah ibn Shaqiq commented: "I felt some uneasiness in my heart about what he had said, so I went to Abu Hurairah to ask him about that, and he confirmed what Ibn 'Abbas had said."

Validity of combined prayers after their legal excuse ceases to exist: In *al-Mughni* it is stated: "If someone performs both prayers at the time of the earlier *salah* and then his reason for doing so ceases to exist after he has completed the *salah* and before the time of the next *salah* begins [i.e., the next *salah* being the one which he had just prayed during the earlier time], then what he has done is sufficient for him and he need not repeat the second *salah* at its proper time. Since he performed the *salah* in a proper manner, he is free from any extra obligation due to that action. He fulfilled his obligation during a circumstance in which he had some legal excuse, and his action is not invalidated by the fact that this excuse no longer exists. This is similar to the case of a person who performe *tayammum*, and after he finishes his *salah*, he finds water."

Prayer on a ship, train or plane: A *salah* on a ship, train, plane, and so on, is valid and there is no dislike for such an act as it makes life easier for the one performing it. Ibn 'Umar says: "I asked the Prophet *sallallahu alehi wasallam* about *salah* on a ship and he said: 'Pray standing upon them unless you fear that you will be drowned [i.e., the boat might capsize].'" This is related by ad-Daraqutni and by al-Hakim. The later grades it *sahih* according to the criteria of al-Bukhari and Muslim.

'Abdullah ibn Abi 'Utbah reports: "I accompanied Jabir ibn 'Abdullah and Abu Sa'id al-Khudri and Abu Hurairah on a boat, and they prayed standing in a congregation, with one of them as their imam, although they could have gone ashore [if they had so desired]." This is related by Sa'id ibn Mansur.

Some supplications for the traveler

It is preferred for the traveler to say, upon leaving his house:

"In the name of Allah, the Exalted! We have trusted in Allah. There is no power or might, save with Allah. O Allah, I seek refuge

بسم الله توكلت على الله . ولا حول ولا قوة

إلا بالله : اللهم إنى أعوذ بك أن أضل أو

in Thee from being misguided and
from misguiding others, or that I
stray from Your path or cause
others to stray from Your path, or
that I am wronged or that I do
wrong to others, or that I act
foolishly or have someone act
foolishly with me."

أُضِل ، أو أزل أو أُزل ، أو أظلم أو أُظلم
أو أجهل أو يُجهل عليّ .

Then, the person may say whatever he wishes of the supplications which
have been recorded from the Prophet, *sallallahu alehi wasallam.* Here are
some of them:

'Ali ibn Rabi'ah narrates: "'Ali was brought a riding animal. When he
put his foot in the stirrup, he said: 'In the name of Allah.' Then, when
he sat on it, he said: 'Praise be to Allah. Glory be to the One Who made
this subservient to us for we were not able to make [it subservient] and
it is to our Lord that we will return*.' He then praised Allah three times
and extolled His greatness three times and then said: 'Glory be to You;
there is no God but Thee. I have wronged my soul, so forgive me. No
one forgives sins, except You.' Then, he laughed. I said to him: 'Why
do you laugh, commander of the faithful?' He replied: 'I saw the Messenger of Allah doing the same and then laughing. I asked him: "What
makes you laugh, O Messenger of Allah?" He said: "The Lord is pleased
with His slave who says: 'O Lord, forgive me,' and He says: 'My slave
knows that no one forgives sins, save I.'" This is related by Ahmad and
Ibn Hibban, and by al-Hakim who says it is *sahih* according to the criteria
of Imam Muslim.

Al-'Azdi reports that Ibn 'Umar taught him that the Messenger of Allah
would extol Allah's greatness three times while seating himself on his
camel for a journey. Then he would say:

"Glory be to the One who made
this subservient to us for we were
not able [to make it subservient].
It is to our Lord that we shall return. O Allah, we ask of Thee, in
this journey of ours, righteousness
and piety and to (be able to) perform such deeds that are pleasing
to You. O Allah, make this journey of ours easy for us and make
its length short for us. O Allah,

سبحـان الـذى سخـر لنا هذا وما كنا له
مقـرنين وإنا إلى ربنا لمنقلبون : اللهم إنا
نسألك فى سفرنا هذا البر والتقوى ، ومن
العمل ما ترضى : اللهم هوّن علينا سفرنا

---

*Qur'an 43:13

companion on this journey and the One who looks after our family and property in our absence. O Allah, I seek refuge in Thee from the difficulty of traveling and the unhappiness in what I see and in finding that something harmful has happened when I return to my property and family."

هذا واطو لنا بعده : اللهم أنت الصاحب في السفر ، والخليفة في الأهل : اللهم إني أعوذ بك من وعثاء السفر وكآبة المنقلب ، وسوء المنظر في الأهل والمال .

When he would return from his journey he would add:
"Returning [are we] repentant, serving and praising our Lord."

آيبون تائبون عابدون لربنا حامدون .

This is related by Ahmad and Muslim.

Ibn 'Abbas reports that when the Prophet desired to travel, he would say: "O Allah, You are my companion in my travels and the One Who looks after my family [while I am gone]. O Allah, I seek refuge in You from unworthy travel companions and an unpleasant situation upon my return. O Allah, make the distance short for us and the travel easy for us."
When he desired to return, he would say:

"We are returning, [while] repenting to Allah, worshipping our Lord and praising Him."_

آيبون تائبون عابدون لربنا حامدون .

When he would enter upon his family, he would say:

"We are repenting to our Lord. We hope that none of our sins would remain."

توباً توباً لربنا أوباً لا يُغادر علينا حَوْباً .

This is related by Ahmad, at-Tabarani, and al-Bazzar with a *sahih* chain.

'Abdullah ibn Sarjas reports that, when the Prophet had to travel, he would say:

"O Allah, I seek refuge in You from the difficulty of the journey, and sorrow on return, and disorder after things are set right, from the cry of the oppressed, and from seeing harm having come to our property and family."

اللهم إني أعوذ بك من وعثاء السفر وكآبة المنقلب . والحَوَر بعد الكَوَر ، ودعوة المظلوم ، وسوء المنظر في المال والأهل .

And when he returned he would make a similar supplication, but instead of saying: "from seeing harm having come to our property and family," he would mention family first and then property. This is related by Ahmad and Muslim.

Ibn 'Umar reports that when the Prophet went out for a battle or a journey, and night came upon him, he would say:

"O Earth, my Lord and your Lord is Allah. I seek refuge in Allah from your evil and the evil of what is on you and the evil of what has been created upon you and the evil of what walks upon you. I seek refuge in Allah from lions and large black snakes, and from snakes and scorpions, and from the evil or all that inhabit the land, and the evil of a father and what he has fathered."

يا أرض ربى وربك الله ، أعوذ بالله من شرك وشر ما فيك وشر ما خُلق فيك وشر ما دب عليك ، أعوذ بالله من شر كل أسد وأسود ، وحية وعقرب ، ومن شر ساكن البلد ، ومن شر والد وما ولد .

This is related by Ahmad and Abu Dawud.

Khaulah bint Hakim as-Sulimiyah reports that the Prophet *sallallahu alehi wasallam* said: "Whoever stops at a stopping place should say: 'I seek refuge by the perfected word of Allah, the Exalted, from the evil of what has been created,' then nothing will harm him until he leaves that stopping place." This is related by the group, save al-Bukhari and Abu Dawud.

'Ata ibn abi Marwan states from his father that Ka'b took an oath by the One who opened up the sea for Moses that Suhaib related to him that whenever the Messenger of Allah *sallallahu alehi wasallam* saw a city which he wished to enter, he would say:

"O Allah, Lord of the seven heavens and what they shade, Lord of the seven earths and what they carry, Lord of the satans and those that they misguide, Lord of the winds and what they blow away, I ask of You for the good of this city and the good of its inhabitants and the good of what is in it. I seek refuge in You from its evil and the evil of its inhabitants and the evil of what is in it."

اللهم رب السموات السبع وما أظللن ، ورب الأرضين وما أقللن ، ورب الشياطين وما أضللن ، ورب الـرياح وما ذرين ، أسألك خير هذه القرية وخير أهلها وخير ما فيها ، ونعوذ بك من شرها وشر أهلها وشر مافيها .

This is related by an-Nasa'i, ibn Hibban, and al-Hakim who calls it *sahih*.

Ibn 'Umar says: "We would travel with the Messenger of Allah, and when he would see the city that he wished to enter, he would say: 'O Allah, give us blessings from what is in it,' three times. And, 'Allah, give us provisions from its harvest and make us beloved to its inhabitants and make the pious people of its inhabitants beloved to us." This is related by at-Tabarani in *al-Ausat* with a good chain.

'Aishah says: "Whenever the Messenger of Allah came to a place that he wished to enter he would say: 'O Allah, I ask of you of the good of this place and the good of what you have collected therein. O Allah, grant us provisions from its harvest and protect us from its diseases. Make us beloved to its inhabitants and make the pious people of its inhabitants beloved to us.' This is related by ibn as-Sani.

Abu Hurairah reports that when the Prophet *sallallahu alehi wasallam* was on a journey and daybreak approached he would say: "Let one listen and witness the praise of Allah and His good favor toward us. Our Lord, accompany us and show us favour [as we] seek refuge in Allah from the hell-fire." This is related by Muslim.

THE FRIDAY PRAYER (*Salatul Jumu'ah*)

The virtues of *Jumu'ah*: Friday (*Jumu'ah*) is the best day of the week.

Abu Hurairah reports that the Messenger of Allah *sallallahu alehi wasallam* said: "The best day on which the sun rises is Friday. [On Friday] Adam was created and on that day he entered paradise and on that day he was expelled from paradise. And the Hour will come to pass on Friday." This is related by Muslim, Abu Dawud, an-Nasa'i, and at-Tirmidhi who calls it *sahih*.

Abu Lubanah al-Badri relates that the Prophet said: "The most prominent of the days [lit. the leader of the days] is the day of *Jumu'ah* and the most honored in Allah's sight, and it is more honored in Allah's sight than the day of breaking the fast or the day of sacrifice. It has five significant merits: Allah created Adam on this day; on this day Allah sent Adam down to the earth; on this day, Allah caused Adam to die; on this day, there is a time during which if anyone asks anything of Allah it will be granted to him unless he asks for something which is forbidden; and on this day, the Hour will be established. There are no angels close to Allah or sky or earth or wind or mountain or sea who are not worried concerning the day of *Jumu'ah*." This is related by Ahmad and Ibn Majah. Al-Iraqi says its chain is *hasan*.

Supplications during Friday: One should do one's best to make supplications during the last moments (or hours) of *Jumu'ah*.

'Abdullah ibn Salam relates: "I said, and the Messenger of Allah was sitting: 'We find in the Book of Allah that on Friday there is an 'hour' in which, if a believing slave prays to Allah for something, his prayer is (indeed) accepted and he is granted what ever he prays for.' The Messenger of Allah pointed toward me and said: 'Or part of an hour.' I said: 'You have spoken the truth: or part of an hour.' I asked: 'What hour is it?' He replied: 'The last hour of the day.' I remarked: 'That is not a time of salah?' He responded: 'Certainly [it is]; if a believing slave offers salah and then sits, he will not be sitting, save due to the salah, and he will be in salah.'" This is related by Ibn Majah.

Abu Sa'id and Abu Hurairah report that the Messenger of Allah said: "On Jumu'ah there is a time that if a believing slave asks Allah during it for some good, [Allah will definitely] give it to him, and that time is after the 'asr salah." This is related by Ahmad. Al-'Iraqi calls it sahih.

Jabir reports that the Messenger of Allah said: "The day of Jumu'ah has twelve hours, and during one of the hours, you will not find a Muslim slave [of Allah] asking Allah for something, but that He will give it to him. Seek it in the last hour after the 'Asr salah." This is related by an-Nasa'i, Abu Dawud, and by al-Hakim in al-Mustadrak, and he calls it sahih according to Muslim's criteria. Ibn Hajar says that its chain is hasan.

Abu Salamah ibn 'Abdurrahman reports that some companions of the Prophet gathered and mentioned the "hour on Jumu'ah." They left and did not differ on the fact that it is the last hour of Jumu'ah. This is related by Sa'id ibn Mansur in his Sunan and al-Hafiz Ibn Hajar calls it sahih.

Ahmad ibn Hanbal says: "Most of the ahadith concerning the hour in which the supplication is always responded to state the hour to be after the 'asr prayer, and some state it to be after the sun passes the meridian."

There is a hadith recorded by Muslim and Abu Dawud which states that Abu Musa heard the Messenger of Allah say concerning the special hour on Jumu'ah: "It is between the time that the imam sits [i.e., upon the pulpit] and the time that the salah is completed." All the same, this particular hadith is defective because its chain is broken and it is mudtarib.[70]

Making many prayers and salutations upon the Prophet sallallahu alehi wasallam during the night[71] and the day of Jumu'ah:

Aus ibn Aus reports that the Prophet said: "The most virtuous of your days is Jumu'ah. On that day, Adam was created and on that day he died, (on that day) the horn will be blown and the people will be dumbfounded! Increase your prayers upon me as your prayers upon me will be presented

---

[70]Mudtarib means that it is related through so many different and contradictory chains or with so many different and contradictory texts that there is no way to determine the correct chain and text of the hadith. Due to this preponderance of doubt, it is considered a type of weak hadith.—J.Z.

[71]Unlike English usage, "the night of Friday" refers to the night that precedes the day of (Jumu'ah), i.e. Thursday night in English.—J.Z.

to me." The people said: "O Messenger of Allah, how will our prayers be presented to you when you have passed away?" He said: "Allah has prohibited the earth from eating the bodies of the Prophets." This is related by the five, except for at-Tirmidhi.

Ibn al-Qayyim says: "It is preferred to pray for (Allah's blessings on the Prophet during the day and night of *Jumu'ah* as the Prophet said: 'Make many prayers upon me during the day of Friday and the night of Friday.' The Messenger of Allah is the leader of mankind, and *Jumu'ah* is the best of the days of the week. Prayers upon him during that day are a privilege [he deserves] which belongs to no other. This act also has another wisdom to it and that is that all of the good that has passed onto this [Muslim] *ummah*, in this life and the hereafter, has passed through him. Allah has gathered the good of this life and the next life for this *ummah*, and the greatest honor and success will be granted to them on Friday. On that day, they will be granted their houses and palaces in paradise and that is the day they will be given more when they enter paradise. It is a day of celebration for them in this life. It is also a day in which Allah fulfills their needs and answers their prayers and requests in this world. They are aware of all of that and are able to attain it because of the Prophet and it is through him [that they received these teachings]; therefore, in gratitude and appreciation for the great blessings we received through him, we should make many prayers upon him during the day and night of *Jumu'ah*."

Recitation of *Surah* al-Kahf: It is preferred to recite *surah* al-Kahf during the day and night of *Jumu'ah*.

Abu Sa'id al-Khudri reports that the Prophet said: "Whoever recites *Surah* al-Kahf on *Jumu'ah* will have illumination from the light from one *Jumu'ah* to the next." This is related by an-Nasa'i, al-Baihaqi, and al-Hakim.

Ibn 'Umar reports that the Prophet said: "Whoever recites *Surah* al-Kahf on *Jumu'ah* will be blessed with a light that will rise from underneath his feet to the peak of the sky. This will be a light for him on the Day of Resurrection, and he will be forgiven for what is between the *Jumu'ah* [and the next] *Jumu'ah*." This is related by Ibn Mardwwiyah with a faultless chain.

It is disliked to raise one's voice while reciting it in the mosque. Shaikh Muhammad 'Abdu issued a verdict that mentioned reciting *Surah* al-Kahf aloud among the many disliked matters on Friday. He also mentioned the following: singling out Friday as a day of fasting, singling out its night as a night to perform *salatul tahajjud*, reciting *Surah* al-Kahf during it with a specific manner of melody which disturbs those who are offering *salah*, while the people in the mosque are not listening because of their being engaged in conversation with others. Therefore, one should be careful about such a recital.

Performing *ghusl*, beautifying one's self, using the *miswak*, and using perfume for any gathering and especially for *Salatul Jumu'ah*:
It is preferred for anyone – man or woman, an elderly or young person, a traveler or a resident – who desires to attend the *salatul Jumu'ah* or any gathering of the people, to cleanse and to wear best attire. One should perform *ghusl*, put on one's finest clothing, apply perfume[72], and to brush one's teeth. The following *ahadith* are recorded on this matter:

Abu Sa'id reports that the Prophet said: "Every Muslim should have a *ghusl* on Friday and wear his best clothing, and if he has perfume, he should use it." This is related by Ahmad, al-Bukhari, and Muslim.

Ibn Salam reports that he heard the Prophet say, while he was upon the pulpit on Friday: "It would do no [harm] to anyone if he were to buy two gowns for Friday other than his work clothes."[73] This is related by Abu Dawud and Ibn Majah.

Salman al-Farsi reports that the Prophet *sallallahu alehi wasallam* said: "A man who performs *ghusl* on Friday, purifies [himself] what he can and uses dye [for his hair] or perfumes himself in his house, goes to the mosque, and does not cause separation between two people [who are already seated], prays what Allah has prescribed for him, and then listens quietly while the imam speaks, all his sins between that Friday and the next Friday will be forgiven." This is related by Ahmad and al-Bukhari, while Abu Hurairah used to say: "And for three more days as for every good deed Allah grants tenfold reward." The sins mentioned in this *hadith* are the minor sins as Ibn Majah recorded, on the authority of Abu Hurairah in the words: "For one who has not committed major sins."

Ahmad records, with a *sahih* chain, that the Prophet said: "It is obligatory upon every Muslim to perform *ghusl*, apply purfume and use the *miswak* on *Jumu'ah*.[74]

Abu Hurairah reports that one Friday the Prophet said: "O gathering of Muslims, Allah has made this day an 'id for you, so make *ghusl* and use

[72]Women may wear subtle perfumes which others cannot smell.
[73]Al-Baihaqi recorded from Jabir that the Prophet had a special cloak that he would wear on the two 'ids and *Jumu'ah*. This *hadith* shows that it is preferred to set aside special clothing, other than that which one usually wears, for *Jumu'ah*.
[74]It is due to *ahadith* like this one that some scholars are of the opinion that the *ghusl* on Friday is obligatory. In a *hadith* in *Sahih Muslim*, Ibn 'Abbas said that the *ghusl* has been abrogated. Allah knows best. Incidentally, the *ghusl* is not obligatory on one who does not attend *salatul Jumu'ah*. This statement is based on a *hadith* recorded by al-Baihaqi, on the authority of Ibn 'Umar, which states: "Any man or woman who comes to *salatul Jumu'ah*, he or she need not make *ghusl*." This is reported by an-Nasa'i who says its chain is *sahih*.

the *miswak.*" This is related by at-Tabarani in *al-Ausat* and *al-Kabir* with a chain whose narrators are trustworthy.

Going early to *Salatul Jumu'ah*: It is preferred for one to go early to the *salatul Jumu'ah*, unless he is the imam. 'Alqamah says: "I went with 'Abdullah ibn Mas'ud to the mosque and we found that three people had arrived there before us. [Ibn Mas'ud] said: 'The fourth of four, and the fourth of four is not far from Allah, for I have heard the Messenger of Allah say: "The people will be seated on the day of resurrection according to how they came to the *salatul Jumu'ah*: the first, then the second, then the third, then the fourth and the fourth of four is not far from Allah.'" This is related by Ibn Majah and al-Mundhiri.

Abu Hurairah reports that the Prophet said: "Whoever makes *ghusl* on *Jumu'ah* like the *ghusl* one makes due to sexual defilement, and then goes to the mosque, it will be as if he had sacrificed a camel. If he goes during the second hour, it will be as if he had sacrificed a cow. If he goes during the third hour, it will be as if he had sacrificed a horned lamb. If he goes during the fourth hour, it will be as if he had sacrificed a hen. And if he goes during the fifth hour, it will be as if he had sacrificed (something like) an egg. When the imam comes, the angels will be present to listen to the rememberance." This is related by the group, save Ibn Majah.

Ash-Shaf'i and a number of scholars are of the opinion that the "hours" refer to the hours of the day; therefore, it is preferred for the people to start attending the mosque right after dawn. Malik is of the opinion that it refers to portions of the hour before the sun passes its meridian and afterward. Some hold that it refers to portions of the hour before the sun passes its meridian. Ibn Rushd says: "That is the most apparent meaning as going [to the mosque] after the sun passes the meridian is obligatory."

Stepping over others' necks in the mosque: At-Tirmidhi reports that the people of knowledge dislike that one should "step over the necks of the people" on *Jumu'ah* and they were very strict in this regard. 'Abdullah ibn Busr says: "A man came and he was stepping over the necks of the people while the Prophet was delivering *khutbah* of *Jumu'ah*. He said to him: 'Sit down. You have harmed the people and have come late.'" This is related by Abu Dawud, an-Nasa'i, Ahmad, and Ibn Khuzaimah, and others call it *sahih*.

This ruling does not apply to the imam or one who finds an opening and cannot reach it, save by going over the people. If one wants to return to his place after leaving it due to some necessity, he may do so on the condition that he does not harm the people. 'Uqbah ibn al-Harith relates: "I prayed the *'asr* in Medinah behind the Prophet and then he stood and hurried off, stepping over the people, to go to some of the apartments of his wives. The people were afraid because of his rushing away in this manner. When he came out and found them amazed at leaving them in such a hurry, he said: 'I remembered some gold that was in my possession and I hated that it should remain with me, so I ordered it to be distributed.'" This is related by al-Bukhari and an-Nasa'i.

Nawafil before salatul Jumu'ah:

It is a *sunnah* to offer supererogatory prayers before *al-Jumu'ah* until the imam arrives. After the imam's arrival, one should no longer offer any *salah*, save for the prayer of greeting the mosque (*tahayyatul masjid*) which may be performed quickly during the *khutbah* unless one comes at the end of the *khutbah* and would not have the time [i.e., before the actual *salah* begins] to perform *tahayyatul masjid*.

Ibn 'Umar used to perform a long prayer before *al-Jumu'ah* and then two *rak'at* after it, and he said that the Prophet used to do so. This is related by Abu Dawud.

Abu Hurairah reports that the Prophet *sallallahu alehi wasallam* said: "Whoever makes *ghusl* on the day of *Jumu'ah* and then goes to the mosque and prays what has been prescribed for him, and remains quiet while the imam delivers the *khutbah*, and then prays with the imam, he will have forgiven for him what is between that *Jumu'ah* and the next and an additional three days." This is related by Muslim.

Jabir reports that a man came to the mosque on *Jumu'ah* while the Prophet was delivering the *khutbah*. The Prophet inquired of him: "Did you offer the *salah*?" The man replied: "No!" He told him: "Pray two *rak'at*." This is related by the group. In one narration it states: "If one of you comes to the mosque on the day of *Jumu'ah* and the imam is delivering the *khutbah*, he should pray two *rak'at* and make them quick." This is related by Ahmad, Muslim, and Abu Dawud. In another narration, it is stated: "If one of you comes to the mosque on the day of *Jumu'ah* and the imam has already arrived, he should offer two *rak'at*." This is related by al-Bukhari and Muslim.

Feeling drowsy while in the mosque: It is preferred for one who is in the mosque to change place if he feels sleepy. The movement may remove some of his drowsiness and help wake him up. This rule is true for Fridays and any other day.

Ibn 'Umar reports that the Prophet *sallallahu alehi wasallam* said: "If one of you becomes sleepy while he is in the mosque, he should move from his place to another place." This is related by Ahmad, Abu Dawud, al-Baihaqi, and at-Tirmidhi who calls it *hasan sahih*.

THE FRIDAY PRAYER AS AN OBLIGATION

The scholars are in agreement that *salatul Jumu'ah* is an individual obligation and it is two *rak'at*. Allah says in the Qur'an: "O you who believe, when the call for the *salah* of *Jumu'ah* is proclaimed, hasten unto the remembrance of Allah, and leave off business (and trading). That is best for you if you but knew."[75]

The obligatory nature of *salatul Jumu'ah* is also obvious from the *hadith* recorded by al-Bukhari and Muslim from Abu Hurairah that the Prophet said: "We are the last [of the people to come] but the first on the day of resurrection. They received their books before us and we got ours after them. This day was obligatory upon them, but they differed concerning it, and Allah guided us. The people, therefore, follow us: the Jews tomorrow and the Christians the day after tomorrow."

Ibn Mas'ud reports that the Prophet noticed some people staying away from *al-Jumu'ah* and said: "I had the notion to order someone to lead the people in prayer, and then to go and burn the houses of those who stayed away from *al-Jumu'ah*." This is related by Ahmad and Muslim.

Abu Hurairah and Ibn 'Umar report that they heard the Prophet *sallallahu alehi wasallam* say: "Those who are not attending the Friday *salah* should change their ways; otherwise, Allah, the Exalted, will seal their hearts and they will be reckoned the heedless." This is related by Muslim, and by Ahmad and an-Nasa'i from ibn 'Umar and ibn 'Abbas.

Abu al-Ja'd ad-Damari reports that the Prophet said: "Whoever misses three Friday prayers in a row out of negligence will have a seal put over his heart by Allah." This is related by the five, and Ahmad and Ibn Majah have something similar from Jabir, while Ibn as-Sakin has graded it to be *sahih*.

Upon whom *salatul Jumu'ah* is obligatory: *Salatul Jumu'ah* is an obligation upon every free, adult, sane, resident Muslim who has the ability to attend the *salah* and does not have a valid excuse to miss it. *Salatul Jumu'ah*, however, is not obligatory on the following:

(1) Women and children. Concerning this category there is no difference of opinion.

(2) The person who is ill and faces hardship if he goes to the mosque, or who fears that his illness will be increased by going to the mosque, or whose recovery will be delayed. This also includes the person who is nursing a very ill person if, especiallay, the ill person cannot manage in the absence of the nursing person.

Tariq ibn Shihab reports that the Prophet *sallallahu alehi wasallam* said:

---

[75]Qur'an 62:9

"*Al-Jumu'ah* is a duty upon every Muslim in the community, save four: a slave, or a woman, or a child, or a person who is ill." An-Nawawi says that its chain is *sahih* according to the conditions set by al-Bukhari and Muslim. Ibn Hajr says that more than one person has graded it *sahih*.

(3) For the traveler, even if he is staying at a certain place during the time of the beginning of *salatul Jumu'ah*, it is not obligatory. This is based on the fact that the Prophet *sallallahu alehi wasallam* traveled and did not perform the *salatul Jumu'ah* but only prayed the *zuhr* and *'asr* together during the time of the *zuhr* prayers. The caliphs after him and others also acted in a similar manner.

(4) One who is in debt and cannot repay his debt and therefore fears that he will be imprisoned, and one who fears that he will be harmed by an oppressive ruler: Ibn 'Abbas reports that the Prophet *sallallahu alehi wasallam* said: "Whoever hears the call to the *salah* and does not respond to it [i.e.,by coming to the *salah*], there will be no prayer for him unless he has an excuse." The people inquired: "O Messenger of Allah, what is a [valid] excuse?" He answered: "Fear or illness." This is related by Abu Dawud with a *sahih* chain.

(5) Environmental restraints like rain, mud, extreme cold, and so on. Ibn 'Abbas said to the *mu'adhdhin* on a rainy day: "When you say 'I testify that Muhammad is the Messenger of Allah,' do not say 'Come to the prayer,' but say 'Pray in your houses.'" The people objected to that and he told them: "One better than me did so [the Prophet *sallallahu alehi wasallam*]. *Al-Jumu'ah* is an obligation but I dislike that you should go out walking in the mud and slush." Abi Malih reports that his father had witnessed the day of *Jumu'ah* with the Prophet and it was raining and the people were troubled by their shoes so he ordered them to pray in their stopping places. This is related by Abu Dawud and Ibn Majah.

All of these people are not obliged to pray the Friday *salah* although they are obliged to pray the *zuhr*. Should one of them pray *salatul Jumu'ah*, it will still be valid for him or her and he will no longer be obliged to pray the *zuhr*. And the women during the time of the Prophet *sallallahu alehi wasallam*, attended the mosque and used to pray *al-Jumu'ah* with him.

The Time of the *Salatul Jumu'ah*: The majority of the companions and successors were of the opinion that the time of *al-Jumu'ah* is the same as that of the *zuhr*. Ahmad, al-Bukhari, Abu Dawud, at-Tirmidhi, and al-Baihaqi record from Anas that the Prophet *sallallahu alehi wasallam* would pray *al-Jumu'ah* when the sun had passed its meridian. Ahmad and Muslim record that Salamah ibn al-Akua' said: "We would pray *salatul Jumu'ah* with the Prophet when the sun had passed the meridian, and when we returned [from the *salah*], we would be following our shadow." Al-Bukhari says: "The time of *al-Jumu'ah* is when the sun passes its meridian." Similar narrations have been recorded from 'Umar, 'Ali, an-Nu'man ibn Bashir, and 'Umar ibn Harith. Ash-Shaf'i says: "The Prophet *sallallahu alehi wasallam*, Abu Bakr, 'Umar, 'Uthman, and the imams after them all prayed the Jumu'ah when the sun had passed its zenith."

The scholars of the Hanbali school and Ishaq are of the opinion that the time for *al-Jumu'ah* is from the beginning of the time for *salatul 'id* to the end of the time for the *zuhr*. They base their opinion on Ahmad, Muslim, and an-Nasa'i who record from Jabir: "The Prophet would pray *al-Jumu'ah* and then we would take our camels to rest until the sun passed its zenith." This *hadith* clearly states that they prayed *al-Jumu'ah* before the sun passed the meridian. They also cited as proof the *hadith* of 'Abdullah ibn Saidan as-Salmi who said: "We prayed *al-Jumu'ah* with Abu Bakr, and his *khutbah* and *salah* were before noon. Then we prayed with 'Uthman and his *khutbah* and *salah* lasted until after the sun had passed the meridian, and no one scolded either for it." This is related by Ahmad, who cites it as a proof, and by ad-Daraqutni. Ahmad adds: "And [something] similar to that has been related from ibn Mas'ud, Jabir, Sa'id, and Mu'awiyyah. They all prayed before the sun passed the meridian and no one objected to what they did, and that was the consensus. The majority of the scholars, however, interpret the *hadith* of Jabir as implying that one should pray the *salah* early in its time, when the sun has passed the meridian, and not wait until the weather gets cool. The prayer and the resting of the camels was right after the sun passed the meridian. As to the report from 'Abdullah ibn Saidan, these scholars consdier it weak. Ibn Hajar writes about him: 'He is one of the major *tabi'in* [i.e., of the generation after the companions], and his integrity is not well-established. 'Adi says: "He is somewhat majhul, i.e. unknown as a trustworthy person." Bukhari observes: "His report is not to be trusted, especially when he is contradicted by people who are more credible (*qawi*) than him as Ibn abi Shaibah relates from Suwaid ibn Ghaflah that the later prayed with Abu Bakr and 'Umar after the sun had passed the meridian and its chain is strong.'"

The number of people required for *al-Jumu'ah*: There is no dispute among the scholars that a congregation is a necessary condition for the validity of *al-Jumu'ah*. This is based on the *hadith* of Tariq ibn Shihab who reports that the Prophet said: "*Al-Jumu'ah* is an obligation (*wajib*) upon every Muslim in the community." However, the scholars do differ on how many people are required for *al-Jumu'ah*. There are fifteen different opinions on this question and they are mentioned by Ibn Hajar in *Fath al-Bari*. The strongest opinion is that *salatul Jumu'ah* is valid if there are two or more people present since the Prophet is reported to have said: "Two or more constitute a congregation."

Ash-Shaukani says: "The other prayers are considered to be made in congregation if there are two people present. The same applies to *Jumu'ah salah*, unless there is a reason for it to be different. There is no evidence to show that [for the purpose of the congregation] its number should be larger than that for the other prayers. 'Abdul Haqq says: 'There is no confirmed *hadith* on the number of people needed for *al-Jumu'ah*.' Similarly, as-Sayuti holds: 'There is no confirmed *hadith* which states a particular number [for the *Jumu'ah salah*].'" This is also the opinion of at-Tabari, Dawud, an-Nakha'i, and Ibn Hazm.

The place for al-Jumu'ah: It is valid to perform the *Jumu'ah salah* in any country, city, mosque, any building in a city, or in any space in a city as it also is valid to have it performed in more than one place. 'Umar wrote the following to the people of Bahrain: "Offer the *Jumu'ah salah* wherever you may be." This is related by Ibn abi Shaibah. Ahmad holds its chain to be good. This includes both the cities and countryside.

Ibn 'Abbas says: "The first Friday *salah* that was performed in Islam, after the Friday *salah* in the mosque of the Messenger of Allah *sallallahu alehi wasallam* in Medinah, was in Jawa'i, a village in Bahrain." This is related by al-Bukhari and Abu Dawud.

Al-Laith ibn Sa'd reports that the people of Egypt and of the surrounding sea-shore would perform the *Jumu'ah salah* during the time of 'Umar and 'Uthman according to their orders. Some of the companions of the Prophet attended *jumu'ah* prayer with them. Ibn 'Umar saw the people in the areas between Makkah and Medinah performing the *Jumu'ah* prayers, and he did not object to their action. This is related by 'Abdurrazzaq with a *sahih* chain.

Conditions Stipulated By The Jurists for the Friday Prayer

Some of the conditions under which the *jumu'ah salah* becomes obligatory have already been mentioned (i.e., it is obligatory for a free, sane, adult male resident who does not have a valid excuse which would excuse him from attending the prayer). It was also mentioned that a congregation is a condition for the Friday *salah*. This is what the *sunnah* of the Prophet teaches us and what Allah holds us responsible for. Concerning the other stipulations which some of the jurists stipulate for the *Jumu'ah salah*, none of them has any basis to which we may refer, or any evidence to support it. It will be sufficient here to simply quote the author of *ar-Raudah an-Nadiyah* who writes:

[The Friday *salah*] is like the rest of the prayers and there is nothing in it that differs from them, unless there is some evidence to the contrary. This statement refutes those who stipulate, as a necessary conditions for Friday prayer, the presence of a well-established imam and a congregational mosque in the area as well as a certain number of people attending the congregational prayer. There is no evidence whatever that those conditions are even preferred – not to speak of being obligatory, or for that matter, being a necessary condition for the Friday *salah*. If two people pray the *Jumu'ah* in a place where there is no one else but them, they would have performed their prescribed duty. If one of them delivers the *khutbah*, they would be following what is *sunnah*; and if they leave the *khutbah*, then it is only the *sunnah* which they have neglected, (not something which was obligatory). But for the *hadith* of Tariq ibn Shihab which clearly requires every Muslim to offer it in congregation and the fact that the Prophet *sallallahu alehi wasallam* always performed it in a congregation, offering it individually, like the rest of the prayers, would have been quite acceptable. Concerning the statement "from four people to the ruler of the area," that is certainly not the Prophet's statement nor of any of his companions... In fact, [this is] a statement of al-Hassan al-Basri. As to various statements and psuedo-juristic opinions concerning this noble worship, the Friday prayer, which Allah has prescribed once a week as one of the signs of Islam, a little consideration should suffice to show their superfluity and error. One of these is the amazing statement that *khutbah* is equivalent to two *rak'at* of *salah*, and if one misses it, then his *jumu'ah* is not valid. They seem to be quite ignorant of what has been related from the Prophet through a number of chains which support each other that "if a person misses one *rak'ah*, then he is to perform another *rak'ah* and his *salah* would be completed." Have not other *ahadith* reached them that are valid in such matters? Some say that one cannot perform the *Jumu'ah* unless there are three people with the imam and others hold that four people are needed, while yet others stipulate seven people! Still others say nine, and some think twelve, twenty, thirty, and there are even some who think forty, fifty, seventy, and every number that is between those numbers! Some hold that many people have to be present without specifying a particular number, while others state that *al-Jumu'ah* may only be performed in a city in which there is a "congregational mosque." Some are convinced that there have to be so many thousand people living in the area. Some hold that there has to be a congregational mosque and a public restroom. Yet others propose that the prayer is not obligatory unless there is a well-known and established imam; if such an imam cannot be found or if his credibility is doubtful, then the Friday *salah* is neither obligatory nor legitimate. ...No such statement can be found [in the book of Allah or in the *sunnah*] to support what they claim to be the conditions or pre-requisites of the *Jumu'ah*... Whoever comes with such gibberish must be refuted for the only criterion is the Book of Allah and the *Sunnah* of His Messenger. As Allah says in the Qur'an: "If you dispute concerning any matter, refer it to Allah and the Messenger[76]"; "The answer of the believers, when summoned to Allah and His Messenger, in order that he may judge between them is no other than this: they say: "We hear and we obey,"[77]; "But no, by thy Lord, they can have no (real) faith, until they make thee judge in all disputes between them, and find in their souls no resistance against thy decisions, but accept them with the fullest conviction."[78] Those verses and others similar to them are the clearest evidence that one must return to the rule of Allah and His Messenger if there is any dispute. The rule of Allah is the Book of Allah. The rule of the Messenger, after his passing away, is his *sunnah* and nothing other than that. Also, Allah did not endow any of his slaves – even if he reaches the highest degree of knowledge and has accumulated what no one else has – with the right to make any statement concerning this religion without any authority from the Book or the *Sunnah*. Likewise, if a *mujtahid* (jurisconsult) should take liberty of proposing an opinion without substantiating it, then it is not permissible for anyone to follow him in that, regardless of who he may be. I, as Allah knows, am always greatly astonished by this type of writers and their writings which supposedly provide guidance in one's creed and practice but which are filled with gibberish. This is not limited to only some of the schools among the different schools of law, or only certain areas from among the different areas, or only certain eras from among all of the eras [it is found in all of these schools of law, areas, and eras]! In fact, the later people follow the earlier people [in such things] as if they were following the *umm al-kitab* [mother of the Book], although, [they follow] distorted teachings...

---

[76]Qur'an 4:59
[77]Qur'an 24:51
[78]Qur'an 4:65

The Friday *khutbah*

Ruling concerning *khutbah*: The majority of the people of knowledge are of the opinion that *khutbahtul Jumu'ah* is obligatory and they support this by the confirmed *ahadith* which state that the Prophet always made the *khutbah* with the *Jumu'ah*. In their support they also quote the saying of the Prophet: "Pray as you see me pray," and the Qur'anic verse: "O you who believe, when the call is proclaimed for *salatul jumu'ah*, hasten unto the remembrance of Allah."[79] This verse contains an order to hasten unto the remembrance, which implies it is obligatory, and (the scholars) interpret the remembrance of Allah to include the *khutbatul Jumu'ah*. Ash-Shaukani refutes the first argument by saying that *hadith* simply states the action of the Prophet *sallallahu alehi wasallam* and does not necessarily prove that such an action is obligatory. As to the verse, he regards it as simply a command to be present at the *salah* which is obligatory and excludes *khutbah*... Regarding their argument relating to the commandment to "hasten unto the rememberance of Allah," he says it refers to *salah* only, which is the real cause for making haste. There is, however, an agreement that the Friday *salah* is obligatory while there is a dispute over whether or not the *khutbah* is obligatory. Ash-Shaukani concludes by saying that apparently the correct view is the one held by al-Hassan al-Basri, Dawud az-Zahiri and al-Juwaini, that the *khutbah* is only a highly recommended act.

The greeting of the imam: The imam should greet the people when he comes upon the pulpit, followed by the *adhan* which is to be made when he sits. The imam should face the people during the *adhan*.

Jabir reports that when the Prophet mounted the pulpit, he would greet the people. This is related by Ibn Majah and in its chain is Ibn Lahiya[80], and al-Athram has recorded it in his *Sunnan* from ash-Sha'biy, on the authority of the Prophtet, in *mursal* form. Ata' and others also reported in *mursal* form that when the Prophet walked to the top of the pulpit, he would turn to the people and say: "Peace be upon you." According to ash-Sha'biy: "Abu Bakr and 'Umar used to do that [also]."

As-Sa'ib ibn Yazid informs: "The first *adhan* to *salah* made on the day of *Jumu'ah* was made when the imam sat upon the pulpit during the time of the Prophet, Abu Bakr, and 'Umar. Then, during the time of 'Uthman, since there were many people, he instituted a third *adhan*[81] outside the

---

[79]Qur'an 62:9

[80]Ibn Lahiya is known to be a weak narrator of *hadith*. His books were destroyed in a fire and after that time he had to relate *hadith* from his faulty memory.—J.Z.

[81]A third call meaning besides the first *adhan* and the *iqamah* for the beginning of the prayer.—J.Z.

mosque. The Prophet only had one *mu'adhdhin*." This is related by al-Bukhari, an-Nasa'i, and Abu Dawud. In another narration, it is stated: "During the time of 'Uthman, there were many people, so 'Uthman ordered the people to make a third call to *salah* on the day of *Jumu'ah*, outside of the mosque, and that practice has continued."

Ahmad and an-Nasa'i record: "Bilal would make the *adhan* to *salah* when the Prophet *sallallahu alehi wasallam* sat upon the pulpit, and he would make the *iqamah* when the Prophet came down from the pulpit."

'Adi ibn-Thabit relates from his father on the authority of his grandfather who said: "When the Prophet ascended the pulpit, he would face his companions." This is related by Ibn Majah. Concerning this latter *hadith*, although there is some doubt about it, at-Tirmidhi says: "The people of knowledge from among the companions and others follow that and they prefer that the imam face the people when delivering the *khutbah*."

Contents of the *khutbah*: It is preferred that the Friday *khutbah* include praises of Allah, the Exalted, prayers upon the Prophet, admonitions, and Qur'anic recitations.

Abu Hurairah reports that the Prophet *sallallahu alehi wassallam* said: "Every speech that does not begin with the praises of Allah is defective." This is related by Abu Dawud. Ahmad has something similar to it.

In another version, it is stated: "The Friday *khutbah* that does not contain the testimony ["There is no God except Allah, and Muhammad is His Messenger] is like the defective hand." This is related by Ahmad, Abu Dawud, and at-Tirmidhi.

Ibn Mas'ud reports that the Prophet would say in his opening testimony: "All praise be to Allah, we seek His aid and we seek His forgiveness and we seek refuge in Allah from the evil of our souls. Whomever Allah guides, no one will be able to mislead him. Whoever He leaves astray will have no guidance for him. And I testify that there is no God except Allah and that Muhammad is His slave and His Messenger whom He sent with the truth and as a warner before the Hour. Whoever obeys Allah and His Messenger will be guided aright, and whoever disobeys them will only harm his own self and he will not harm Allah, the Exalted, at all."

Ibn Shihab was asked about the Prophet's opening testimony during his *khutbah* on the day of *Jumu'ah*, and he said something similar to that except that he stated: "Whoever disobeys them has gone astray." Abu Dawud related both of these reports.

Jabir ibn Samurah says: "The Messenger of Allah would deliver his *khutbah* standing, would sit in between the two *khutbahs*, would recite some verses, and would remind the people [about Allah]." This is related by the group, save al-Bukhari and at-Tirmidhi.

Jabir also related that the Prophet *sallallahu alehi wasallam* would not make his admonitions on Friday too long, but give a very short *khutbah*. This is related by Abu Dawud.

Umm Hisham bint Harithah ibn an-Nu'man says: "I learnt [*Surah*] Qaf of the Glorious Qur'an from the Prophet for he recited it upon the pulpit every Friday when he addressed the people." This is related by Ahmad, Muslim, an-Nasa'i, and Abu Dawud.

Ya'la ibn Umayyah reports that he heard the Prophet recite, while on the pulpit: "And they cry: O Malik!..." (az-Zukhruf: 77). This is related by al-Bukhari and Muslim.

Ibn Majah records from Ubayy that the Messenger of Allah recited: "Blessed is He..." [*Surah* al-Mulk] on Friday while he was standing. In *ar-Raudah an-Nadiyah*, it is stated: "Thus the required *khutbah*, in terms of Islamic law, should be modeled after the Prophet's *khutbah* exhorting people to do good and warning them against dire consequences of the evil. This is the spirit of the address which the Islamic law has instituted. As to the other contents of the *khutbah*, like praising Allah, saying prayers upon His Messengers or reciting a portion of the Qur'an, none of these is its main purpose, which is to admonish people... It has been customary among the Muslims [in the light of the *sunnah*] that if one wanted to make some sort of proclamation, he would begin with praises of Allah and prayers upon His Prophet, or something of that nature. Still, that is not the purpose of the *khutbah*; indeed, the purpose is that which is said after praises of Allah and prayers for the prophet. If a person delivers a *khutbah* and confines it to only praising Allah and saying prayers upon the Prophet, his *khutbah* would hardly be acceptable. Any person with common sense could understand that.

It is the admonitory aspect of the Friday *khutbah* which the *ahadith* emphasise, and if a *khatib* makes an admonition, he fulfills the purpose of *shari'ah*; if he precedes his *khutbah* with praises of Allah and prayers upon the Prophet and during his admonitions he uses Qur'anic verses, then he does it in a complete and satisfactory manner."

Posture during and between the *khutbahs*: It is proper for the imam to stand for the two *khutbas* and to sit for a short while in between them.

Ibn 'Umar said: "When the Prophet *sallallahu alehi wasallam* would deliver the *Khutbatul Jumu'ah*, he did so standing, and then he would sit, and then he would stand [again, for the second *khutbah*] as the people do today." This is related by the group.

Jabir ibn-Samura said: "The Prophet would deliver the *khutbah* while standing, and then he would sit, and then he would stand and speak again. Whoever says that he gave the *khutbah* while sitting has lied. Verily, I prayed with him more than two thousand prayers [including the five daily prayers]." This is related by Ahmad, Muslim, and Abu Dawud.

Ibn abi-Shaibah records that Tawus said: "The Prophet gave the *khutbah* while standing and so did Abu Bakr, 'Umar, and 'Uthman. The first one to give *khutbah* while sitting upon the pulpit was Mu'awiyyah," Ibn abi-Shaibah also records from ash-Sha'biy that Mu'awiyyah used to deliver the *khutbah* while sitting, when he became overweight. Some of the scholars say that it is obligatory to deliver the *khutbah* while standing and it is also obligatory to sit in between the two *khutbahs*. They cite the example of the Prophet and his companions who always did so; however, the fact that they consistently performed an act is not sufficient to prove that it is *fard* (obligatory).

It is preferred to raise one's voice, to keep the *khutbah* short, and to the point: 'Ammar ibn Yasir reports that he heard the Messenger of Allah say: "Prolonging *salah* and shortening one's *khutbah* is a sign of one's understanding of the religion. So, prolong the prayer and shorten the *khutbah*." This is related by Ahmad and Muslim. Shortening the *khutbah* and prolonging one's *salah* shows one's understanding of religion, for such a person is able to comprehend and express much in a few words.

Jabir ibn Samurah says: "The Prophet's *salah* was of a moderate length and so was his *khutbah*." This is related by the group, save al-Bukhari and Abu Dawud.

'Abdullah ibn abi Aufa reports: "The *salah* of the Messenger of Allah was long and his *khutbah* was short." This is related by an-Nasa'i with a *sahih* chain.

Jabir informs: "When the Prophet delivered the *khutbah*, his eyes became red, his voice rose, and his anger increased as if giving a warning to the enemy." This is related by Muslim and Ibn Majah.

An-Nawawi says: "It is preferred for the *khutbah* to be in an eloquent and proper Arabic, and it should be an organized speech that the people can understand. It should not be a speech, which is over the heads of the people, nor should it be shallow or contain foul language as that would defeat its purpose. Its words should be chosen carefully to make them attractive and meaningful."

Giving his views on the subject, Ibn al-Qayyim says: "The *khutbah* of the Prophet reinforced the fundamental articles of faith, like belief in Allah, the Exalted, His angels, His books, His messengers, and the meeting with Him. He would mention the paradise and the hellfire and what Allah, the Exalted, has promised to His devoted servants and the people who obey Him and what Allah has promised to His enemies and the miscreant. While listening to his *khutbah*, the hearts would be filled with belief in Allah, His oneness, and His majesty. His *khutbahs* were not like speeches of those who speak only of matters of concern of common folk, lamenting earthly life and frightening people of the approaching death. Such speeches cannot inspire faith in Allah or strengthen belief in His oneness or move people by allusion to His mighty works in history, nor can they kindle in hearts intense love for Allah, making the listeners look forward eagerly to the time they will meet Him! The people who hear such speeches gain no benefit at all, except that they will die and that their wealth will be distributed and their bodies will be turned to dust. Woe to such poets, what sort of faith is fostered by such sermons, and what sort of *tawhid* do they teach or knowledge disseminate? If we study the *khutbahs* of the Prophet *sallallahu alehi wasallam* and his companions, we find them embued with perspicuous guidance, *tawhid*, attributes of Allah, explaining the basic articles of the faith, inviting people to Allah, and drawing their attention to His providential care that makes Him so beloved to His slaves. His *khutbahs* referred to Allah's dealings with others in the past so as to warn his listeners against His wrath and exhort them to remember Him, thank Him and win His pleasure and love. Those who heard these *khutbahs* were inspired with the love of Allah and they looked forward eagerly to meeting their Lord. As time went by, the example of the Prophet was forgotten and other things prevailed. The main purpose of the *khutbah* was forgotten. The eloquent and nice words that moved the hearts became rare in speeches. The main thrust of the *khutbah* was neglected. The hearts were no longer touched and the basic purpose of the *khutbah* was lost."

The imam interrupting his *khutbah* for some reason: Abu Hurairah reports: "The Prophet was delivering a *khutbah* and al-Hassan and al-Hussain [his grandsons] came and they were wearing two red shirts and they were tripping while walking. The Prophet came down from the pulpit and picked them up and placed them in front of himself, and then he said: 'Allah and His Messenger have told the truth. Verily, your wealth and children are a trial. I looked to these two children walking and tripping, and I could not be patient, so I cut off my *khutbah* and went to pick them up.'" This is related by the five.

Abu Rifah al-'Adwi says: "I went to the Prophet while he was delivering a *khutbah*, and I said: 'O Messenger of Allah, this strange man has come to ask about his religion as he does not know what his religion is.' The Prophet turned to me and left his speech, he came to me and he was given a wooden chair with four iron legs, and he started to teach me what Allah had taught him and then he went back to complete his *khutbah*." This is related by Muslim and an-Nasa'i.

Ibn al-Qayyim writes: "The Prophet would interrupt his *khutbah* due to some reason, or to respond to a question from some of his companions.

Sometimes he would descend from the pulpit due to some need and then return and complete his *khutbah*, as he did when he picked up al-Hassan and al-Hussain. He took them and then returned with them to the pulpit. Sometimes he would interrupt his *khutbah* to say things to certain people, [e.g.,] 'Sit, so and so,' 'Pray, so and so.' [Sometimes] he ordered them to take care of certain things during his *khutbah*."

It is forbidden to speak during the *khutbah*: The majority of the scholars are of the opinion that it is obligatory to be silent during the *khutbah*, and one is not to indulge in conversation during the *khutbah*, not even if it is to order one to do some good or to stop some evil, and this rule applies whether or not the person sitting in the mosque can actually hear the *khutbah*.

Ibn 'Abbas reports that the Prophet *sallallahu alehi wasallam* said: "Whoever speaks in *Jumu'ah* while the imam is delivering the *khutbah* is like a donkey who is carrying books, and for those who tell him to be quiet, there is no [reward] for the *Jumu'ah*." This is related by Ahmad, ibn abi-Shaibah, al-Bazzar, and at-Tabarani. Ibn Hajar said in *Bulugh al-Maram*: "There is no fault in its chain."

'Abdullah ibn 'Amr reports that the Messenger of Allah said: "There are three types of people who attend the *Jumu'ah*: one, a man who is present but speaks [during the speech], and that is his portion of the prayer; two, a man who is present and makes supplications – in his case, Allah may give him what he asks, if He wishes, or He may not give him what he asks, three, a person who is present and observes silence and does not step over the necks of the Muslims nor harm anyone – for him, there is expiation from that *Jumu'ah* until the next *Jumu'ah* plus an additional three days as Allah has said: 'He that does good shall have ten times as much to his credit.'[82]" This is related by Ahmad and Abu Dawud with a good chain.

Abu Hurairah reports that the Prophet said: "If, during the *Jumu'ah* while the imam is delivering *khutbah*, you tell your companion to be quiet, then you have spoken needlessly." This is related by the group, save Ibn Majah.

Abu ad-Darda' says: "The Prophet was upon the pulpit and was addressing the people and he recited a verse, and next to me was Ubayy ibn-Ka'b and I asked him: When was that verse revealed?' He refused to talk to me until the Messenger of Allah came down from the pulpit and then he said to me: 'You have nothing from your *Jumu'ah*, except your useless talk.' When the Prophet had finished, I went to him and informed him of what had happened, and he said: 'Ubayy has told the truth. If you hear

---

[82]Qur'an 6:160

your imam speaking, be quiet until he is finished.'" This is related by Ahmad and at-Tabarani.

Ahmad and ash-Shaf'i are reported to have made a distinction, concerning this ruling, between one who can hear the speech and the one who cannot hear the speech, saying that speaking is forbidden for the former and not for the latter, although it is preferred for the latter also to be silent.

At-Tirmidhi records that Ahmad and Ishaq made an exception for replying to a salutation and responding to a sneeze while the imam is delivering the Friday *khutbah*. According to ash-Shaf'i: "If a person sneezes [during the *khutbah*] and someone says: 'May Allah bless you,' I wish I could have accomadated it since such a reply is a *sunnah*. In my view it is *makruh* that a person should greet someone with *salam* [while they are listening to the *khutbah*]. [What makes it worse is] that his *salam* is not returned, even though saying *salam* is a *sunnah* while responding to it is a *fard*.

Indulging in conversation when the *khutbah* is not being delivered, is permissible. Tha'labah ibn abi-Malik says: "We would be talking on *Jumu'ah* while 'Umar was sitting on the pulpit and when the call to *salah* was finished 'Umar would stand and no one would utter a word until he had completely finished both of his *khutbahs*. When the *iqamah* was made and 'Umar came down from the pulpit, the people would then speak." This is related by ash-Shaf'i in his *Musnad*.

Ahmad records, with a *sahih* chain, that while the *adhan* was being made, 'Uthman ibn-'Affan would be sitting on the pulpit, apprising the people of their situation and the prices of some commodities.

Catching One *Rak'ah* or Less of the *Jumu'ah*: Most of the people of knowledge are of the opinion that if a person catches only one *rak'ah* of al-*Jumu'ah*, then that *rak'ah* will be valid and the person need only make up the one *rak'ah* that he misses.

Ibn 'Umar reports that the Prophet *sallallahu alehi wasallam* said: "Whoever catches only one *rak'ah* of the *salah* and then adds to it the other one, his prayer will be complete." This is related by an-Nasa'i, Ibn Majah, and ad-Daraqutni. In *Bulugh al-Maram*, Ibn Hajar says that its chain is *sahih* although Abu Hatim says that the strongest opinion is that it is *mursal*.

Abu Hurairah reports that the Prophet *sallallahu alehi wasallam* said: "Whoever catches one *rak'ah* of the prayer has indeed caught the whole prayer." This is related by the group.

Whoever catches less than one *rak'ah* of the *salah* has not caught the *Jumu'ah* and he is to pray four *rak'at* of the *zuhr salah* according to the majority of the scholars.

Ibn Mas'ud says: "Whoever catches one *rak'ah* from al-*Jumu'ah* is only to add another one to it. Whoever misses both *rak'at* is to pray four *rak'at*." This is related by at-Tabarani with a good chain.

Ibn 'Umar says: "If one catches from the Friday *salah* one *rak'ah*, then he is to add another one to it. If he catches only the sitting [at the end of the prayer, following the bowing], then he is to pray four [*rak'at*]." This is related by al-Baihaqi. Such is the opinion of the Shaf'i, Maliki, and Hanbali schools, and Muhammad ibn al-Hassan. Abu Hanifah and Abu Yusuf say that if one catches the *tashahud* with the imam, then he has caught *al-Jumu'ah*. He should pray two *rak'at* after the imam makes the *taslim*, and his Friday *salah* would be complete.

Offering the *salah* in a crowded area: Ahmad and al-Baihaqi relate from Sayyar that 'Umar was giving an address and said: "The Messenger of Allah built this mosque and we were with him [i.e., the emigrants and the helpers], and if it becomes very crowded, a person among you is to make the prostration on the back of his brother." When, he saw some people praying in the street, he said to them: "Pray in the mosque."

***Nawafil* before and after *al-Jumu'ah*:** It is a *sunnah* to pray four *rak'at* or two *rak'at* after *al-Jumu'ah*: Abu Hurairah reports that the Prophet *sallallahu alehi wasallam* said: "Whoever is to pray after the *Jumu'ah* should pray four *rak'at*." This is related by Muslim, Abu Dawud, and at-Tirmidhi.

Ibn 'Umar says: "The Prophet would pray two *rak'at* in his house on the day of *Jumu'ah*." This is related by the group.

Ibn al-Qayyim says: "After the Prophet finished the *Jumu'ah*, he would enter his house and pray two *rak'at*, and he ordered those who prayed the *Jumu'ah* to pray four *rak'at* after it.

Our sheikh Ibn Taimiyyah says: 'When he prayed in the mosque, he would pray four [*rak'at*], and when he prayed in his house, he would pray two *rak'at*.' I say: this is what the *hadith* is pointing to. Abu Dawud records from ibn 'Umar that when he prayed in the mosque, he would pray four *rak'at*, and when he prayed in his house, he would pray two *rak'at*. Also, in the two *Sahihs* it is reported from ibn 'Umar that the Prophet would pray two *rak'at* in his house after the Friday *salah*."

If one prays four *rak'at*, then, according to some, he is to pray them all connected, while others hold that he is to pray two *rak'at*, make the *taslim*, followed by another two *rak'at*. It is preferred to pray them in one's house. If one prays them in the mosque, he should change his place of prayer after the Friday *salah*.

Concerning any *sunnah* prayer before the Friday *salah*, Ibn Taimiyyah writes: "The Prophet *sallallahu alehi wasallam* never offered any *salah* after the *adhan* and before the Friday *salah*, and no one has ever related such an act from him. During the Prophet's time, there was only one *adhan* and that was made when the Prophet sat upon the pulpit. Bilal would make the *adhan* and then the Prophet would give the two *khutbahs*. Next, Bilal would make the *iqamah* and the Prophet would lead the people in *salah*. It is not possible that the Prophet would have made a *salah* after the *adhan* nor anyone else among the Muslims who prayed with the Prophet could have done so. And we have no evidence to show that the Prophet, *sallallahu alehi wasallam*, prayed in his house before going out to the mosque on Friday. He did not specify any time for any *salah* before the Friday *salah*. What he said was meant to exhort those going early to the mosque on Friday to engage themselves in prayer. He said: 'Whoever goes out early and walks and does not ride to the mosque and prays what has been prescribed [by Allah] for him...' That has been related from the Prophet's companions. When they would reach the mosque on Friday, they would pray whatever amount was easy for them. Some of them prayed ten *rak'at* and some prayed twelve and some only eight and others less than that. For this reason most of the scholars are of the opinion that there is no *sunnah* prayer with a specified number of *rak'ah* or time, before *al-jumu'ah*, for there is nothing either in the actions or statements of the Prophet to support or confirm it.

Salatul Jumu'ah and Salatul 'Id

Occurring on the same day: If the day of *'Id* occurs on *Jumu'ah*, then *salatul Jumu'ah* is no longer an obligation upon those who performed the *salatul 'Id*.

Zaid ibn Arqam says: "The Prophet *sallallahu alehi wasallam* prayed the *salatul 'id* and then he gave an exemption concerning the *Jumu'ah*, saying: 'Whoever wishes to pray it may pray it.'" This is related by the five and al-Hakim. Ibn Khuzaimah calls it *sahih*.

Abu Hurairah reports that the prophet *sallallahu alehi wasallam* said: "Two festivals have occurred together on this day of yours. For whosoever desires, this will suffice for his *salatul Jumu'ah*, but we are going to perform *salatul Jumu'ah*." This is related by Abu Dawud.

It is preferred for the imam to perform the *Jumu'ah* so anyone who wishes to perform it may do so as well as those who were not able to attend the *'id* prayer. The Prophet *sallallahu alehi wasallam* said: "We are going to perform the *salatul Jumu'ah*."

According to the Hanbali school, the *zuhr* is obligatory upon anyone who does not attend the *salatul Jumu'ah* because he has performed the *'id* prayer. Nevertheless, it apparently is not obligatory as there is a *hadith* in *Sunan Abu Dawud* in which Ibn az-Zubair says: "*'Id* and *Jumu'ah* occurred on the same day so he joined them and prayed two *rak'at* at an early time, and did not add anything to it until *'asr*.

'ID PRAYERS
(SALATUL 'IDAIN)

The prayers of the two 'ids was prescribed in the first year after the migration. It is a *sunnah mu'kkadah* as the Prophet *sallallahu alehi wasallam* always performed these prayers and he ordered the men and women to go out to attend them.

Grooming for the two 'ids: It is preferred to make the *ghusl*, perfume one's self and don one's best attire on the occasions of the two 'ids.

Ja'far ibn-Muhammad relates from his father on the authority of his grandfather who reported that the Prophet would wear a Yemeni cloak on every 'id. This is related by ash-Shaf'i and al-Baghawi.

Al-Hassan as-Sibt says: "The Messenger of Allah ordered us to wear the best clothes we could find for the two 'ids and to apply the best perfume we could find and to sacrifice the best animal we could find." This is related by al-Hakim and in its chain is Ishaq ibn Barzakh whom al-'Azdi declares to be weak while Ibn Hibban says he is trustworthy.

Ibn al-Qayyim writes: "The Prophet used to wear his most beautiful clothes for them and he had a special cloak that he would wear on the two 'ids and *Jumu'ah*.

Eating on the two 'ids: One is to eat before going to the *salah* for *'idul fitr*, (the end of Ramadan) but not do so on the occasion of the *'idul adha* (commemmorating Prophet Ibrahim's sacrifice). For *'idul fitr*, it is a *sunnah* to eat an odd number of dates before going to pray *salatul 'id* while for *'idul adha* the eating should be delayed until one returns from the 'id prayers and then he may eat of his sacrifice if he has sacrificed an animal.

Anas reports: "The Prophet would not go out on the festival of breaking the fast until he had eaten an odd number of dates." This is related by Ahmad and al-Bukhari.

Buraidah reports: "The Prophet would not go out on the day of breaking the fast ('idul fitr) until he had eaten and on the day of sacrifice ('idul adha) he would not eat until he had returned [from salah]." This is related by at-Tirmidhi and Ibn Majah, and also by Ahmad who added: "And he would eat from his sacrifice."

In al-Muwatta' it is recorded from Sa'id ibn al-Musayyab that the people were ordered to eat before they go out on the day of breaking the fast.

Ibn-Qudamah said: "I do not know of any difference of opinion over the fact that one should hasten in eating [eat early] on the day of breaking of the fast."

Going out to the musalla (place of prayer): Salatul 'id can be performed in the mosque but it is preferred to perform in a place outside the city as long as there is no excuse or reason to do otherwise (e.g., rain and so on) as the Prophet would pray the two 'ids in the outskirts of Medinah and he never prayed it in his mosque, except once and because it was raining.

Abu Hurairah reports that it was raining on the day of 'id, so the Prophet led them in salatul 'id in the mosque. This is related by Abu Dawud, Ibn Majah, and al-Hakim, and its chain contains an unknown narrator. Al-Hafiz says in at-Talkhis: "Its chain is weak," and adh-Dhahabi asserts: "This hadith is rejected."

Women and children going out to attend 'id prayer: Shari'ah requires women and children to go out and attend the salatul 'idain. This includes married, single, young, old, or menstruating women.

Umm 'Atiyah reports: "We were ordered to go out with the single and menstruating women to the two 'ids in order to witness the good and the supplications of the Muslims. The menstruating women would be separate from the others." This is related by al-Bukhari and Muslim.

Ibn 'Abbas says that the Prophet would take his wives and daughters to the two 'ids. This is related by Ibn-Majah and al-Baihaqi.

Ibn 'Abbas further reports: "I went out with the Prophet on the day of breaking the fast or of the sacrifice, and he prayed and gave a khutbah, and then he went to the women and admonished them, reminded them of Allah, and ordered them to give charity." This is related by al-Bukhari.

Taking different routs to and from musalla: Most of the people of knowledge are of the opinion that it is preferred for a person to go to the salah by one route and then to return home through another route, regardless of whether he be the imam or a member of the congregation.

Jabir reports: "On the days of *'id*, the Prophet would take different routes." This is related by al-Bukhari.

Abu Hurairah says: "When the Prophet went to *salatul 'id*, he would return through a different route." This is related by Ahmad, Muslim, and at-Tirmidhi.

It is permissible to return through the same route by which one goes to the *musalla*. Bakr ibn Mubashir says: "I used to go with the companions of the Prophet to the *musalla* on *'idul adha* and on *'idul fitr*, and we passed through a specific valley in Medinah until we came to the place of *salah* and prayed with the Messenger of Allah, and then we would return to our houses through the same valley." This is related by Abu Dawud, al-Hakim, and by al-Bukhari in his *Tarikh*. Ibn as-Sakin says that its chain is acceptable.

The time of *'Id* prayers: The time for *salatul 'id* begins from the time the sun is three meters above the horizon until the sun reaches its meridian.

Ahmad ibn Hassan al-Bana' records that Jundub said: "The Prophet prayed the *'idul fitr* prayer while the sun was [approximately] six meters[83] above the horizon and the *'id* of the sacrifice while the sun was three meters above the horizon."

Ash-Shaukani says: "That is the best of what has been related concerning the specific time of *salatul 'idain* and the *hadith* shows that it is preferred to hasten in praying *salatul adha* and to delay the *salatul fitr*."

Ibn Qudamah says: "It is a *sunnah* to pray *salatul adha* early in order to allow more time for the people to perform the sacrifice, and the *salatul fitr* is to be delayed in order to give people time to pay *zakat al-Fitr*. I know of no difference of opinion on this point."

The *adhan* and *iqamah* for *salatul 'idain*: Ibn al-Qayyim writes: "When the Messenger of Allah went to the *musalla* (place of prayer), he would perform the *salah* without any *adhan* or *iqamah* and without saying *'as-salatu jami'ah'* (prayer in congregation). The *sunnah* is not to do any of that."

Ibn 'Abbas and Jabir both report that there was no *adhan* on the day of the breaking of the fast or on the day of sacrifice. This is related by al-Bukhari and Muslim. Muslim records that 'Ata said: "Jabir informed me that there is no *adhan* for the *'id* of breaking the fast, neither when the imam arrives nor afterward. And there is no *iqamah* or call of any kind."

Sa'd ibn abi-Waqqas reports: "The Prophet prayed *salatul 'id* without any *adhan* or *iqamah*. He would deliver two *khutbahs* standing and would seperate them by sitting between them." This is related by al-Bazzar.

---

[83]Literally "two *rumah*" and each *rumah* is approximately three meters.

The *takbir* during *salatul 'idain*: The *'id* prayer consists of two *rak'at* during which it is *sunnah* to pronounce the *takbir* seven times, after the opening *takbir* and before the Qur'anic recital in the first *rak'ah*. During the second *rak'ah*, one makes *takbir* five times after the *takbir* which is customarily made for standing after the prostration. One is to raise one's hands during each pronouncement of the *takbir*. This is based on a report transmitted from 'Umar and his son Abdullah.

'Amr ibn Shu'aib reports from his father on the authority of his grand-father that the Prophet would make twelve *takbirat* during the *'id* prayer, seven in the first *rak'ah* and five in the second. He did not pray before or after the *'id*. This is related by Ahmad and Ibn Majah. Ahmad says: "I follow that."

Abu Dawud and ad-Daraqutni report that the Prophet said: "The *takbirat* during the [*'id* of] breaking the fast are seven in the first *rak'ah* and five in the second, and the Qur'anic recital comes after them in both the *rak'at*." This is the strongest opinion and it is the opinion of the majority of the people of knowledge from among the companions, the successors, and the *imams*. Ibn Abdul-Barr commenting on the number of *takbirat*, says: "It has been related through many good chains that the Prophet made seven *takbirat* in the first *rak'ah* and five in the second. Such has been related from 'Abdullah ibn 'Amr, Ibn 'Umar, Jabir, 'Aishah. Abu Waqid, and 'Amer ibn 'Auf al-Mazni. Nothing that has been related from him, either through a stonger or weaker chain, differs from that, and it was the first to be practiced."[84]

As to the pause between *takbirat*, it is said that the Prophet would be silent for a short period of time between the *takhirat*, and nothing has been related from him concerning exactly what he said during that pause; however, at-Tabarani and al-Baihaqi relate, with a strong chain, that Ibn Mas'ud would praise and extol Allah, the Exalted, and make prayers upon the Prophet during such intervals.[85] The same has been recorded from Hudhaifah and Abu Musa. Pronouncing the *takbirat* are a *sunnah* even though the *salah* is not invalidated if one neglects them, either intentionally or out of forgetfulness.

Ibn Qudamah says: "I know of no difference of opinion on that point." Ash-Shaukani states that the strongest opinion is that if one does not per-form the *takbirat* out of forgetfulness, he is not to perform the prostrations of forgetfulness.

---

[84]The Hanafi school holds that in the first *rak'ah* three *takbirat* are to be made after the open-ing *takbir*, but before the recital.

[85]Ahmad and Ash-Shaf'i hold it is preferred to extol and glorify Allah during these intervals between *takbirat* and to say words like: *Subhan allah*, *Al-hamdulillah*, and *La ilaha illalahu wallahu akbar*.

Prayer before or after *salatul 'id*: It is not established that there is any *sunnah* prayer before or after the *'id* prayer. The Prophet never performed any such prayer, neither did his companions upon arrival at the *musalla* (prayer place).

Ibn 'Abbas reports: "The Messenger of Allah went out to the site of the *'id* prayer and prayed two *rak'at* [i.e., the *'id* prayer] without praying anything before or after it." This is related by the group.

It is reported that Ibn 'Umar did the same and he stated that this was the practice of the Prophet.

Al-Bukhari records that Ibn 'Abbas disliked that one should perform a prayer before *salatul 'id*. Concerning voluntary prayers at such a time, Ibn Hajar has stated in *Fath al-Bari* that there is no evidence to show that it is not allowed, unless it is at the times in which it is disliked to pray on any day.

For whom the performance of *salatul 'id* **is valid:** The *'id* prayer is valid for men, women, children, travellers, residents, people in congregation, and people praying individually. It is also valid if performed in a house, mosque, or a distant place designated for the *salah*, and so on.

Whoever misses *salatul 'id* with the congregation may pray two *rak'at*. In *Sahih al-Bukhari* we find in the chapter entitled: "If one misses *salatul 'id* he may pray two *rak'at* and the same is the case for the women or people in their houses or in the countryside. This is based on the Prophet's words: 'O Muslims, this is our festival.'" Anas ibn Malik ordered his protege Ibn abi-'Utbah, [who lived] in a remote area, to gather his family and children and to pray [the *'id* prayer] like the people in the city and with *takbirat* similar to theirs. 'Ikrimah said: "The people of the country should gather for the *'id* and pray two *rak'at* as the imam does." 'Ata says: "If you miss the *'id* [*salah*], pray two *rak'at*."

The *khutbah* **of** *salatul 'id*: The *khutbah* after *salatul 'id* is a *sunnah* and so is listening to it. Abu Sa'id says: "On the *'id* of breaking the fast and of the sacrifice, the Prophet would go to the *musalla* (prayer place) and begin with the *salah* and when he finished, he would face the people while the people were sitting in rows, and he would admonish them, advise them, and exhort them [to do good deeds]. And if he wished to send off an army or order something, he would do so and then leave." Abu Sa'id then says: "The people continued to act likewise until I went out with Marwan, while he was the govenor of Medinah, for one of the two *'ids*. When I arrived at the place of prayer, I found a *minbar* that was built by Kathir ibn as-Salt.[86] When Marwan went to mount it before the prayer,

---

[86]The Prophet *sallallahu alehi wasallam* did not use a *mimbar* for the *'id khutbah*. (editor)

I pulled him by his clothes. He pushed me away and gave the *khutbah* before the *salah*. I said to him: 'By Allah you have changed [the order].' He said: 'O Abu Sa'id...what you know is gone.' I said: 'By Allah, what I know is better than what I don't know.' He said: 'The people would not stay with us after the *salah* so we made the *khutbah* before the *salah*.'" This is related by al-Bukhari and Muslim.

'Abdullah ibn as-Sa'ib said: "I prayed the *'id salah* with the Messenger of Allah and when he finished the *salah* he said: 'We will be delivering a *khutbah*. Whoever wishes to stay for the *khutbah* may stay. Whoever would like to leave, may leave.'" This is related by an-Nasa'i, Abu Dawud, and Ibn Majah.

Whatever has been recorded suggests that there are two *khutbahs* for the *'id* and the imam sits between them [i.e., like the *khutbatul Jumu'ah*]. Such reports are considered weak. An-Nawawi says: "There is nothing at all substantiated about there being more than one *khutbah*."

Ibn al-Qayyim writes: "The Prophet would begin all of his *khutbahs* with the praise of Allah and there is no *hadith* from him that states that he began his *'id khutbahs* with *takbir*.

Ibn Majah recorded in his *Sunan* from Sa'id, the *mu'adhdhin* of the Prophet, that the Prophet would say the *takbir* during his *khutbahs* and even more so during the *'id khutbahs*. Still, this does not prove that he began his *khutbah* with it! The people differ over the beginning of the *'id* and the *khutbah* for *salatul istisqa'* (prayer for rain). Some say that they are to begin with *takbir*. Some say that the *khutbah* for *salatul istisqa'* begins with praying for forgiveness while others say it begins with praises of Allah." Shaikh al-Islam Ibn Taimiyyah says: "That is correct as the Prophet said: 'Every affair that does not begin with the praise of Allah is deficient.' The Prophet began all of his speeches with praises of Allah. Concerning the statement of many jurists, i.e., he began the 'prayer for rain' by asking forgiveness from Allah and the *'id* speech with *takbir*, there is absolutely no proof for it in the Prophet's *sunnah*. In fact the *sunnah* contradicts that statement as he began all of his speeches with the praises of Allah."

Making up a missed *'id* prayer: Abu 'Umair ibn Anas reports: "My Ansari uncles from among the companions of the Messenger of Allah said to me: 'The moon for the month of Shawwal was hidden from us and, therefore, our companions fasted. Then at the end of the day, riders came and they bore witness to the Prophet *sallallahu alehi wasallam* that they had seen the moon the previous night. The Prophet ordered the people to break their fasts and to go out to the site of the *salatul 'id* on the next day.'" This is related by Ahmad, an-Nasa'i, and Ibn Majah with a *sahih* chain. In this *hadith* there lies evidence for those who say that if the people miss *salatul 'id* due to some excuse, then they may go out and pray it the next day.

Playing, amusements, singing, and eating on the days of *'id*: Recreation, amusements, and singing, if they stay within the moral bounds, are permissible on the days of *'id*.

Anas reports: "When the Prophet came to Medinah they had two days of sport and amusement. The Prophet said: "Allah, the Exalted, has exchanged these days for two days better than them: the day of breaking the fast and the day of sacrifice." This is related by an-Nasa'i and Ibn Hibban with a *sahih* chain.

'Aishah says: "The Abyssinians were preforming in the mosque on the day of *'id*. I looked over the Prophet's shoulders and he lowered them a little so I could see them until I was satisfied and left." This is related by Ahmad, al-Bukhari, and Muslim.

Ahmad, al-Bukhari, and Muslim also record that she said: "Abu Bakr entered upon us on the day of *'id* and there were some slave girls who were recounting [in song the battle of] Bu'ath in which many of the brave of the tribes of Aus and Khazraj were killed. Abu Bakr said: 'Slaves of Allah, you play the pipes of the Satan!' He said it three times. The Prophet said to him: 'O Abu Bakr, every people have a festival and this is our festival.'" In al-Bukhari's version, 'Aishah said: "The Messenger of Allah, entered the house and I had two girls who were singing about the battle of Bu'ath. The Prophet lied down on the bed and turned his face to the other direction. Abu Bakr entered and spoke harshly to me, 'Musical instruments of the Satan in the presence of the Messenger of Allah!' The Messenger of Allah turned his face to him and said: 'Leave them.' When Abu Bakr became inattentive I signaled to the girls to leave. It was the day of *'id* and the Africans were performing with their shields and spears. Either I asked him or the Prophet asked if I would like to watch them [I don't recall now]. I replied in the affirmative. At this the Prophet made me stand behind him and my cheek was against his. He was saying: 'Carry on, O tribe of Arfadah,'[87] until I tired. The Prophet asked: 'Is that enough for you?' I replied: "yes," so he said: 'Leave [then].'"

Ibn Hajar writes in *Fath al-Bari*, "Ibn as-Siraj related from Abu az-Zinad on the authority of 'Urwah from 'Aishah that the Prophet said that day: 'Let the Jews of Medinah know that our religion is spacious [and has room for relaxation] and I have been sent with an easy and straight forward religion.'"

Ahmad and Muslim record from Nubaishah that the Prophet *sallallahu alehi wasallam* said: "The days of *tashriq* (i.e., the days in which the *'id*

---

[87]Arfadah: an epithet used for the people of Abyssinia.

is celebrated) are days of eating and drinking [non alcoholic drinks] and of remembering Allah, the Exalted."

The excellence of good deeds in the first ten days of Dhul-Hijjah: Ibn 'Abbas reports that the Prophet *sallallahu alehi wasallam* said: "No good deeds done on other days are superior to those done on these days [meaning the ten days of Dhul-Hijjah]." The companions asked: "O Messenger of Allah, not even *jihad* in the way of Allah?" He said: "Not even *jihad*, save for the man who puts his life and wealth in danger [for Allah's sake] and returns with neither of them." This is related by the group save Muslim and an-Nasa'i.

Ahmad and at-Tabarani record from Ibn 'Umar that the Messenger of Allah said: "There is no day more honorable in Allah's sight and no acts more beloved therein to Allah than those in these ten days. So say *tahlil* ["There is no God but Allah"], *takbir* [Allah is the greatest] and *tahmid* ["All praise is due to Allah"] a lot [on those days]."

Ibn 'Abbas says about the *'ayah*, "Remember Allah during the well known days,"[88] that it refers to the first ten days of Dhul-Hijjah. This is related by al-Bukhari. Sa'id ibn Jubair would push himself very hard [to do good deeds] during these ten days.

Al-Auza'i says: "It has reached me that a deed on one of the ten days is similar to fighting in the way of Allah, fasting during its days and guarding during its nights, except for him who becomes a martyr." As to its source, he adds: "A man from the tribe of Bani Makhzum related that to me from the Prophet."

Abu Hurairah relates that the Prophet said: "There are no days more loved to Allah for you to worship Him therein than the ten days of Dhul-Hijja. Fasting any day during it is equivalent to fasting one year and to offer *salatul tahajjud* (late-night prayer) during one of its nights is like performing the late night prayer on the night of power. [i.e., *Lailatul Qadr*]." This is related by at-Tirmidhi, Ibn Majah, and al-Baihaqi.

Congratulating one another on the days of *'id*: It is commendable to congratulate one another on the days of *'id*.

Jabir ibn Nafir reports: "When the companions of the Prophet met each other on the day of *'id*, they would say to each other, '*taqabbal minna wa minka* [May Allah] accept it from us and you.'" Ibn Hajar said that its chain is *hasan*.

Takbirat during the days of *'id*: It is a *sunnah* to pronounce the *takbirat* on *'id* days. Concerning the *'id* of breaking the fast, Allah says "you should complete the prescribed period and that you should glorify Allah

---

[88]Qur'an 2:203

[i.e., say *takbirat*] for having guided you and that you may give thanks."[89]

Concerning the *'id* of the sacrifice, Allah says: "that you may remember Allah during the well known days;"[90] and: "He has made them subject to you, that you may glorify Allah for His guidance to you."[91] The majority of the scholars say that the time for the *takbirat* during the *'id* of breaking the fast is from the time one goes to the *'id* prayer until the *khutbah* begins. Weak *ahadith* have been recorded stating this, but there are also authentic reports from Ibn 'Umar and other companions that they did so. Al-Hakim says: "This *sunnah* has been practiced by *ahl-il hadith*. Malik, Ahmad, Ishaq, and Abu Thaur [have made statements concurring that practice]."

Some say that the *takbirat* are from the night before the *'id*, when the moon is seen, until the person goes to the *musalla* and the imam arrives. The time for the *takbirat* during the *'id* of the sacrifice is from the day of 'Arafah until the time of the *'asr* on the thirteenth of Dhul-Hijjah.

Ibn Hajar writes in *Fath al-Bari*: "None of that has been confirmed from the Prophet. The most authentic report from the companions is that 'Ali and Ibn Mas'ud would make the *takbirat* from the day of 'Arafah to the *'asr* of the last day of Mina. Ibn al-Mundhir and others reported it. Ash-Shaf'i, Ahamd, Abu Yusuf, and Muhammad follow that report and it is also the view of 'Umar and Ibn 'Abbas."

There is no specific time for the *takbirat* during the days of *tashriq* (three days after *'idul adha*). In fact, it is preferred to pronounce *takbirat* during every moment of those days.

Al-Bukhari recorded: "During 'Umar's stay at Mina, he would say *takbirat* in his tent [so loud] that the people in the mosque would hear it and then they would start doing it also and the people in the market place would do the same and all of Mina would resound with the *takbirat*. Ibn 'Umar used to say the *takbirat*, during those days of Mina, after the prayers and while on his bed, in his tent, while sitting and while walking during all of those days. Maimuna would say the *takbirat* on the day of sacrifice. The women used to say *takbirat* behind Abban ibn 'Uthman and 'Umar ibn 'Abdulaziz along with the men in the mosque during the days of *tashriq*." Al-Hafiz ibn Hajar said: "These reports show that the *takbirat* are made during all the times of these days, after *salah* and all other times. Some say the *takbirat* are made only after the *salah*, and some say they are to be made only after the *fard* prayers and not after *nawafil*, others declare them to be for men and not for women, while some say that they are only to be said in congregations and not individually, while others reserve them only for those who perform the *salah* on time and not for those

---

[89]Qur'an 2:185
[90]Qur'an 2:203
[91]Qur'an 22:37

who are making up a missed prayer, and some say only for residents and not travellers, whereas others think they are only for the people of the city and not for the people of the countryside. Apparently al-Bukhari is of the opinion that it is for all people and the reports that he has transmitted support his opinion."

These *takbirat* can be made in many different forms. The most authentic form is that which has been recorded with a *sahih* chain by 'Abdurrazaq from Salman, who said: "They made *takbirat* with: '*Allahu akbar, Allahu akbar, Allahu akbar kabeera.*'" From 'Umar and ibn Mas'ud the following is related: "*Allahu akbar. Allahu akbar. La ilaha illallah. Allahu akbar. Allahu akbar wa lillahil-hamd**."

---

*Translation: Allah is the greatest, Allah is the greatest. There is no God but Allah. Allah is the greatest, Allah is the greatest. All praise belongs to Allah.

www.ingramcontent.com/pod-product-compliance
Lightning Source LLC
Chambersburg PA
CBHW020859090426
42736CB00008B/431